GOTH'S DARK EMPIRE

GOTH'S DARK EMPIRE

Carol Siegel

Indiana University Press ◆ Bloomington and Indianapolis

This book is a publication of

Indiana University Press
601 North Morton Street
Bloomington, IN 47404-3797 USA

http://iupress.indiana.edu

Telephone orders   800-842-6796
Fax orders   812-855-7931
Orders by e-mail   iuporder@indiana.edu

The paper used in this publication meets the minimum requirements of
American National Standard for Information Sciences—Permanence of
Paper for Printed Library Materials, ANSI Z39.48-1984.

Manufactured in the United States of America

Library of Congress Cataloging-in-Publication Data

Siegel, Carol, date-
  Goth's dark empire / Carol Siegel.
    p. cm.
  Includes bibliographical references and index.
  ISBN 0-253-34593-6 (cloth : alk. paper) — ISBN 0-253-21776-8 (pbk. : alk. paper)
  1. Goth culture (Subculture) I. Title.
  HQ796.S457 2005
  306'.1—dc22
                                    2004029641

1 2 3 4 5 10 09 08 07 06 05

TO GERHARD

CONTENTS

ACKNOWLEDGMENTS

My gratitude goes out first to all the Goths who invited me into their world and guided me through its magnificent darkness. Without your help, encouragement, trust, and corrections of my misperceptions, this book would never have been. And special thanks to the anonymous Goth at the book signing for *New Millennial Sexstyles* who exhorted me to undertake this project. I hope I have honestly represented the concerns that all of you expressed and have faithfully transmitted your ideas about your subculture.

Thanks are also due to the many students who have taken my classes in Contemporary Youth Cultures and Film Studies, and my special seminar on the history of the Gothic over the past four years. Please forgive me for not listing you all here, and know that I appreciated all your ideas and suggestions about Goth and Deleuze.

As always I thank my San Francisco friends and family, and in particular Jamie O'Toole, Chris Toomey, and Mary Stewart for their enthusiastic accompaniment on three Goth-hunting expeditions in The City. And Scott Candey for opening the dark doors to me on the first of these journeys of discovery.

For reading parts of this manuscript and offering helpful suggestions, I thank Joe Austin, Ellen E. Berry, Michael Bibby, Shelli Fowler, Laura Frost, Lauren Goodlad, Virginia Hyde, Ann Kibbey, Michael Kramp, Katherine Olson, Tim Shary, Juanita Smart, Noel Sturgeon, and Patricia White. And for especially useful general discussion of the project with me, I am grateful to November Rose Anderson, Paul Brians, Joan Burbick, Doug Cunningham, Dee Anne Finken, Joanna Frueh, Denise Garrett, Will Hamlin, John Hegglund, Paula Kamen, Kristin Kohl, Karmen MacKendrick, Eric Petracca, T. V. Reed, Elizabeth Sargent, Robert Schimelfenig, Noel Sturgeon, and Garry Watson.

For his wonderful work as a teaching assistant and for being the absolute best research assistant anyone could ever have, I will always be grateful to Don Anderson. I also thank him for providing the discography.

My thanks to Robert Sloan, my editor at Indiana University Press, for once again making the publication process a joy for me, and to Shoshanna Green for her invaluable help in preparing the manuscript.

I am grateful to Washington State University Vancouver for providing me with a semester's sabbatical in fall 2003 to allow me time to write the penultimate draft of the book, and to Washington State University's English Department for its award of the Buchanan Distinguished Professorship, which provided financial support for a large portion of the travel and research materials for this project, as well as the research assistantship.

Part of chapter 1, "Perils for the Pure," was selected for inclusion in Joe Austin's collection of papers presented at "Youth, Popular Culture, and Everyday Life," a conference at Bowling Green State University, February 8–10, 2002, and I thank him for permission to reprint it here.

I thank Duke University Press for permission to publish here, as part of chapter 3, "That Obscure Object of Desire Revisited," material that also appears in the collection *Undead Subcultures*.

My essay "Curing ~~Boys~~ Don't Cry: Brandon Teena's Stories," published in *Genders* 37 (2003), appears in revised form as part of chapter 4. For her permission to reprint that material, I thank the journal's editor, Ann Kibbey.

GOTH'S DARK EMPIRE

INTRODUCTION

I. Death, Pleasure, and the Frenzy of the Invisible, Or Why Take Goth Seriously?

I begin this extended look at the subculture called Goth with an allusion to Linda Williams's landmark feminist study of pornographic films, *Hard Core: Power, Pleasure, and the "Frenzy of the Visible,"* because, just as Williams did when she addressed that topic fifteen years ago, I am entering an area of inquiry that has attracted an enormous amount of attention in popular media but relatively little serious scholarly study. Moreover, like Williams, I must confront the dominant view among American academics that this subject is at best embarrassingly silly and at worst another dismal sign of the degeneracy of our times. And just as Williams set out to examine the Foucauldian "knowledge-pleasure" produced as "the frenzy of the visible" through the convergence of "a variety of discourses of sexuality" within pornography (36), I set out to examine the Deleuzoguattarian becomings[1] that are produced through the discourses of sexuality that converge within Goth. The greatest difference between the objects of my study and those of Williams's is that in this case they are, in effect, invisible.

It may seem odd to refer to Goths as effectively invisible, because immediately after the 1999 shootings at Columbine High School in Littleton, Colorado, the press erroneously, but very insistently, attributed the tragedy to the Goth subculture. As a result of the moral panic that followed, anyone with the slightest interest in youth cultures, rock and roll cultures, or popular media has probably heard of Goths by now. But until very recently Goth was nearly invisible within the academic world in the sense that, despite the presence of Goths in most of our classes, few academics had much to say about them. Although Goth emerged as a named subculture at the end of the 1970s, cultural studies scholars did not turn their attention to it for another twenty years, and still there is only one book-length study of Goth in this field. Where one might most expect Goths to be discussed, in overviews of Gothic traditions in literature and art, they have rarely been mentioned.[2]

Despite the omnipresence of Goths in America throughout the 1990s, almost all the serious attention they have received has been from British scholars concentrating on Goth in Britain, which, like other permutations and off-shoots of British Punk, can differ markedly from the American subculture that shares the name. The only explanation I have been able to find for American academics' lack of interest in Goth is that they have, for the most part, seen the subculture's radical engagements with gender and sexuality as an ephemeral trend, a superficial experimentation with images rather than substance typical of the sort of expression of youthful rebellion deemed nearly meaningless by scholars because it is structured almost entirely by niche marketing to bored young consumers, who move on to the next trend advertised on MTV so quickly that to study any of these trends individually would seem foolish. I disagree with this assessment of Goth because I agree with Michel Foucault, Gilles Deleuze, and Félix Guattari that physical pleasures—particularly the consensual sadomasochism (S/M) I find intrinsic to most Goth subcultures—can function as radical technologies of resistance to the oppressive regimes of sexual normalcy upon which the maintenance of consumer capitalism depends, a topic I will take up in the first chapter.

This study will focus throughout on how an array of styles, practices, and aesthetics described as Goth by substantial numbers of people who also identify themselves as Goths make possible ways of thinking that depart from mainstream American values, as constructed by corporate advertising and the rhetoric of political conservatism. This construction predictably centers on acquiring corporately produced or marketed consumer goods, especially cars and houses, as well as clothing and cosmetics intended to create a specific appearance associated by advertisers with health, youth, and success. What passes for success here depends upon disciplining desire in the Foucauldian sense, or territorializing it, as Deleuze would have it, so that it serves the goals of consumer capitalism in corporate America. As I intend to show, when popular interpretations of psychology are used to justify legislation in the name of feminism, it is frequently the case that these goals are inadvertently served, especially when intensities disruptive of social order are suppressed because they are believed to endanger vulnerable young girls. In contrast, subcultures considered Goth(ic) by their participants valorize intense physical sensation and intellectual pleasure and, in the interest of promoting these, foster two modes of expression that Deleuze sees as crucial to successful existence: the production of carefully hand-crafted visual styles and the cultivation of new eroticisms.

Throughout the book, and especially in chapter 3, I will argue that Goth should be read as a celebration of S/M practices as liberatory, but here I will pause only to explain why I consider the connection of Goth to S/M impossible to ignore. In the early 1990s I decided to explore a segment of what would later be called third-wave feminism through investigation of specific youth subcultures. This work was motivated by the growing gap, well documented in writings by third-wave feminists, between the majority of feminist theorists of my own generation and young people with radical perspectives on sexuality and gender, including clashing opinions about the potential of S/M to disrupt gender binarity. Because of my own interest in rock and roll cultures and their overlap with subcultures organized around putatively perverse sex practices, I began by meeting with fans of what was then a rapidly rising band, Nine Inch Nails.[3]

What interested me most about Nine Inch Nails, a music project controlled by frontman Trent Reznor, was that Reznor is the first male artist in any genre since Leopold von Sacher-Masoch to represent himself publicly as a heterosexual masochist and subsequently to achieve tremendous popular success. What I soon discovered was that almost all the self-described "hardcore" Nine Inch Nails fans I encountered also called themselves Goths. After conversing with over one hundred and sixty of them, I had been supplied with ample evidence that, contrary to the common belief among the middle-aged, teenagers do listen to the lyrics of songs. These young people not only recognized that the music they loved concerned itself with sadomasochism, but they also approved of the stories they believed the songs were recounting about S/M practices.[4]

As Simon Reynolds notes in his excellent study of the reception of rock music, *Blissed Out*, teenage fans characteristically scrutinize lyrics of songs they love and struggle to interpret each line as if it were part of an incomplete narrative (15). As with Gothic "fragments" like Coleridge's "Kubla Khan," the audience is understood to be invited to supply a narrative that will contain and thus make sense of the images provided. Interestingly, almost all the young people with whom I spoke felt sure that the songs "Sanctified" and "Sin," from Nine Inch Nails' 1989 debut album, *Pretty Hate Machine*, which went platinum that year, referred respectively to Reznor's initiation into female-dominant sadomasochism and his experience of being "fisted." They read another 1989 song, "Twist," as referring to S/M knife play, and all understood the 1994 hit song "Closer" as a song about the pleasures of bondage (an interpretation helped by the song's tremendously popular video). In 1998 at a Johns Hopkins Center for Talented Youth Humanities Day presentation I did on Gothic conventions in contemporary rock and roll, middle school students, including several Goths, spontaneously referred to an animal-masked female figure in the "Closer" video as "the dominatress." Over one hundred of the young people with whom I spoke correctly identified numerous images of S/M and bondage equipment in Nine Inch Nails' music videos and other promotional materials, using not general descriptors like "gag" but specific terms of S/M culture, as in the frequent observation, "Trent is wearing a ball gag." Apparently, then, Goth youth culture stylings have been connected to the practice of ritual S/M, at the very least by a common understanding of objects and rituals.

This commonality was reinforced in Portland as well as in many other cities, such as New York, Chicago, Los Angeles, and San Francisco, in the 1990s and at the beginning of the twenty-first century by the frequency with which Goth performances and so-called fetish nights shared venues in the club scene. Because of all this, I am surprised by the view of many outside analysts of the Goth scene that the use of S/M paraphernalia and images by young Goths was innocent of any sexual connotation. The voices from the academy further astounded me by declaring that the Goth youth cultural products had no significant connection to real Gothic literature.

If "real" in this context means Gothic literature as its current prominent theorists most commonly understand it, then this may be true. For example, Mark Edmundson's *Nightmare on Mainstreet: Angels, Sadomasochism, and the Culture of Gothic* offers a psychoanalytically orthodox explanation of the prevalence of Gothic stylings among the young. Beginning from the standard therapeutic assumption that sadomasochism is in its essence a way of avoiding real love and commitment, he reads both traditional Gothic literature and current trends as indicative of their respective generations' wholesale turning away from affectionate bonding to embrace nihilistic isolation. He predicts that, if the popularity of the Gothic and of its corollary S/M were to continue, we would soon find ourselves inhabiting a culture in which "[e]quality in love, as well as in politics and social life generally, would no longer be a tenable ideal" (131). "There would be no conception of love, no room to wish for the happiness of others, for their pleasure, their growth into imaginative prowess and complexity of character" (133). Edmundson goes so far as to lament that while "[e]arly terror Gothic was the literature of revolution," current Gothic is "out of step with the facts" in a nation that "has grown more and more stable" (17, 32), so that the fear of the exterior world it foments has become exaggerated and inappropriate—at least if one ignores the eco-disasters unfolding daily.[5] His conclusion is that authentic expressions of the Gothic are absent from Goth youth cultures.

One might expect more appreciation for Goth's undermining of gender norms from a less conservative critic, one who does not refer contemptuously to Foucauldianism, "feminist tracts," and the "60's movement to so-called liberation" as forces that are threatening to destroy that "stable" culture Edmundson deems good enough to warrant preservation (14, 64). But if we leave aside Edmundson's rather alarming ignorance of Goth youth culture (he confidently describes Madonna as a leading musician in the Goth rock genre, 46) and his obvious moral disapproval of Gothic literature of any era, we are left with a vision of the relation of contemporary Goth to literary forms previously labeled Gothic not unlike that presented by Fred Botting in *Gothic*, an introduction to the genre in Routledge's New Critical Idiom series.

Botting's discussion of late-twentieth-century Gothic films and books ignores what would seem to be obvious favorites of young people, like the seminal Goth films *Edward Scissorhands* (1990) and *The Crow* (1994). In Botting's view Francis Ford Coppola's 1992 film *Dracula* indicates "the end of Gothic," because the form has now been "divested of its transgressions, horrors, and diabolical laughter, of its brilliant gloom and rich darkness" (180). Of course, the inhabitants of what many websites proclaim "the world of Goth," thickly populated as it is with transgressive, horrific, darkly comic, and diabolical artifacts, would declare otherwise, but neither Botting nor Edmundson recognizes any significant continuity between Goth youth culture and classic Gothic literature.

In his textbook for the Cambridge University Press series Contexts in Literature, *The Gothic Tradition* (2000), David Stevens demonstrates a superior ability to observe the world around him, especially through a section on "Gothic Whitby," site of both Bram Stoker's writing of *Dracula* and contemporary "regular gothic festivals" (40). His short book also provides a concise section on Goth music, concluding quite arguably that "[r]evivals in gothic rock music continue to come and go, although not with the same intensity as experienced in the late 1970s and early 1980s" (38). Perhaps his conclusion that audience engagement faded after the intensity of the early 1980s is wishful thinking on his part since, although he strives for a balanced presentation, he describes both Goth music and the closely related Darkwave as frighteningly ideal vehicles for "extreme right-wing political movements" (39). Given how viciously conservative about sexuality and gender neo-Nazis have shown themselves to be and the almost universal association among young music fans of Goth with transgression of sexual and gender boundaries, it seems strange to conclude, as Stevens does, from a single quote from a fascist newspaper, that neo-Nazis must find Goth music appealing. Once again, actual Goths as we can see them in communities from Whitby, England, to Portland, Oregon, seem invisible.

As Michael Moynihan and Didrik Søderlind make clear throughout their controversial[6] journalistic account of the Norwegian Black Metal movement and related music cultures, *Lords of Chaos: The Bloody Rise of the Satanic Metal Underground* (1998), not only is Goth only tangentially related to Black Metal, through the self-placement of both styles within the larger category Darkwave, the fans and bands involved in creating Black Metal are far from uniformly racist or fascistic. Simply observing the audiences on Goth club nights should confirm this view. In terms of public style and behavior, Goth is the antithesis of the hard-edged fascist mode among contemporary young people, a fact I will explore most extensively through my final chapter's discussion of Goth's role in the construction of new Asian American masculinities.

My surprise at the pervasive lack of recognition of the Goth subculture in academic writing was largely due to how impossible I found Goth to ignore. My own introduction to the late 1980s resurgence of Goth came through casual talk with students and young friends involved in the local club scenes in places I lived, taught, and spent recreational time: San Francisco; Berkeley; New Orleans (where I first encountered Goth as a subculture locally overlapping Rave in the period from 1987 to 1988, when I taught at Loyola University there[7]); New York; Chicago; Portland, Oregon (my current residence); Seaside, Tillamook, and Cannon Beach, Oregon; Seattle, Tacoma, Olympia, and Vancouver, Washington, as well as Washington State University's main campus in Pullman; and the nearby college community in Moscow, Idaho. However, I did not think very much about the meanings that might be attached to this popular form of identification within the club scene until one evening in the mid-1990s, just at dusk, when I was walking to the downtown club district in Portland.

As I passed over the pedestrian bridge above the freeway, I saw a group of Goths streaming like black smoke down under the freeway overpass. The poetic beauty of this moment, and its mystery—what were they planning to do under the street?—brought to mind, by way of contrast, how, as a young woman, I used to rather obnoxiously intone lines from the "Unreal City" section of T. S. Eliot's "The Waste Land" whenever I found myself among what I saw as the zombie capitalist commuters in San Francisco's financial district descending into the BART subway stations at rush hour: "so many, / I had not thought death had undone so many." At that time I felt myself, like Eliot, to be part of a world whose reality contrasted with the deathly dreaming of people who ignored basic human drives in favor of chasing a symbol, money. Their passage was out of the world of actual value into that of group delusion. But here in Portland's literally underground Goth movement was a spectacle that suggested an alternative to the life-in-death that is the bland conformity demanded as the price of participation in American corporate culture. Here were people who designed their appearances, including a generous use of permanent markers like facial piercings and tattoos, to make blending into the mainstream impossible. Yet they also marked themselves as dead, with corpse-white makeup, deeply shadowed eyes, and, in some case, ripped and stained clothing made to look like the cerements on disinterred bodies.

Had death also, though so differently, undone them? If so, in what sense? Certainly they had an intimate relation to death. My own youthful sense of self was constructed along lines dictated by my assimilation of the rhetoric of sexual liberation expressed in sixties favorites, such as Norman O. Brown's 1959 *Life against Death*, in which refusal to submit to the deathly demands of an oppressive culture means coming alive sexually, and vice versa. So it was both exciting and unsettling to me to see the Goths' perversely eroticized embrace of death. Here, it seemed, was a new take on the old sexual revolution.

The sexual revolution was, in my view, the most significant event of the twentieth century. In the broadest sense, we might attribute the sexual revolution of the nineteen-sixties and seventies to a general sense that it had become possible to have sex without consequences that threatened one's life, thanks to the development of antibiotics that cured all well-known venereal diseases (sexually transmitted diseases that antibiotics would not kill were not widely known or understood by the public in this period) and the invention of the birth control pill, followed rapidly by other highly effective means of birth control, and culminating with the legalization of abortion. For many people who were sexually active during this time, these changes in the technologies of reproduction and disease prevention meant no less than that, for the first time in human history, anyone—and, especially notably, any woman—could expect to survive exercising sexual freedom, none the worse physically.

Common wisdom holds that for the generations that became sexually active after the discovery of AIDS, sexual "excess" was once again seen as the road to certain, horrible death. If Goth is part of a new sexual revolution, it must address this change. For, as Gavin Baddeley observes, "the Gothic is, at root, about extremes of experience and an appetite for excess" (63). However, it is hard to understand Goth as central to a new sexual revolution unless we recognize that, long before the advent of AIDS awareness, the freedom the sexual revolution brought had soured for many, as dozens of feminist discussions of the putative failure of the sexual revolution claim.

If, in the sixties and seventies, being alive meant being sexually alive, that condition was also seen by Leftists as the very essence of rebellion in a culture within which, as Foucault famously shows in volume 1 of his *History of Sexuality*, sexuality has been understood since the nineteenth century to be "the general and disquieting secret that pervades our conduct and our existence," and "both the hidden aspect and the generative principle of meaning" (67, 155). To the sexual rebels, as a consequence, being sexually limited or inhibited by one's own feelings or circumstances meant being in effect dead, and that deadness was a state many understood to be forced upon them by a sexist culture. However, in terms of the mainstream's sexual economy, counterculture sex radicals were as good as dead from the moment we emerged as a political force in the sixties, because we were neither marriage material, as they understood it, nor shamed victims.[8] We were dead to their world.

Popular horror novelist and early Goth favorite Anne Rice has been one of the foremost chroniclers of this phenomenon, especially in her first novel, the best-selling *Interview with the Vampire* (1976). Since the AIDS pandemic, it has been difficult to read the novel's obsessive treatment of erotic predation and blood-borne infection outside the context of the fears of sexuality aroused, or more precisely reawakened, by that crisis. However, that Rice wrote the story prior to AIDS is important for many reasons, including that its sexual symbology can be understood as a bridge between the discontents that for many people accompanied the sexual revolution and the fulfillment of their direst prophecies of its consequences, as those prophecies were fulfilled with the onset of the pandemic.

Louis, the sensitive, gloomy focus character of the novel, emblematizes those miserable wretches who saw themselves as seduced and abandoned by the sexual revolution. He has been given no instruction in how to live the new, vampiric life into which he has been plunged because of another's erotic attention, as he constantly complains throughout the text. And he is tormented by the unleashing of his own dark, predatory desires, which he cannot satisfy without making other souls as alienated from the ordinary daylight world as he is himself. His lamentation of this situation sounds uncannily like that of the many people—a cultural force to which I shall return later—who now insist that the reason the sexual revolution did not offer real liberation is that what humans truly need is emotional intimacy, not orgasmic release.

His sometime lover, the unrestrained, exuberantly amoral Lestat, figures those annoying people (myself among them) who seemed perfectly content with the freedoms the sexual revolution offered. We can recognize in him the stereotypical conscience-less consumer of pornography and cruiser of discotheques, who so infuriated more sensitive souls throughout the seventies. In Claudia and Armand, the children "made" (that is, into vampires) too soon, and thus hopelessly perverse in their exercise of their dark powers, we can see not only anticipation of the wave of anti-pedophilia paranoia that would begin in the 1980s, but also the traditional way in which sexual conservatives have obfuscated their own fears of sexuality, by expressing anxiety about the danger sexual freedom poses to the young. Rice's novel works as a depiction of a way of life at once unbearable and irresistible, for despite the bitter unhappiness of Louis's reminiscences even his interviewer succumbs to the lure of vampirism.

I was reminded of Rice's novel when reading Jane Gerhard's fascinating history of the intersections of the women's movement and the sexual revolution, *Desiring Revolution* (2001). As her wealth of sources makes abundantly clear, for most American women the sexual revolution was fraught with "risks, which, while they might lead to excitement, might also lead to disappointment," by which her informants seem to mean failure to attain marital security (79). In second-wave feminist writings, Gerhard uncovers a veritable archive of sexual dissatisfaction, frustration with available options for the expression of sexuality, and a recurring, and to my mind bizarrely impossible, desire to somehow realize a female heterosexuality utterly independent of men or male sexuality. The call for (hetero)sex on women's own terms becomes a lament not unlike that of Louis, Rice's reluctant vampire, who can neither return to the daylight world of his virginal/prelapsarian innocence nor "take back the night" in any way that will render him an agent rather than a victim. His own sense of morality, or rather the cultural discourses that construct his sense of good and evil, tells him that the only positions open to him are endless subjection to the will of wrongdoers or else becoming one of the predators he despises. This dilemma resonates eerily with the cultural feminist insistence in the late seventies that "for sex to be consistent with feminism, it had to reflect women's values by prioritizing intimacy, nongenital touching, and emotional nurturing" (Gerhard, 186). Gerhard's sources remember, as do I, that within cultural feminism, orientation toward orgasm as a goal was discouraged, and we were all urged to transform even our private fantasies so that all values associated with masculinity, patriarchy, and violence, all of which were always conflated, would be purged (Gerhard, 186). Sex as it had been known was already redefined as death for some of us before AIDS ended phase one of the sexual revolution.[9]

Goth first appeared to me as a mode of being sexually undead—and loving it. Goths seemed mournful, as anyone might well be who has been kicked out of what the American majority recognizes as decent and proper existence, but not overly conflicted about their outcast status. Instead, as I will discuss in chapter 1, which focuses on Goth's engagement with abstinence education, they accepted that sex involves desires whose satisfaction, even within fully consensual circumstances, can cause physical or emotional harm to oneself and others. They accepted that people are imperfect and the world is dangerous. But in the face of those dangers, they chose to be visibly different in ways that challenge sexual and gender norms. And they accepted the consequences of that visibility. Moreover, their enactments of mournfulness were rarely truly lugubrious. Rather, as Baddeley argues, "'[c]amp' is an important concept to anyone who wishes to understand the Gothic aesthetic" (11). And it is most fully demonstrated through Goths' tendency to make "a mockery of conventional wisdom," especially about sexual morality and gendered identity (12). Therefore it seemed to me time for theorists of gender and sexuality within academe to choose to see Goth, and not leave analysis of this revolutionary subculture to the popular media.

After the Columbine massacre, many journalistic articles and a number of books appeared warning parents and educators about Goth. A guidebook for parents and teachers produced by the Religious Right, *Unglued & Tattooed: How to Save Your Teen from Raves, Ritalin, Goth, Body Carving, GHB, Sex, and 12 Other Emerging Threats*, by Sara Trollinger and Mike Yorkey (2001), is a particularly depressing example. Various newspaper articles and many more websites offered a sort of educative counter-attack. Kerry Acker's 2000 contribution to the Need to Know Library series, *Everything You Need to Know about the Goth Scene*, is representative of the most unthreatening, if not the most accurate, of these reassuring texts. But enough damage had been done to the image of Goth that it faded from its previous commercial prominence. If it had ever been a subculture we might have felt justified in studying seriously, it seemed to be one no longer. One of the shocks attendant upon the release of Michael Moore's film *Bowling for Columbine* (2002) is that the film never mentions Goth. Although, as I will discuss in chapter 4, other films that might have been expected to reference Goth, such as *Boys Don't Cry*, have in effect erased it from the cultural record, Goth's omission from Moore's film on the school shootings is simply amazing. This is one of the strongest indications that, only three years after the tragic event, Goth was already becoming an irrelevant historical blip even to those who care about the future, the kind of short-lived craze that ultimately tells us little beyond what we already know: young people follow fads, fads are appropriated by entertainment corporations, and then the young move on.

Those who hold this attitude cannot be characterized as merely dismissing what they cannot understand. That Goth cultures waned post-Columbine, swirling down the popular cultural drain so fast it was hard to get more than a glimpse of them, could not have been more dramatically illustrated than it was by the lack of any mention of this once powerful youth culture in the *Village Voice* 2001 "Back to School: Guide to New York." Subsequent *Voice* "Guides" continued to leave Goth out of their reports on local music-centered youth cultures, and the Goth category once prevalent in most music listings in the alternative press has similarly disappeared.

In the period from 1995 to 1998, as I talked with almost two hundred young people who self-identified as members of alternative music communities for my book on changes in concepts of sexuality and gender, *New Millennial Sexstyles*, not one single young person who appeared to me to be a Goth corrected my impression of his or her identity. Instead, many excitedly explained to me what it meant to them to live the Goth lifestyle. When, in 2000, I returned to speak to more young people, this time specifically looking for Goths, very few with whom I initiated conversation self-identified as Goth, although many confessed that others perceived them to be Goths. A succinct explanation for this change is provided by Sue Widdicombe and Robin Wooffitt's Foucauldian assertion that because "category ascriptions are . . . a form of social control," when "respondents resist the relevance of a subcultural categorization" they are "resisting the potential applicability of culturally available knowledge" to themselves (210).[10] And, like Widdicombe and Wooffitt, I think such refusal to identify with a group to which the respondent's style strongly suggests affiliation is especially likely when the group in question is generally associated with violence (104–106).

Evidence that Goth still exists underground, and comes up to the surface for air more than occasionally, is provided by several recent publications, including Mick Mercer's impressive *21st Century Goth*, a hefty two-hundred-and-fifty-six-page guide to Goth websites. And, of course, Goths also exist as figures to mock, as is evidenced by the bobbing-head Goth girl doll, "Raven," and the "Emily" line of products (t-shirts, bags, address books) sold in would-be hip boutiques. But, as most websites that provide guides for Goth nights, clubs, shops, and activities reflect, the number of businesses serving Goths steadily dwindles.

Many such guides are posted on www.sfgoth.com, a website for online Goths in San Francisco, my hometown. During an excursion to check out the local Goth scene in July of 2001, I discovered that the "Dead Club Listing," a record of recently defunct Goth clubs (http://www.sfgoth.com/black/index.html), extensive as it was, did not fully reflect the rapidity with which the terrain of San Francisco Bay Area Goth was shrinking. For instance, Gargoyle on Haight Street, still a Goth emporium when the listing was updated, shortly before my trip, had shrunk to a bead store, as my Goth guide for the day, Carrie, discovered to her horror. Several places listed in a guidebook created for the 1997 Goth Convergence and updated three months prior to my trip had already closed. No Goths were visible on Market Street, San Francisco's main artery for foot traffic, in the afternoon or evening. Goths came out only at night and only in the SoMa (South of Market) area, a former warehouse district that was defined by S/M clubs and related businesses in the seventies and then gentrified in the eighties to serve the art gallery scene. Berkeley had very few recognizable Goths, despite the huge record emporiums, Rasputin's and Amoeba, both featuring Goth/Industrial sections. The *San Francisco Bay Guardian* made no mention of Goth, except in an advertisement for Rasputin's whose description of the CD *Metal Dreams Volume 3*, by "various artists," read, "*Metal Dreams Volume 3* is a stellar collection of classic heavy metal power ballads that span several sub-genres of metal including Goth, Power, Thrash, Electronica, and Progressive metal." How deeply into the darkness Goths had fallen. And by 2003, when I began the final draft of this book, the situation had deteriorated further. Yet in the beginning of 2004, apparently due to the commercial success of the Goth band

Evanescence, Goth once again began to rise. Goths reappeared about town in the light of day.

Through it all, I remain intrigued by Goth. One reason for my persistent interest in Goth is Goth's own persistence, although sometimes in rather vitiated form, in spite of all that has been done officially to suppress it. While moral panics, according to Sarah Thornton and many subsequent theorists of popular culture, often do seem to encourage youth interest in demonized subcultures,[11] Goth's current resurgence cannot be explained as a delayed reaction to post-Columbine negative press, which might be assumed to have ultimately rendered Goth more appealing to especially rebellious youth. Goth is far older than the cresting of its dark wave in the 1990s has led many to believe, as I shall demonstrate in chapter 2 through discussion of Gothicism in the early novels of Angela Carter. The one aspect of Goth that remains consistent is its relation to the dominant culture, always defiant, always reflecting back darkly, always making possible new ways of seeing.

II. A Little Night Music, or What Exactly Is Goth?

> "I am so impure."
>
> —Nine Inch Nails, "Reptile"

> "Because of AIDS, we couldn't think about sex without
> thinking about death, so we had to eroticize death."
>
> —Anonymous female, age 36 (2000)

It is hard to distinguish early manifestations of Goth as a particular style, since everything from The Cramps' clownish fusion of Punk and horror to Kiss's stadium shock rock could retrospectively be described as Goth by some fans. For example, in Julien Temple's 2000 documentary on The Sex Pistols, *The Filth and the Fury*, John (Johnny Rotten) Lydon describes the style of Sid Vicious when he joined the band as Goth. To many Gen-Xers and also rock historians, amateur and professional, Goth began in the 1970s with bands like Joy Division representing the "art" side and theatrical acts like Alice Cooper's representing the "pop" side. As Baddeley points out, "certain sounds would become recognizable trademarks [of Goth rock] in the 1980s—deep, icy vocals, tribal beats, mesmeric melodies—but the defining characteristics would remain thematic or visual rather than musical, and a bewildering range of bands who evoked bizarre, melancholy or macabre moods would find themselves dubbed 'Goth'" (202).[12] So it may make more sense for anyone not deeply invested in identifying as Goth to think of it as a style, if we can take "style" to mean a manner of becoming, in the sense Deleuze uses the word. Deleuze opposes "becoming" to "being," the latter signifying fixed identity, the former shifting identifications. He asserts that style is the mode through which identities are expressed, because "there is no subject, there are only collective assemblages of enunciation" (Deleuze and Guattari, *Kafka*, 18). What he calls minoritarian style—in other words, that which departs from the sign systems expressive of the majority's consensus—is the style that inhabits becoming. Goth style is minoritarian.

My most succinct definition of Goth style is, perhaps inevitably, derived from my own counterculture past. Thinking of what happens when one first begins to feel Goth brings to mind for me the t-shirts and greeting cards that suddenly appeared in San Francisco gift stores in the late seventies decorated with a cartoon of a winking woman saying things like "Damn! I forgot to get married and have children." Whereas back in the day my generation hoped to die before we got old, my own attraction to Goth as a mode of becoming rather than simply an object of study began with the sudden recognition that, as far as American mainstream culture was concerned, I, along with all the other counterculture radicals, was already—damn!—dead. "We are the ones who in today's conformist moral order are bygone" (Deleuze, *Desert Islands*, 79). To me, then, Goths are people who try to do something interesting, and usually something sexually exciting, with that sense of being dead to the straight world. In the sense that Goth appropriates the mainstream's designation of everything that does not fit into its systems of signification as dead or deathly, Goth cultures are death cults extraordinaire.

Also instructive about "the famous Gothic fascination with death" is the participant's account furnished by Henry Jenkins as part of his courageous post-Columbine defense of Goth to the U.S. Congress. He quotes an informant:

> Most people don't realize that, when goths talk or obsess over the topic of death, they're talking about their own final experience on Earth. The Gothic attitude is that death is our last ride, and we only get one chance at it. It is to be revered and a natural part of being human, not feared and hidden from view. The Gothic focus on death has nothing to do with murder or the experience of others.

She goes on to discuss her mother's relief at finding that for her daughter and her daughter's friends Goth identification did not seem to include S/M activity. Still she does say that, in her experience, Goths are "into exploring their own pain" psychically, finding it "much nobler to glory in your own pain than to go out and harm other people because you're not happy." Here, then, is yet another permutation of masochistic practice combined with high valuation of death within Goth cultures.

I speak of Goth cultures in the plural because determining whether or not a person, art product, commodity, or subcultural group should be considered Goth is not easy. Definitions of Goth from those outside Goth cultures, of any sort, are fairly straightforward, although ultimately so general as to be confusing. To outsiders Goths are people, usually young, who dress in black clothing and may also dye their hair black. They listen to depressing, slow, and discordant music with unpleasant lyrics, read horror fiction, and watch films about vampires. Since Columbine, non-Goths are likely to suspect anyone under thirty who wears a dark trench coat of being a (potentially murderous) Goth.

People who are understood by others to be Goths can be even more confusing. Most serious musicians, as opposed to poseurs attempting to ride the wave of a trend, who have been called Goths have resisted the label, preferring to be considered "dark." The same is now increasingly true of individuals whose appearance suggests Goth affiliation of some sort. Obviously most American young people who might have been content to be labeled Goth prior to the Columbine disaster are more wary of that designation now that such a declaration of identity is likely to mean expulsion from school and a subsequent life under the eye of local law enforcement. And it does not help the intermittently undertaken projects to rehabilitate Goth's image that S/M themes are ubiquitous in the work of bands considered Goth or Goth forerunners, because mainstream culture continues to associate S/M with psychopathology and fascism.

For psychoanalytic theory and the actual practice of psychiatry and psychology, S/M remains problematic. All but the most progressive therapists place it either on or over the border of what they label pathology. In this case, as in all others concerning the diagnosis and interpretation of human desires, I agree with Deleuze, as he writes with Claire Parnet in *Dialogues II*, that "[t]here is no blossoming of desire, wherever it happens—in an unremarkable family or a local school—which does not call established structures into question. Desire is revolutionary because it always wants more connections and assemblages. But psychoanalysis cuts off and beats down all connections, all assemblages—it hates desire, it hates politics" (78–79). Like Foucault, as well as Deleuze and Guattari, I see psychology as the great overcoder of sexual feeling, always obscuring our bodies and pleasures beneath narratives of illness. To decode Goth in a different mode, I turn to Deleuze and Guattari.

III. Styling a Politics of New Pleasures: Deleuzian Goth

At this point it seems important to say a bit about my methodology in undertaking this study of Goth, especially because, currently, one of the greatest divisions among scholars of youth and subcultures seems to be between, on the one hand, those who apply theory to the cultures without much regard for what participants in the cultures have to say about themselves, and, on the other, participant-observers whose interpretations begin with serious and respectful attention to the statements of those in the scene. As David Muggleton argues, from the latter position, "[t]oo often 'big theories' have been relied upon (Marxism, the sociology of deviance, semiotics, etc.), which picture those involved in subcultures as passive pawns of history, their lives shaped by grand narratives beyond their control" (3). Muggleton finds hopeful the development of "a new cohort of academic taste-makers for whom the deficiencies of established theories are likely to be thrown into sharp relief by their own personal experiences as, say, punks or clubbers" (4). I concur that this new development is likely to put an end to the sort of attitude—which Muggleton and I both regard with horror—expressed at the conclusion of Dick Hebdige's seminal study, *Subculture: The Meaning of Style,* by his infamous remark that "[i]t is highly unlikely . . . that the members of any of the subcultures described in this book would recognize themselves reflected here" (139). I also applaud Muggleton's determination to base his interpretations of subcultures on "the subjectively held meanings, values and beliefs of the subculturists themselves" (10). Still, I disagree with Muggleton by believing that there is no intrinsic conflict between applying so-called high theory to subcultural artifacts as a means of understanding subcultures and attending respectfully to the ways participants in those cultures define themselves.

For those of us to whom high theory is important primarily because it helps us articulate our own experiences of the world, there is no conflict between theorizing and truly taking in what people have to say about their lives. Since, as I discuss extensively throughout *New Millennial Sexstyles,* I now have a large number of young friends involved in the Goth subculture, I circulated sections of this book among them and was pleased to find that the sections that they liked most and found most accurately representative of their experience were nearly always those in which I applied Deleuzian theory to Goth style.[13] As numerous philosophers and critical theorists whose work I will discuss in the course of this study believe, Foucault, Deleuze, and Guattari do not disregard agency, and to read them as if they did, as the New Historicists often have done, goes against the purpose of their intentionally revolutionary texts.

Moreover, Muggleton overestimates the importance of his informants' assertions of an individuality that they see as precluding identification within a socially constructed cultural category, such as Punk or Goth. How different his results would have been had he set out, as I did, to talk to young people who began the conversation by asserting their identification with a specific subcultural group, and then gone on to analyze these assertions using theories of identity construction as his interpretive framework.[14] Muggleton seems

to me at his analytical best when he does apply theory: for instance, drawing on sociological theories of liminality to explain the "rejection of sharply
drawn boundaries and resistance towards [the] restriction" of a label by youthful participants in subcultures (73). I think he is right to attribute to the "in-
herently liminal tendencies [of subcultures] what would otherwise remain
somewhat contradictory statements of the kind made by another informant,
Paula—'even then, though, I didn't like people calling me a goth, even though
I was'" (73). Goth is filled with contradictions and we need to apply theory to
understand, and draw conclusions from, the information provided by participants. I believe that Muggleton would have done well to think about what
the "aesthetic-Romantic cultural traits . . . which find their expression in flux,
plurality, and heterogeneity," and which he sees as characteristic of "style
subcultures such as punk, goth, skinhead, hippy, etc." (5), might have to do
with Deleuze's theorization of becoming versus being. Deleuze's discussion,
in *Difference and Repetition*, of the superiority of "individuation" to "subjectivity" as a concept for understanding human identity seems especially relevant (331). Deleuze and Guattari's philosophy is ideally suited to analyzing
the subculture that calls itself Goth.

Foucault's preface and Mark Seem's introduction to Deleuze and Guattari's *Anti-Oedipus* provide a useful starting point for examining why Deleuze
and Guattari are so crucial to understanding Goth and to explaining how the
very element of Goth that causes many serious scholars to dismiss it as an
ultimately meaningless youth culture—its emphasis on style—actually functions to deterritorialize the pervasive depression of contemporary youth in
the politically dominant industrialized countries, thus creating the sort of
new bodily pleasures that Deleuze and Guattari, as well as Foucault, see as
central to the transformative askesis that enables us to think "otherwise," and
ultimately to enact resistance to the dominant powers of our society, which
function to structure our lives in ways beneficial to the State. To avoid a
lengthy exegesis of their complex philosophy and keep this introduction to
the point, I am limiting citation from Deleuze and Guattari here almost entirely to their very pertinent text *Nomadology*, which also appears as a section
of *A Thousand Plateaus*. Deleuze and Guattari see nomads as existing outside the organization (territorialization) of matter into units of meaning that
constitutes the official State. The quintessential figures of resistance to the
territorialization inscribed on human bodies and the holistic body of Earth
by Imperial forces, they are, thus, the ultimate anti-fascists.

In his preface to the work, Foucault sums up *Anti-Oedipus*'s intention in
a way that seems to me applicable to all Deleuze's writings with Guattari:
"the major enemy, the strategic adversary is fascism . . . and not only historical fascism . . . but also the fascism that causes us to love power, to desire the

very thing that dominates and exploits us. . . . one might say that *Anti-Oedipus* is an *Introduction to the Non-Fascist Life*" (xiii). Mark Seem's introduction elaborates on this theme, explaining that to Deleuze and Guattari, "[d]epression and Oedipus are agencies of the State, agencies of paranoia, long before being delegated to the family. . . . Everyone has been oedipalized and neuroticized at home, at school, at work. Everyone wants to be a fascist" (xx). He comes to this conclusion because, within the regime of discipline (that is, the systematic internalization of prohibitions through surveillance and the medicalization of confession), we all learn "to desire our own repression" and that of others (xx). The hierarchical, fixed-gender Freudian family model has become the paradigm for human relations. And within this paradigm, as Sylvia Plath so brilliantly noted in her poem "Daddy," with its famous line "Every woman adores a fascist," power can be attained only by organizing desires in support of the phallus as transcendent signifier, that is, by supporting a system of oppression in which subjectivity is defined by lack, and being itself is defined by submission to the always unattainable ideal of definitively impenetrable masculine dominance.

Therefore, as Seem notes, "[t]he first task of the revolutionary [according to Deleuze and Guattari] is to learn from the psychotic how to shake off the Oedipal yoke and the effects of power, in order to initiate a radical politics of desire freed from all beliefs," releasing "forces that escape coding, scramble the codes, and flee in all directions: *orphans* (no daddy-mommy-me), *atheists* (no beliefs), and *nomads* (no habits, no territories)" (xxi, emphasis Seem's). In order for the political goals of *Anti-Oedipus* to be realized, Seem believes, we must understand that Deleuze and Guattari call "for a radical reversal of the relationship between individuals and tools or machines" and recognize "that such a reversal must be governed by a collective political process, and not by professionals and experts. The ultimate answer to neurotic dependencies on professionals is *mutual self-care*" (xxii, emphasis Seem's).

Perhaps one reason that both Seem and Foucault introduce *Anti-Oedipus* by emphasizing its anti-authoritarianism, and in specific its anti-fascism, is that Deleuze and Guattari, as admirers of the blood-knowledge philosophies of D. H. Lawrence, ardent believers in ending the reign of the intellect over the body, and enthusiastic commentators on the deterritorializing effects of masochistic practices, insistently raise the question of how to embrace darkness without going fascist—also a central question of Goth, as I will discuss shortly. As Deleuze and Guattari put it in *Nomadology*, directly after celebrating the "tribe-race" of "nomad thought" as a means of escaping identity construction dependent on the concept of "a universal subject within the horizon of an all-encompassing Being" and in service to an Imperial State, "Immediately, we clearly see the dangers, the profound ambiguities that in-here in this enterprise, as if each effort and each creation faced a possible infamy. For what can be done to prevent the theme of a race from turning into a racism, a dominant and all-encompassing fascism, or into a sect and a folklore, micro-fascisms?" (48).

Baddeley's description of the Gothic aesthetic informing contemporary Goth makes clear the affinity between this movement and the nomadic mode that Deleuze and Guattari find both so appealing and so dangerous:

> Gothic is sophisticated barbarism. It is a passion for life draped in the symbolism of death. It is a cynical love of sentiment. It is a marriage of extremes such as sex and death. It uses darkness to illuminate. It believes duty is vain, and vanity is a duty. It is the compulsion to do the wrong thing for the right reasons. It is a yearning for the black days of a past that never was. It denies orthodox reality and puts faith in the imaginary. It is the unholy, the uncanny, the unnatural. (Baddeley, 19)

Here the stylistic departure from rationalism promises relief from relentless binarity, even as it threatens, like fascism, to overwhelm the belief in human rights that arose from the Enlightenment.

Another motivation of Seem's and Foucault's emphasis on the anti-fascist purpose of Deleuze and Guattari's texts may be their need to counter the denigration of the pursuit of pleasure as apolitical that has become a constant feature of discourses of both the Left and the Right. Leftists in the United States and abroad regularly deplore the decadence of people who give a high priority to pleasure. Thus the Left casts hedonism as the contrastive opposite of political engagement. The Right places pleasure on the opposite side of the political dichotomy from duty and sees commitment to it as synonymous with a refusal to recognize that political responsibility must be properly exercised. Maybe this is why popular interpreters of the U.S. Constitution now seem confused by its reference to our right to pursue pleasure, placed as it is amidst rhetoric that remains revolutionary. Foucault and Seem labor to remind us that in articulating a politics of pleasure, Deleuze and Guattari are resisting fascism.

The first academic study of Goth, *Goth: Identity, Style, and Subculture,* also investigates the possibility of a politics of pleasure. Cultural studies professor and Birmingham Goth scene participant-observer Paul Hodkinson begins this book by describing ways that the participants in Goth subculture depart from the models of subcultural identity developed by the Birmingham school of cultural studies. He contends—accurately, I believe—that while Goth is a trans-global phenomenon and involves many aspects of performative identity construction, Goth, wherever it may be found, remains clearly recognizable as such (17–19). His most daring claim is that within Goth, style *is* substance, since for Goths "a set of shared tastes and values which is distinct from those of other groups and reasonably consistent, from one participant to the next, one place to the next, one year to the next" creates their subcultural identity and generates an inclusive and liberally tolerant community wherever Goths find themselves (30).

The primary values of Goths are expressed through visually perceptible aspects of personal style: dress, coiffure, jewelry, and tattoos and other body modifications. Goths are determined to face down death, as it were, and they achieve this almost entirely through the eroticization or even the simple valorization of appearances and objects associated with morbidity and decay: for instance, black lipstick and dull blue or gray nail polish. And as Hodkinson discusses, Goth's feminized androgyny is created through a "subcultural style" that obscures the usual markers of gender difference through adherence to such stylistic choices and through male cross-dressing (55). Hodkinson recognizes that consumption of goods does much to define Goths: "As well as tending to take precedence over place, gender, class and other structural foci for identity, the goth scene tend[s] to be its participants' most important leisure or consumer-related affiliation" (72–73), and "[t]o a significant extent, it [is] through ownership and use of consumer goods that goths [claim] their subcultural capital, differentiating themselves subtly from one another and more overtly from groupings and individuals outside the subculture" (132). Since he seems to believe that no culture that participates in networks of commerce can be deemed truly resistant, he cautions against reading the Goth subculture as one of resistance. However, he insists that the Goth scene has not been co-opted by corporate commercialism, nor has their movement been appropriated to serve the ends of what Deleuze and Guattari call the Imperial State.

In Hodkinson's view, it is Goth that appropriates capitalism for its participants. Craftsmanship is far more important to Goth commerce than marketing, as Goths have so far proven quite resistant to consumer goods not produced by artisans identified with their subculture. Deleuze and Guattari "define the artisan as he who is determined in such a way as to follow a flow of matter" (*Anti-Oedipus*, 100). That is, artisans do not impose a predefined order on things; instead, they respond to inherent flows. The predilection in Goth art for waves, arabesques, and shadings, and, in their wood and bone sculptures, for shapes clearly determined by the materials, speaks to this. And as Hodkinson demonstrates, the Goth marketplace creates and circulates goods for the most part independently of non-Goth means of distribution. Unlike the roles commonly played by consumers in the late-capitalist State, Goths' "independent creativity" and their "active appropriation" of consumer goods intended for other purposes than the ones they serve in the Goth subculture both work to construct an "assemblage of style" which strongly "emphasizes the important role for its participants themselves in the ongoing development of their shared style" (137).

This is particularly evident in the case of music, which remains a defining element of the Goth subculture. Vast networks of distribution for the musical productions of independent Goth groups, mix tapes of Goth music compiled by individual Goths, and CD compilations similarly made outside the regulations of the music industry brought the Goths Hodkinson studied together, serving as pretexts for events and a method of building community (142). As Deleuze and Guattari discuss, music is "on the side of the nomadic" in its resistance to structuring mechanisms of the State (*Nomadology*, 88). The ongoing internet music file-sharing revolution, which may yet bring down the entertainment industry's conglomerate monopolies, partakes of the nomadic attitude toward private property.

Like many before him, including Mick Mercer, Hodkinson finds the internet an indispensable "facilitating network" for the development of Goth identity (176). He remarks that "goth websites also gave individual participants the potential to involve themselves in the construction of their subculture" (178). For Goths their self-generated subculture governs all else: "There is little doubt that for Goths the most important activities were going out to events and socializing with other members of the subculture" (Hodkinson, 85). Goths are often physically nomadic, as almost all commentators on their cultures note. Hodkinson describes them as "likely to travel hundreds of miles" to visit other clubs and scenes related to their subculture (105). On the internet Goths locate community in commonality rather than in geographical proximity. Deleuze and Guattari's text *Nomadology* provides many illuminating ideas in relation to these Goth practices.

One might well begin by looking at Deleuze and Guattari's description of the Gothic aesthetic, as it was first exemplified by twelfth-century cathedrals, as a manifestation of the nomadic. I will quote this description at some length because this form of architecture is so highly valued by today's Goths that elements from it appear as a definitive markers of the subcultural sensibility in artifacts as diverse as Goth anime, such as *Vampire Hunter D*, in which even space ships tend to have Gothic cathedral form; Goth cinema, such as the films of Tim Burton; Goth novels, such as the works of Poppy Z. Brite and Patrick McGrath; and Goth web art.

> Ever farther, ever higher . . . But the difference is not simply quantitative, it marks a qualitative change: the static relation, form-matter, tends to fade into the background in favour of a dynamic relation, material-forces. It is the cutting of the stone that turns it into a material capable of holding and coordinating forces of thrust. . . . the vault is no longer a form, but the line of continuous variation of the stones. It is as if Gothic conquered a smooth space . . . " (*Nomadology*, 22–23)

This stretching out along lines of flight, infinite variation of elements without hierarchical interrelation, is characteristic of any Goth gathering, where authority, if it has any meaning at all, is imagined only as something to resist. Deleuzian lines of flight are paths toward new and transformative connection; they make becoming, rather than fixed being, possible. That the largest Goth gathering of each year is called the Goth Convergence is not incidental. As Deleuze and Guattari note, "Packs, bands, are groups of the rhizomic type, as opposed to the arborescent type which centers around organs of power" (13). This distinction is extremely important in that within Deleuzian theory the tree structure is the basis of the Imperial State and all fixed forms. Rhizomatic connections are those that enable nonhierarchic relation. The rhizome is the precondition of the nomadic. Goth movement, on the dance floor or through larger spaces, is a drifting together, then apart. Deleuze and Guattari say, "the nomadic trajectory . . . distributes people . . . in an open space, one that is indefinite and noncommunicating. . . . The nomad distributes himself in a smooth space, he occupies, inhabits, holds that space; that is his territorial principle" (50–51). Thus also the Goth, which is presumably why Hodkinson chose to place at the center of his study the annual migration of English, American, and European Goths to the Whitby Gothic Weekend.

One of the most charming aspects of Hodkinson's book is its descriptions of "Gothing up," or dressing for such events as a group, accompanied by photos of the results—which, as he claims, are distinctive in each separate Goth's case and yet also convey a clear sense of shared identification. But since everyone is not as easily charmed as I am by nonconformity, I recognize, as does Hodkinson, that the look of Goth is largely responsible for the hostile criticism it has received. Even more troubling to Goth's academic fans, including Hodkinson and myself, is the association of such stylings with the culturally ephemeral, fads and crazes, rather than subcultural formations to be taken seriously. Here style is substance, Hodkinson argues; however, his argument seems to me weakened by his insistence, throughout the study, that "we should not treat the goth style, or any particular elements of it, as symbolic of any particular structural, psychological or political circumstances or goals" (61). This statement, unusual in the context of the numerous published and web-posted political and philosophical writings by self-described Goths, could be accounted for by the general cautiousness of his approach to theories of subcultural resistance to hegemony.

Hodkinson's reluctance to attribute resistance to Goth seems rooted in the term's specialized (Marxian) meaning within Centre for Contemporary Cultural Studies (CCCS) scholarship on "spectacular cultures." As described in Hebdige's *Subculture*, and in many subsequent works by CCCS scholars, subcultural styles can and should be read as spectacles of resistance to the dominant culture. Hebdige argues that "[s]tyle in subculture is . . . pregnant with significance [because] its transformations go 'against nature,' interrupting the process of 'normalization.' As such, they are gestures, movements toward a speech which offends the 'silent majority,' which challenges the principle of unity and cohesion, which contradicts the myth of consensus" (18). Hodkinson and Muggleton both take this to mean that Hebdige believes the styles function as signs unconsciously displayed by participants who can resist only subconsciously. Muggleton argues that "valid" analysis of subcultures must be based on compatibility between the theory or theories used as framework and "the common-sense reality of social actors," which latter he posits as identical to their statements about themselves and their scene (11). But must reading a spectacle of resistance in the cultural artifacts through which style is expressed necessarily mean one discounts the ways that participants in a subculture describe their motives for participation? Yes, if one agrees with Muggleton, as Hodkinson seems to do, that "it is individuality that is the basis of subcultural affiliation," and that participants' claims to individuality mean that subcultures are "apolitical forms rather than gestures of resistance" (147–48).

Muggleton somewhat contradicts his own position as one who transmits the self-definition of the subculturists when he decides to reject all the criteria for assessing Punk authenticity offered by the Punks he interviews because he considers that to participate in their attempt to construct an ideal standard of Punk would "privilege the views of only certain members whose lifestyle coincides with the analysis's conception of what 'core' resistance should be" (153). True enough, but in the absence of any agreed-upon definition of Punk authenticity, one is left with nothing but the assertions of individuality that have such weight for him. Punk becomes by default an apolitical movement.

Feminist theorists, myself included, have long been familiar with such dilemmas, as the popularization of feminist ideas has resulted in such oddities as women who oppose reproductive freedom and advocate female subordination to males within marriage claiming that they are feminists, generally because they want a social benefit associated with feminism, such as protection from workplace sexual harassment. We, however, have addressed these definitional struggles differently than Muggleton and Hodkinson do, insisting that feminism is appropriately defined by the views of the majority of feminists who have made their views known through political work explicitly identified as feminist by its participants, including all manner of publication. My approach to Goth is similar. I take seriously the statements of Goths whose definitions of their subculture depart from those of the majority of self-identified Goths, as represented by the young people with whom I have spoken for this project and those who express their views in print and on the internet. But I do privilege this majority. Since the majority describe themselves as resistant to the dominant culture, as I shall discuss in the pages that follow, I deem Goth a resistant subculture. While my readings of Goth will most often here be accomplished through readings of texts (including music and film), my attention to them was always directed and my interpretation of them guided by information provided in the direct statements of Goths with whom I spoke or corresponded personally or whose writings are available on the World Wide Web. Consequently I feel that while my approach does have many affinities with Hebdige's, my conclusions do not ignore or belittle the majority of actual Goths' constructions of their subculture(s).

My strongest area of disagreement with Hodkinson concerns his repeated claims that the fetish wear popular among Goths does not necessarily indicate that his fellow Goths have any sexual inclinations that might be deemed deviant, although such assertions are invariably accompanied by his disclosure of the "transgression of boundaries of gender and sexuality" for which Goths are infamous (197). A few Goths with whom I have spoken in recent years have made the same claims as Hodkinson. If Goth boys wear skirts and fishnet stockings, if they paint their nails and eyelids, they do not do so as transvestites or to suggest feminine identification but merely because this is more comfortable and attractive to them than conventional male attire. They say that the comfort and utility of this style is so great that they maintain it despite vicious attacks from unofficial gender police who misunderstand.

I remain unconvinced that fetish styles are adopted merely for comfort, not only because I never heard such talk from Goths prior to the post-Columbine moral panic in which they were all labeled dangerous deviants, but also because Goth seems to me, as it does to many Goths, including Jenkins's informant, to have a history that predates its official naming and that roots it in generations of rebellions against sexual norming. Mick Mercer's guides to Goth on the web include pages of references to Goth-oriented S/M and fetish societies, 'zines, and discussion groups. The vast majority of Goths with whom I spoke about their fetish wear expressed interest in S/M or involvement in its practice. Others, like Jenkins's informant, spoke of the style's symbolic representation of an enjoyment of their own pain (also known as masochism) that they expressed through solitary activities. That Hodkinson's informants most often told him the opposite is something for which I cannot account.

I can only assert that my conclusions about the relation of S/M to Goth, just like Hodkinson's, are the result of observation of Goths interacting in social scenes and of conversations with individuals who identified themselves to me as Goths. When I asked Goths of my acquaintance what they thought of the way Hodkinson's assertion about the significance of their attire contradicted their own, their most frequent explanation was that they themselves would deny that their garb had sexual connotations if they were asked about it in an interview, rather than in casual conversation with a friend. Some also admonished me to be aware that since Hodkinson was already self-identified as a Goth, he would naturally avoid attributing to the majority of Goths any sort of perversity that not all might share or wish to make public. This latter idea makes sense to me as an explanation of how Hodkinson can make the apparently contradictory claims that Goths show tolerance of marginalized sexualities but do not present themselves as having such sexualities. (Is their tolerance purely abstract? Are they open to putative perversity among Goths, although most never encounter any?)

My own reading of Goth, generated more safely from my position on its margins because of my less Gothic appearance, takes into account the symbolic messages conveyed by what Hodkinson rightly calls its essential "dark twisted" style (36). Goth emerged as a music style with a name at the end of the 1970s (most critics say with the release of Bauhaus's "Bela Lugosi's Dead," 1979), at the same time as the young in Western culture entered an era of previously unprecedented despair. The failure of social welfare programs, the return of the conservative political agenda in the world's most powerful nations, the explosion of homelessness and extreme poverty among women and children, the economic shifts that have eroded the middle class and polarized nations into the corporate wealthy against the impoverished and disenfranchised, the AIDS pandemic, the public backlash against sexual freedom, and the near collapse of the natural environment (including the onset of global warming and the disintegration of the ozone layer) seem to me factors that probably contributed to what the American Psychiatric Association has labeled an epidemic of teen depression, too often resulting in suicide.[15] Not only is Goth's darkness explicable to a great degree as a result of the situation of youth in these dark days, it seems an answer. Through its visual style, Goth responds to the dominant discourses of a culture that is in the process of failing its most vulnerable members. Richard Davenport-Hines gives this condensed history:

> Punk had followed the decade of love with the sounds of, clothes and gestures of destructive fury; but Goths sought a different sort of excess, luxuriating in death, mystery and desolation. They found both elation and shame in reducing violence, extremism, atrocities and death to aesthetic images. Their elders' sense of purpose seemed to them purposeless. Their black clothes and unnaturally pallid skin were influenced by the dawning of cybernetics. Their robotic allegiances were neither to the promotional hype of the information age nor to the omnipotence of Schwarzenegger as the Terminator, but to the old premonitions, traceable back to *The Golem*, Frankenstein's monster and the drones of *Metropolis*, that machines are neither invulnerable nor infallible. (365–66)

Goth provides a valuable retreat for young people who cannot avoid despair but do not want to give up on pleasure. As Jenkins's informant puts it, Goth exists because "[p]eople want a safe space to explore the more depressing aspects of the world they live in. They don't want to feel guilty for not being happy all the time, they don't want to be told to get on Prozac, and they don't want to force themselves to put on masks for the benefit of the people around them." In place of the denial of the future that characterizes mainstream American life, Goth offers a very special kind of masochistic delight in knowing the worst, as I shall discuss at length in the pages that follow, and shall focus on in chapter 5.

What is valuable about Goth for the rest of us is suggested by this comment by Deleuze on how Foucauldian historiography helps us think otherwise than in the Imperial mode: "It is because the articulable has primacy that the visible contests it with its own form, which allows itself to be determined without being reduced. . . . [T]he primacy of the statement will be valuable only in this way, that it brings itself to bear on something irreducible" (*Foucault*, 50). One might also productively look to Deleuze and Guattari's *What Is Philosophy?*: "We are not in the world, we become the world by contemplating it. Everything is vision, becoming" (169). The look of Goth, its style-as-substance, can thus be understood as a potentially very powerful force of resistance, a way of generating affects that can stand against State institutions of control and the discourses of power they authorize. Goth cannot *tell* us how to live both darkly and against fascism, but it can *show* us.

I.◆

PERILS FOR THE PURE
Goth Cultures and Abstinence Programs

In an epilogue to his history of Gothic rock and roll music and cultures, *The Dark Reign of Gothic Rock*, Dave Thompson speculates that because the 1990s second wave of Goth began in America, it has been characterized by a harsh, infuriated seriousness that the original movement lacked (242). Thompson seems bemused by what he perceives as an American tendency to treat rock and roll as a form of revolution. Why are American teens so humorlessly angry? What are they angry about? Donna Gaines is more illuminating on this topic. Throughout her classic study of 1980s heavy metal fans, *Teenage Wasteland*, Gaines insists that music cultures function as a kind of religion for young people who are denied realistic preparation for the adult world and instead are subjected to "custodial schooling" and "infantilizing rules and regulations" necessitated by society's failure to teach the young how to protect themselves (259). This is nowhere more evident than in the dominant culture's treatment of young people's sexuality, to which rock and roll cultures are an obvious reaction formation. Trapped within a culture that withholds from them (by design, as I will discuss) almost all useful information about sex, and thus doomed to err in great numbers, as the United State's appalling rate of unwanted pregnancies and venereal diseases among teens reflects, young people form radical countercultures around their musical tastes. And this makes sense because of the nature of music.

As Foucault wisely proclaimed, "One is not radical because one pronounces a few words; no, the essence of being radical is physical" ("Clarifications on the Question of Power," 191). Due to the physicality of human responses to music, the inescapability of feeling its strong rhythms in the body, rock music has become a stronghold of American physical resistance to conservative politics. At this point it seems necessary to stop briefly to address the usual cultural studies position, derived from the Frankfurt School, that this resistance is meaningless because all popular music will inevitably be commodified and thus fuel the very capitalist system it was meant to oppose.[1] Leaving aside Paul Hodkinson's argument, discussed in the introduction, that Goth music has always been primarily distributed through small independent networks controlled by Goths themselves, one can also recognize that even the most corporately controlled rock and roll still has a somatic existence outside the marketplace, where it enters the body's rhythms and creates feelings. Music gets inside of us. "Not only is rock music . . . an integral part of the life of many people, but it is a cultural initiator: to like rock, to like a certain kind of rock rather than another, is also a way of life, a manner of reacting; it is a whole set of tastes and attitudes," and thus the music "offers the possibility of a relation which is intense, strong, alive . . . through which the listener affirms himself" or herself (Foucault, "Contemporary Music and Its Public," 316). Rock and roll, with its long history of association with the rituals of youthful sexual initiation, gets inside the physical movements and postures we associate with freedom of sexual expression.

As anyone looking at a rock and roll performance of any type can easily see, part of the music's intensity comes from its self-conscious symbolism of eroticized rebellion. So the question should perhaps be not whether rock and roll is understood by its fans as rebellious, but whether it can be the vehicle for the overthrow of corporate capitalism and the system of bourgeois sexuality which serves as its foundation. To that question, I must answer that it has not yet succeeded in doing so, but this failure does not mean that we need pay no attention to the function of rock and roll as a technology of resistance for the young. Like Foucault's, "my ethic is . . . to be respectful when something singular arises, to be intransigent when power offends against the universal" ("Is It Useless to Revolt?" 134). And of those who revolt through their musical choices, I can only say, as he does of the criminals, "madmen," and political revolutionaries whose activities put them into opposition to the dominant powers,

> One does not have to be in solidarity with them. One does not have to maintain that these confused voices sound better than the others and express the ultimate truth. For there to be a sense in listening to them and in searching for what they want to say, it is sufficient to say that they exist and that they have against them so much, which is set up to silence them. ("Is It Useless to Revolt?" 133–34)

By focusing on Goth rock and roll cultures, I do not mean to imply that they stand out as the most radical node in the area of resistance to conservative normalization of youthful sexuality; however, Goth is an important object of study for many reasons, including the rapidity with which Goths have been demonized and forced underground at the end of the millennium.[2]

And it is a shame! Foucauldian sex radical that I am, the essence of Goth was expressed for me by the Revolting Cocks' 1993 parodic cover of Rod Stewart's imbecilic 1978 disco anthem, "Da Ya Think I'm Sexy?" Like many covers produced by alternative rockers in the early nineties, this song presents a pointed contrast to the original that suggests the depth of changes in attitudes about sex and love. As Ian Buchanan argues, such revisions within popular music are meaningful because they give "a voice to teenagers [and other subculturists] who, in most senses of the word do not otherwise have one." He sees this sort of revision of popular music as specifically Deleuzian in that they "use the voice it gives them to enunciate themselves differently and in so doing make habitable the objective conditions of their existence . . . set[ting] in motion a becoming-minor—or, what amounts to the same thing, a becoming-public of the otherwise 'private' individual—which as Deleuze and Guattari have said, is the initiation of a line of flight that is an escape" (185).

While this parodic song cannot, of course, be considered representative of all Goth music, it nonetheless helps define a particularly Goth form of deterritorialization. Because the cover is done in the Goth/Industrial mode, using electronic equipment to distort and reassemble samples, as well as to shape the instrumentals and vocals supplied by the band into dissonant noise, it participates in the process Robert Walser rightly attributes to rap: it critiques the values and assumptions of a past musical culture while simultaneously articulating its own, on the level of sound itself (294, 303). Sampling, in particular, literally brings back to life dead youth cultures, and sampling within Goth rock tends to then subject the resurrected sounds to a dissection meant to reveal traces of the sickness these corpse-songs once carried.

Stewart's song, through a narrative of a one-night stand that works out so well that one can assume the pair will continue as lovers, combines an accurate enough portrayal of meat-market discotheque folkways with sugary romance. In fact the song's subtitle is "Sugar, Sugar." Gender stereotypes define the behavior of the two lovers, who are heterosexual, despite disco's association with gay cultures. The girl is appropriately passive: "She sits alone waiting for suggestions." When the man propositions her, she replies with a girlish request for "a dime so I can call my mother." Even the song's descriptions of their bodily responses conform to images of innocent female weakness and passionate male strength: "her heart is gently pounding," while "[h]is heart's beating like a drum." The long, hook-rich refrain exemplifies the repetitive beats of that especially unimaginative and formulaic disco music aimed at the segment of the heterosexual bourgeoisie who, at the time of the song's release, had belatedly decided to experiment with sex with strangers, but generally only as a means of seeking marital partners.

The Revolting Cocks give this insipid song the send-up it deserves in a cover version filled with ominous Industrial noise, a hint of seemingly terrified shrieks following the line "Relax baby now we are alone," and hilarious substitutions for the stupidest lyrics, like "gimme a buck so I can buy a rubber." Guest vocalist Trent Reznor's alternately leering and panting vocals and his sardonic phrasings twist the song's original mood into something dark and strange. But the heart of the cover's darkness can be found in its suggestions of the changes in the physical circumstances of casual sexuality in the eleven years between Stewart's disco days and this song's release.

Today a young person bent on casual sex is more likely to be preoccupied with getting a condom than with calling home to tell lies to a concerned parent, and her sex partner is more likely to be apologetic because he's "out of KY jelly" (as in the Revolting Cocks' chortling rendition) than because he has no milk or coffee, as in Stewart's original. But more importantly, the reason for these changes, the reason that flesh can no longer meet flesh in an innocent, naturalized atmosphere where "all the birds are singing," is that every sexual encounter now carries with it the threat of disease transmission. And this implicitly accounts for the transformation of the happy bopping of Stewart's song into the groaning, crashing, mechanistic dissonance of the Revolting Cocks'. Notable, too, is the later song's lack of moralizing and its refusal to offer any alternative to what it depicts as the near-death experience that bar pickups have become. In classic Goth style, it shows us today's horrific sexscape and then makes the very horror sexy and delightful.

Writing about dark music, in A Thousand Plateaus, Gilles Deleuze and Félix Guattari provide a description useful to understanding Goth music's treatment of sexuality:

> Music is never tragic, music is joy. But there are times when it necessarily gives us a taste for death; not so much happiness as dying happily, being extinguished. Not as a function of a death instinct it allegedly awakens in us, but of a dimension proper to its sound assemblage, to its sound machine, the moment that must be confronted, the moment the transversal turns into a line of abolition. Peace *and* exasperation. (299, emphasis Deleuze and Guattari's)

In an increasingly grim world where spontaneous pleasure—once a near universal youthful dream—seems to be receding ever more rapidly, Goth offers a truly alternative vision because of the courage with which it confronts our new reality principles. But all that may soon come to an end, now that Goth has become the most demonized counterculture of the new millennium. Although it may seem premature to start eulogizing a countercultural movement that is not dead yet, every Goth adores a good funeral and there is something quintessentially Goth about the very concept of decline. So in the spirit of Goth's celebration of dissolution and decay, this chapter begins the task of unearthing the hidden history of Goth's suppression, commemorating its continued resistance, and memorializing its gloriously dark empire.

Goth's darkest hour came on April 20, 1999, when Dylan Kleibold and Eric Harris opened fire on their classmates and teachers at Columbine High School in Littleton, Colorado, killing thirteen and wounding twenty-three. Despite the lack of any evidence that the shooters considered themselves Goths and repeated testimony from surviving classmates that the boys were excluded from the school's reputedly Goth clique, "the Trench Coat Mafia," the mainstream media quickly applied this label to them, and a frenzy of anti-Goth sentiment followed.[3] That relatively few adults outside rock and roll music subcultures had any conception of what Goth might mean to the young in no way impeded the wildfire spread of the idea that the nation's middle and high schools harbored darkly dressed murderous psychopaths called Goths who were likely to kill any other adolescents with whom they came in contact, but especially those whom conservative adults usually consider good kids: athletes and the exceptionally religious. Because of the extreme dangers Goth was deemed to pose, parents and teachers began a campaign to suppress anything associated with it among the young. Their success was reflected in the rapid shrinking and retreat underground of the hitherto enormous and diverse group of intertwined subcultures variously called Goth and Darkwave culture by those who identify with their music, literature, film, fashions, aesthetics, and philosophy.

Obviously those, like myself, who enjoy Goth culture see this as a tragedy. However, the decline of Goth's influence over the young is also to be lamented by those not under its sway, primarily because of the sophisticated and brave willingness to engage with difficult questions about sexuality and gender that Goth has represented since its beginnings. Some comments on Goth and Industrial music and art by Csaba Toth help elucidate how Goth attitudes inflect sexual styles: "They've dealt with their feelings of alienation from society by reinventing themselves as 'monsters'" (96); "They position themselves as reporters or tour guides to the macabre, rarely its victims" (96); "In [the music video] Gothic land of the end of the long cycle (of the post-industrial war boom), boundaries between the 'normal' and the pathologized 'other' collapse, and the 'normal' is often more dreadful than its 'unnatural' opposite" (88). Consequently it is fairly easy to understand why for many people sexual "queerness" of all kinds is associated with Goth, why clubs often combine Goth and fetish nights, and why many shops and online emporia that cater to Goths also sell supplies for bondage and S/M.

As many of the postings that appeared on www.gothic.net after Columbine tell us, a central principle of the Goth scene is open-mindedness, especially about gendered behaviors and characteristics and about sexualities condemned by the mainstream. A "Goth scout" who goes by the name of Voodoo lists some of the "general ideals the vast majority of Goths can agree on": "Most Goths prize individuality and consider tolerance and acceptance of others among the highest virtues." Preston A. Elder reports he has "found that the Goth scene tends not to discriminate on sexual preference." Lady Chaos testifies, "I would say without a doubt that I have yet to meet a more tolerant, open, and non-judgemental group in all my life." Michael S. Burg, a self-identified San Francisco Goth, writes that the subculture's "propensity is . . . towards a community that accepts [all interested young people] in spite of their differences. The only discrimination practiced by goths would be the occasional dress code required by various nightclub owners." Hodkinson emphasizes that Goth deliberately creates an "androgynous environment" which "loosen[s] the links between stylistic facets of gender and the fixed sexual categories of male and female" (55, 48). Although he ultimately judges Goth "transgression of boundaries of gender and sexuality" to be only "partial," Hodkinson finds the rejection of fixed, conventional gender identities one of the most significant features of this subculture (197). If the ordinary world of the young is now a place where they are driven to near madness, suicide, or murder by continual group and administrative policing of gender and sexuality, as numerous Goths and nerds posting in response to Katz's "Voices from the Hellmouth" claim, then the Goth subculture represents an area of escape from what many young people refer to as "norming."

Long before May third of 1999, when an ACLU press release reported that high school students had written in with "literally hundreds of complaints" about violation of their rights based on their Goth dress or demeanor,[4] the forces of normalization had begun an attack on young people who could not or would not conform to what could be called the new morality of the end of the twentieth century. To understand this conflict is to begin to understand Goth, the second wave of which began rising during the same time period.[5]

In Goth's first wave, in the late 1970s and early 1980s, styles that would come to define the movement were adopted by a relatively small number of people in a few major cities, most notably London. These early Goths were usually involved in rock and roll scenes informed by the Punk anti-pop ethic but might also be enthusiasts of Gothic horror literature, especially the works of H. P. Lovecraft and Edgar Allan Poe. Intellectualism was one of the salient characteristics of Goth's first wave, and it was expressed primarily through an emphasis on literature and high art. Dave Thompson credibly argues that "today's Goths, the black-clad, white-faced, ghoulishly grave individuals for whom Bela still remains undead, have little to do with the Gothic Rock that was created and christened in the first frightening years of Thatcher's Britain" (10). In place of the early Goth "ideal of 19th-century Romanticism and beauty," the American Goth wave that began with Trent Reznor's 1989 album *Pretty Hate Machine*'s fusion of Goth and Industrial gave severely disaffected young people a sound expressive of their rage and pain (243).

The second wave of Goth did not directly follow the discovery of AIDS in the early 1980s, as is often speculated, but instead paralleled the rise of abstinence education in the United States, which became dominant in the late 1980s, due to legislators' support of the Christian Right agenda.[6] By the mid-1990s there was hardly a town in America so tiny that it did not have at least a few teenagers with black-dyed hair and black-painted fingernails who referred to themselves as Goths. The association between this style and a refusal to get with the abstinence program is made in innumerable books, magazine stories, television shows, and films of the period. A speech by a character in bestseller writer Laura Lippman's 1999 murder mystery, *In Big Trouble*, nicely sums up the popular concept of Goth identity held by mainstream Americans: "She was part of this very fast crowd, and she did the whole Goth thing. Dyed her hair jet black, if you can imagine. Smoked pot, screwed around" (246). Should we be surprised to learn that this young woman becomes a murderer? Not if we keep in mind that abnormality and dangerousness seem synonymous to the majority of Americans.

In fact, the media's assumption that Dylan Kleibold and Eric Harris were Goths becomes more comprehensible in light of their friend and schoolmate Brooks Brown's discussion of the gender politics he experienced at Columbine High School. "Columbine's culture worshipped the athlete," and boys like himself, Kleibold, and Harris, who were not athletic, were constantly taunted as "faggots" (42–44, 47, 54, 163). The school administration, Brown convincingly claims, allowed the athletes and their followers to violently enforce a rigid code of gender norms, which the administration too seemed to implicitly support: "If a guy was acting in the Columbine drama program, he was immediately labeled 'a drama fag,'" and accordingly persecuted (61). Girls who refused or were unable to conform were labeled "sluts" and "lesbians" and those who favored the male outcasts in any way were attacked as "fag lover[s]" (69, 54). For the young victims as well as for the adults who allowed this situation to persist, music-centered cultures represented a potent form of resistance. Brown writes, "The Punk kids accepted me. They felt like outcasts just like I did, and they identified with music that attacked the establishment and the majority" (43). Although Brown condemns the solution his two friends sought, he recognizes that they acted out of a sense of hopelessness that must be addressed by adults in authority over the young (269). His continual narrative return to his view that, in the name of sexual normality, the Columbine school officials supported athleticism among boys and Fundamentalist Christianity among girls as the only acceptable expressions of identity for each gender, a system that made it impossible for boys like himself and his friends to get dates, suggests more than just the frustration of a young man whose efforts to attain a satisfying sex life are blocked. It also brings into the view of those of us not still in high school what the current intensified adult interest in defining sexual health for the young has wrought.

Because abstinence programs institutionalize the taming of youthful sexuality in the holy name of normality, I turn first to them. A quote from a male friend (age 21 in the year 2000), who wishes to remain anonymous, should indicate what high school Goths, of which he was one, have been up against: "I learned about sex and death at the same time. At school they taught me sex is a very beautiful thing that can kill you." As Janice M. Irvine reports, "At the turn of the twenty-first century, almost one in five students reported that their sex education teachers presented sex as 'something to fear and avoid'" (121). The cover of the April 2002 issue of *Cosmo Girl* illuminates the attitude this sort of instruction can give young women. It features youthful movie star Tara Reid with her breasts bulging under a very tight, thin, white t-shirt with the caption "BE SEXY It Doesn't Mean You Have to Have Sex." Apparently, for some young women, sex is no longer a much anticipated pleasure to be experienced as soon as one can, but instead has become a tedious chore to be avoided, if possible.[7]

Alas, this view often seems to be endorsed by feminism, at least if the sex in question is heterosex. Alice Echols's history *Daring to Be Bad: Radical Feminism in America, 1967–1975* makes the point that by 1989, the year of the book's publication, the ascendance of anti-pornography feminists to the position of media spokeswomen for the movement had erased from public consciousness all recollection of the sort of radical feminist support for sexual freedom evidenced in Shulamith Firestone's pronouncement that a goal of the movement was to make "all forms of sexuality [acceptable] and indulged" (211). Current understandings of what feminist radicalism means have not become any more uniform than they were when Echols's book appeared and immediately became embroiled in controversy, as Jane Gerhard's 2001 study of second-wave feminism, discussed in the introduction, makes clear.

Feminist sex radicals continue to be active in nonacademic publication. For instance, in her regular column in the *Village Voice*, "Pucker Up," sex educator Tristan Taormino discusses her adventures and discoveries as a sex-toy-loving lesbian who adores anal sex, group sex, and exhibitionism, is very attracted to other women and to the female-to-male transsexuals and transvestites who call themselves transmen, and occasionally enjoys a fling with a biological male. In *Bad Girl*, a documentary made in 2001 for Canadian public television but never aired due to the film's sexual explicitness, feminist filmmaker Marielle Nitoslawska interviews a wide variety of women making pornographic or erotic films and shows clips from their productions. But the landscape of feminist thought has not changed dramatically for many others since the twenty-five essays (most by well-known feminist activists) contained in the 1993 book *Making Violence Sexy: Feminist Views on Pornography* advanced the view, "There is no viable pro-pornography feminism" (Dworkin and MacKinnon, 90). That all of these people consider themselves radical feminists can be more than merely semantically confusing.

And what adds to the confusion is that feminist sex radicalism is grossly misunderstood by many academics, including a large number of feminist scholars. Lack of academic feminist interest in Goth should probably be attributed in part to this misunderstanding. The common association of the term "radical feminist" by both academe and the popular press with lesbian separatism, wholesale rejection of conventional feminine affect or appearance, and anti-pornography activism has resulted in confusion among feminists themselves about what radical feminism can mean to us. Since cultural critics recognized the emergence of a third wave of feminism early in the 1990s, numerous young feminist theorists have articulated responses to the "sex wars" that disrupted the previous generation's feminist solidarity.

A book which gives some indication of the magnitude of the current state of confusion over what sexual liberation for heterosexual women now means is Paula Kamen's *Her Way: Young Women Remake the Sexual Revolution*. The majority of Kamen's informants claim that the sexual revolution of the sixties and seventies failed women because it was "conducted entirely according to men's rules" (180). This assessment seems based on a binarism in which women are explicitly associated with a commitment to monogamy, a desire to achieve domestic security through home ownership, preference for oral or manual clitoral stimulation rather than penetration, and a need for the sort of emotional closeness attained through a life-partnership involving lots of communication about feelings. The values and goals attributed to men are mainly implied rather than directly stated, but seem to include desire for a variety of sexual partners and preference for penetrative intercourse. Even in well-researched studies like this one, female sexual freedom often seems to be envisioned somewhat contradictorily as the right to refuse sex or to prioritize emotional commitment. No wonder, then, that the wild zones in which Goths often wander seem to be treated as beneath the notice of many feminist theorists.

Kamen frequently asserts that feminism should provide women with choices and should honor the diversity of our tastes and desires. She praises pro-sex groups like the college campus organization Sluts against Rape, saying that their efforts to sexualize Take Back the Night marches "represent a culmination of the past forty years of sexual organizing for women's sexual control. . . . [They are] organized drives to expand their range of choices, including rejecting unwanted sex and exploring forbidden sexual desires" (189). Still, because of its journalistic focus on her interviewees' views rather than her own, the book relentlessly naturalizes a specific group of choices and desires.[8] Presumably this reflects the view of heterosexuality held by the majority of Kamen's female interviewees. Becoming familiar with potential sex partners through discussion of feelings, experiences, and preferences is referred to, throughout the book, as "a basic human gesture" (220), which, of course, conveys the message that anonymous sex is unnatural and even inhuman. Kamen's interviewees decry "male sexual norms" for making women uncomfortable about "the basic and rational human need of making an emotional connection with sex" and for influencing some women to believe that sexual activity can be compartmentalized and considered apart from "other realms of human experience" (234–35). They define "promiscuity" as "making one's self more available to more partners" (235), implying that women cannot exercise choice under such circumstances and so their "availability" can benefit only men. In contrast, they "define sexual freedom in women's terms" as the connection of sex "to the mind and the spirit" through bonding with a trusted partner who shares one's values, dreams, and life goals (234). The majority of Kamen's informants apparently do not even recognize open marriage or polyamory as valid choices for feminists, as is indicated by their use of the term "cheating" interchangeably with "extramarital sex" (122). Thus, although at one point Kamen states that "[j]ust as lesbians have increased women's awareness of how to have orgasms without the aid of intercourse, gay men also have transformed heterosexuality" (75–76), her interview subjects' concept of the beneficial influence of gay men seems limited to approval of the greater acceptance of anal sex among marital partners. Anything that keeps the husband and wife exclusively sexually focused on each other is lauded by Kamen's informants as consistent with feminism.

Still, some texts produced by women and gay men continue to articulate alternatives to this official feminism. In addition to Taormino's delightful columns, collected in *Down and Dirty Sex Secrets: The New and Naughty Guide to Being Great in Bed* (2003), and the similar sex advice Carol Queen offers in *Real Live Nude Girl: Chronicles of Sex-Positive Culture* (2002), among other books, we have a plethora of hip young advice-givers and raconteurs of sex, the most familiar and widely distributed of whom is probably Susie Bright. One thing all these young women seem to have in common with the very out-of-the-closet gay sex advisor Dan Savage is their support for sexual adventuring with strangers and casual acquaintances. The Donnas' Punk rock hit about touring, "Forty Boys in Forty Nights," joyfully celebrates such a life with such lines as "makin' out all night in Hollywood / you know I'd do 'em all if I could." This brought back for me the mid-seventies when some young feminist radicals like myself and my friends used to go to Castro Street shops and buy t-shirts inscribed "So Many Men, So Little Time." Far from representing surrender to a masculine mode of sexuality that meant abandoning our own desires, these borrowings from gay male culture seemed to us then, and still seem to me now, to be useful to feminism, providing models for coming out as a nondomestic, nontraditional heterosexual woman. Queer-friendly Goth culture provides similar modes of role modeling, so much so that it hardly seems accidental that in San Francisco, Folsom Street, the formerly gay male S/M district now also infamous through its association with Foucault's American adventures in new pleasures, has become the main Goth club area.

It has always been a mystery to me why the idea that Foucault had little to say to women has become a commonplace of academic feminist theory. In a 1983 *Salmagundi* interview about homosexual sexual ways, Foucault asserts, "where freedom of sexual choice is concerned one has to be absolutely intransigent" ("Sexual Choice, Sexual Act," 289). He then responds to the question of whether "radical feminists" are right in believing that male and female sexualities differ because men pursue sensation while women want "support, affection, [and] long-term commitment": "All I can do is explode with laughter" (291). Finally, he goes on to explain that the history of heterosexuality, as a system in which one person seduces while the other attempts to resist, has caused "all the energy and imagination" to be "channeled into courtship," while the homosexual relationship, because its clandestine existence necessitates brief and coded approaches, has traditionally been focused on "intensifying the act of sex itself" (298). In his view, as in my own, the sexual revolution has effected a change, giving heterosex the potential for a different sort of focus, so that not only the body but the mind and the emotions can be engaged intensely in new ways (301). As the father of queer theory, Foucault presented us with what David Halperin calls "the challenge" of creating "relationships that might offer strategies for enhancing pleasure and might enable us to escape the ready-made formulas already available to us—formulas which offer no alternative to purely sexual encounters, on the one hand, and the merging of identities in love, on the other" (81). Foucault, however, did not deny the value of the "purely sexual encounter."

Here is what Amber Hollibaugh has to say in the 1996 Dangerous Bedfellows collection of essays, *Policing Public Sex*, about whether lesbians should continue to pursue purely sexual encounters, even if they might result in HIV infection: "Will an individual be allowed to take life-threatening chances with his or her own life, or another's life, for desire? Is any sexuality, any form of desire worth that much? . . . What is worth living to experience is worth risking everything for" (335–36). Foucault claims that revolt against the dominant powers is never useless because "it is through revolt that subjectivity (not that of great men but that of whomever) introduces itself into history and gives it the breath of life" ("Is It Useless to Revolt?" 133).

What is perhaps the most powerful argument within academe for the positive influence of gay male sexual attitudes on feminist practice does not concern itself, except peripherally, with heterosexual women. However, not only does it take radical feminism as one of its central topics, the entire work exemplifies feminist sex radicalism. Ladelle McWhorter's 1999 *Bodies and Pleasures: Foucault and the Politics of Sexual Normalization* is an autobiographical, philosophical guide to transforming one's life through pleasure, as it is understood in Foucault's work on sexuality. The book seems aimed primarily at a lesbian feminist academic audience. McWhorter concentrates on how Foucauldian askesis remade her sense of bodily presence. Through "intense and reflective self-cultivation" she trained her body so that it was no longer one of "the normalized natural bodies" formed in relation to the "functional norms" of our culture, but instead a site of resistance to the discourses of homophobia that had previously filled her with impotent rage (189, 157). Following what she sees as the central idea of his philosophy, she tells us, "We can't just say no to sexual regimes; if we want to undermine the regimes of power and knowledge that oppress and threaten to dominate us, we have to cultivate a new way of life that stands counter to them and eventually that is just other to them" (190).

I certainly would not want to claim that this sort of resistance is easier for McWhorter than it would be for a heterosexual, or to imply that she is fortunate in belonging to a group so despised and persecuted that she is forced to choose either the living death of compliance or else the revolutionary "self-overcoming through aesthetic pleasures" (a chapter title) that her book promotes. However, as McWhorter herself points out, heterosexuals face different challenges because heterosexual desire's only defense in our sex-phobic culture is that it "contribute[s] to the perpetuation and strengthening of the species" (129). In other words, heterosex is tolerated because it is seen as useful to the group in the largest sense. Thus the heterosexual would-be sex radical must find, and make public, a relationship to the body and its pleasures that does not treat sexual experience as a means to a putatively greater end than pleasure. That this is now occurring in subcultures like Goth seems a hopeful sign. Once again, thanks to feminism's third wave, sex radical women are introducing their subjectivities into history, and maybe this time, because of the now frequently denigrated theory revolution that came before, their subjectivities will not be erased.

However, one cannot underestimate the accomplishments of forces of normalization in demonizing sexual activity of all kinds, nor the extent to which young people have assimilated these messages. A website called masturbateforpeace.com, which appeared at the beginning of the second war with Iraq, suggests the magnitude of changes in young people's concepts of sexuality in the last thirty years. It apparently no longer makes sense to advocate making love not war, since, as put into song by Jane's Addiction, "sex *is* violence."[9] The only safe and good sex seems to be the non-interpersonal kind. What more evidence do we need that the ideals of the sexual revolution are dead, or surviving only among those whose form of rebellion often includes identification with the undead? Goths still seem to recognize that this revolution was about more than just freedom to engage in formerly prohibited sexual activities and that, in fact, it encompassed (and made it possible to imagine) many other sorts of liberation, including opening up to resignification the constricting gender identities sexual conservatism imposes.

The sexual revolution of the nineteen-sixties and early seventies was one of the most widely influential social and cultural movements of the twentieth century. Because managing sexuality is a central aspect of all social organizations from pretechnological tribes to corporations, the sexual revolution's insistence on the importance of putting pleasure before duty profoundly altered the ways millions of people thought about their socially embedded identities and roles. Its challenges to traditional institutions such as marriage and family changed the world as we experience it. It is hard to imagine that the Gay Liberation Movement would have been as successful as it has been without the greater acceptance of diverse forms of sexual expression that the sexual revolution brought. And despite the majoritist feminist view that the movement failed women, its central premise that one's body is one's own to use as one chooses had obvious implications for the development of feminist discourses of choice, not just in reproductive matters, but also in relation to marriage and other forms of life-partnership. In fact, it is in the growing recognition that lesbians should have civil rights equal to those of heterosexuals that the beneficial effects of the sexual revolution on women's struggles for freedom may be clearest.

Less obvious, but still important, is how much this movement did to emancipate adolescents from parental control. In the mid-nineteen-sixties, as the baby boomers, famously the largest generation the world had ever known, clamored for equal access to pleasure, adult efforts at policing the sexual activities of minors began to fail. Related liberatory struggles, such as the Free Speech Movement, released a flow of information about sex. This debunked both officially and unofficially promulgated anti-sex myths that had previously inhibited the young and also justified parental intervention in their children's developing sex lives. Movements that on the surface seem unrelated to sexual liberation, such as the mental patients' rights (or anti-psychiatric) movement, can still be understood as energized by the sexual revolution, as is apparent when one considers Phyllis Chesler's book *Women and Madness*.

In this landmark feminist study, many of the concerns touched on above are conflated, as is evident when Chesler angrily comments, "Celibacy is the official order of the asylum day. Patients are made to inhabit an eternal American adolescence, where sexuality and aggression are as feared, mocked, and punished as they are within the Family" (36). By 1972, the year of this book's publication, sexual freedom, understood as freedom from outside, authoritative interference in one's pursuit of consensual sexual pleasure, had become intrinsic to American liberal, as well as radical, concepts of justice.[10] The violation of the sexual rights of minors was thought of more in terms of restrictions than as the imposition of adult sexuality on "children" in their teens. The tone of Chesler's analogy seems nearly incomprehensible today when virtually all references to sexual activity in adolescence concern its suppression in the interest of protecting the young. What happened?

Once again, Foucault's words seem apropos. Speculating, in 1978, on what would follow the sexual revolution, he predicted the emergence of "a society of dangers, with on the one side, those who are in danger, and on the other those who are dangerous." And while the main focus of this paranoia would be on relations between adults and minors, he foresaw that "[s]exuality will become a threat in all social relations, in all relations between members of different age groups, in all relations between individuals." Ultimately, "what we will have there [in legal and medical institutions] is a new regime for the supervision of sexuality" ("Sexual Morality and the Law," 281). It may make more sense to think about the vigilant official surveillance of Goths at the turn of the millennium as part of this history rather than as a reasonable response to the Columbine shootings. We might even go so far as to think of the Columbine massacre as the occasion for policing Goth, instead of the cause, because of the way Goth developed as a force against the changes conservatives justified by invoking the AIDS threat.

In the early nineteen-eighties, as various governmental agencies released information about the transmission of AIDS, American concepts of sexuality changed once again. We can read the extent of this change from a brief look at a newspaper editorial response to the July 2001 revelation that a sexual affair took place between Representative Gary Condit and Congressional intern Chandra Levy, who subsequently disappeared. The columnist, Susan Reimer, exhorts parents to retain as much control as they can over the sexual behavior of their children in their mid-twenties. She laments, "we cannot dictate the behavior of a 24-year-old. But we can be that little voice in their heads that speaks up whenever they're thinking about doing something they know we wouldn't like." To further this return of an omnipresent parentally introjected conscience, known to old-school Freudians as the overly powerful superego, she recommends that parents "remain in constant supportive contact with their adult children," screening all social activities and keeping an eye out for companions who might lead the adult children sexually astray. When daughters in their mid-twenties show resentment of this constant surveillance, parents must keep in mind that it is for the daughters' own good. One is tempted to ask when parents should stop controlling a child's sex life. When the child is thirty? Forty? Eligible for retirement?

In a less outrageous mode, but in a similar mood, in the July 2001 issue of *Portland Parent* Carol Band advises parents to deceive their teenagers about their own "youthful indiscretions." Band asserts repeatedly that "kids don't really want to know" whether or not their parents had premarital sexual experience, and thus should never be told the truth (14, 16). While parents are urged to "communicate your own values" about sex (17), Band's assumption seems to be that all parents will want their teenagers to be celibate. Moreover, she clearly sees "values" as synonymous with the belief that chastity should be maintained until marriage. Before dismissing this assumption as unrepresentatively conservative, one might want to look at what that venerable liberal organ of sexual information, Planned Parenthood, has to say to the young.

Two pamphlets made available at a Planned Parenthood information table in the lobby of Portland's Arlene Schnitzer Concert Hall before an Ani DiFranco concert July 14, 2001, *Sexually Transmitted Infections* and *Abstinence*, reflect the current liberal position on youthful sexuality. In evaluating these pamphlets, it is important to keep in mind that DiFranco, whose music is released on her own record label, Righteous Babe Records, is an aggressively feminist independent artist whose fans tend to come from the most politically engaged segment of the young. Her fan base substantially represents her own identification with all independent women, especially proud women of color, lesbians, and bisexuals. Unlike, for instance, Britney Spears, whose songs and public statements during the same time period celebrated the power young women can exercise through a careful combination of seductive display and defensive virginity, DiFranco has always presented herself as a sexual, active woman whose control of sexual situations comes from hard-won knowledge, not coy flirtation.

However, as Foucault repeatedly asserts throughout his writings, liberal education itself is a disciplinary technique: "It is democracy—or better still, the liberalism that matured in the nineteenth century—which has developed extremely coercive techniques that in a certain sense have become the counterbalance to a determinate economic and social 'freedom.' Individuals could certainly not be 'liberated' without educating them in a certain way" (*Remarks on Marx*, 171). So we should not be surprised to see liberal organizations, like Planned Parenthood, participating in a movement to contain the adolescent sexuality that might otherwise disrupt social order.

The Planned Parenthood *Sexually Transmitted Infections* pamphlet tells us that "[t]he best approach to battling STIs is to avoid them in the first place! Abstaining from sexual activity is the only 100 percent guaranteed way to prevent most infections." It goes on to advise that "If you are sexually active, *communicate* with your partner. Being open and honest about your sexual history—and trusting that your partner also is open and honest—is very important. You have less chance of contracting an STI if you are sexually intimate with only one person and your partner is intimate only with you" (emphasis Planned Parenthood's). This to an audience who have come to hear a self-proclaimed bisexual who has never advocated either abstinence or monogamy. Reading this pamphlet, as thousands of the hippest young women in the area surged around me heading for the sold-out show, gave me the queasy feeling of being confronted with what I perceive to be mean-spirited lies whose promulgation in that particular place seemed aimed at suppressing the dynamic queer culture DiFranco's presence encourages.

Michael Warner, who rightly associates queer culture with encouragement of a diversity of sexual practices, claims that while conservatives continually posit an opposition between casual sex and romantic love, "[o]ne of [queer culture's] greatest contributions to modern life is the discovery that you can have both: intimacy and casualness; long-term commitment and sex with strangers; romantic love and perverse pleasure. To cast the conflict as one between sex and love is to deny the best insights and lived experience of queers" (73). But such denial now typifies what passes for sex education. The pamphlet *Abstinence* asserts that "[b]eing sexually active makes us vulnerable and responsible in many ways we may not be ready for: the possibility of unplanned pregnancy, the fear of exposure to HIV and other infections, or the expectation to continue having sex. If you don't want to make yourself emotionally and physically vulnerable—especially if you feel pressured to have sex—abstinence can be a way to reinforce your personal boundaries." Among the advantages of abstinence given in a bullet list on the back of the pamphlet is "communicating honestly with your partner." Thus Planned Parenthood formulates a discourse of sexual information based on the belief that sexual activity poses dangers from which abstinence provides a safe haven. The pamphlet's not very subtly delivered message is that no one should have sex outside marriage, especially no one young.

As one might expect, official government-supported abstinence programs are far less subtle. The 1996 welfare reform bill included legislation allocating federal funding for abstinence education that, as Warner notes, focuses on "'teaching the social, psychological, and health gains to be realized by abstaining from sexual activity.'" He follows this alarming quotation from the law by observing, "There is no attempt to spell out what those gains are. It is simply assumed that abstaining from sex is better" (203). And even more troubling, "the law tells states to teach 'that a mutually faithful monogamous relationship in the context of marriage is the expected standard of human sexual activity'" (203). Not only is this "circular reasoning," as Warner maintains ("marriage is normative because it is normative," 204), it implies that any other sort of behavior, or by extension the mere desire for something other than monogamous marriage, is not human, and so those who experience it are not deserving of human rights. In this context the recommendations of Planned Parenthood's pamphlets seem aligned with those of agencies that adamantly oppose recognition of ordinary life as teens live it, and use this willful ignorance to justify condemning teens to unnecessary unhappiness. And girls are not the only targets of this nonsense anymore. As Judith Levine shows, "now, boys are expected to desire as little as girls" (129).

That abstinence could bring its own hazards or that communicating a desire to abstain from sex could be dishonest or manipulative is apparently unthinkable to the Planned Parenthood pamphlets' authors, as is the idea that relationships presumed to be monogamous by one of the partners are no more likely to include full disclosure of sexual histories and current activities than are sexual relationships that both partners acknowledge to be non-exclusive. (Abstinence educators consistently demonstrate a bizarre level of naïveté about the propensity of human beings to lie about their own behavior in order to get what they want sexually.) Abstinence is problematic not only because it can fail to give the emotional protection its proponents claim it will, but also because the protection from disease it offers can last only until sexual activity begins. Entering marriage as a virgin will not protect one from contracting an STD from a dishonest spouse.

The abstinence program now being offered to young people as the cure for all the problems sex may present seems to consist of abstaining from sexual activity until one has found a person whom one expects to become one's life partner. As I discuss in *New Millennial Sexstyles*, among actual young people the message of abstinence programs is often distorted into a prohibition on penetration of the vagina with the penis, as the recipients of this form of sex education take the usual silence on oral and anal intercourse to mean that they are permissible, chaste, and safe activities. Even more practitioners of "abstinence" seem to believe that mutual masturbation is an acceptable component of the chaste life. However, most of these young people and their adult advisors strongly condemn sexual activity of any sort outside a committed, exclusive romantic relationship between heterosexuals. The National Abstinence Clearinghouse, the largest organization supporting this form of miseducation, even warns against "sexual self-stimulation," because of its potential negative impact on later marital relations (Lerner, 36). Absolute avoidance of premarital sexual activity of any sort, followed by married monogamy, is deemed the only true protection against disease and unhappiness. It seems fairly obvious that such advice will have a depressing effect on gay teens. However, not only do the advocates of abstinence typically ignore the program's implication that gays must stay in the closet and marry for cover, they also seem blinded by the anti-sexual biases of our society to the emotional problems that adherence to such a program can create even for heterosexual youth.

If one abstains from sexual activity unless one is in a committed relationship, anyone who experiences sexual desire is likely to feel even more desperate to find such a relationship than young people might otherwise feel. Since our society relentlessly pressures people to pair up into couples, making social interactions for the unpartnered increasingly difficult with every year that passes, the addition of celibacy to single status can be cruel in itself. And obviously, when having a sex life is contingent on attaining a committed relationship, young people will probably have to wait longer for sex than they would if they considered it acceptable to have sex with any attractive and willing partner. But the pain of abstinence goes far beyond adding sexual frustration to loneliness, and prolonging both of these in adolescence and young adulthood.

People who will not have sex unless they are in a committed relationship and who wish to begin having sex must structure their social lives around meeting and getting to know potential life partners. They must avoid activities through which they are unlikely to meet such people, no matter how entertaining the people they would meet may be. Practitioners of abstinence are also compelled to be far more selective than people who are open to casual sex when engaging in any activity that might lead to sexual relations, such as dating, or even flirting.

Instead of having a casual attitude about finding sex partners and engaging in activities they enjoy while looking around, noting who attracts them, and making overtures to those people, the abstinent must constantly concern themselves with possibilities in the distant future. For example, before asking a young man with similar musical tastes if he would like to join her at the Ani DiFranco concert, an abstinent young woman should decide whether he is from her own socio-economic group, has or is likely to attain an acceptable earning potential, and seems ready for a life commitment.[11] Because others generally do not respond well to being dismissed due to their failure to meet such criteria, the sexual abstainer is likely to be criticized by others as overly selective and intermittently berated for having an inflated sense of self-worth.

Because most young people lack the social status and power conducive to having an excessive amount of self-esteem and self-confidence, consistently being told that they are not worth as much as they seem to think is bound to be quite destructive. Young people who are tormented by frustrated sexual desire and by unfulfilled romantic longing for physical intimacy can easily come to feel that their sufferings are due to deep flaws in their own psyches or characters. In conversations with young abstainers I never hear any of them say that they are too selective without hearing them add something along these lines: "I guess there's something wrong with me." Many, no doubt influenced by current discourses of sexuality, speculate that they must have had some sort of sexual trauma, which they have repressed but which has rendered them abnormal and thus unable to achieve happiness.

Even more depressing is the view held by many abstainers that they are alone because they are exceptionally unattractive physically. Again, few young people have had their appearance sufficiently affirmed to be able to consider themselves indisputably good-looking, and agonizing insecurity about physical appearance is a common feature of adolescence. Because advertising and mass entertainment media consistently reiterate that being beautiful causes one to be loved, and because abstinence philosophy defines love as the desire to commit for life to another person, abstainers who are alone frequently attribute their situation to being so ugly that no one wants them. While young people who engage in casual sex usually realize that they are attractive enough to get a lover and see achieving a satisfying long-term relationship as something that has to do more with compatibility than with looks, abstainers, who cannot have any sexual relationship without life-partnering and who have been taught to understand others' attempts to engage them in casual sex as disrespectful, hostile, and even as a form of assault, are more likely to see themselves as universally despised and rejected.

But abstinence not only makes young people feel freakish and at fault for their own loneliness, it also makes them acutely aware of the limitations of their ability to know others. It can drastically intensify alienation. Abstainers must ask themselves very difficult questions about potential sex partners: for instance, they must determine whether a person is genuine, responsible, and trustworthy, rather than merely deciding whether the person is amusing and cute. Thus the very position of abstinence seems destined to make one feel that one has little control over relations with others, for how in the world can you tell through conversation whether a person is honest? It is all very well to say that one should not have sexual relations with anyone who cannot be trusted absolutely, but in real life it is nearly impossible to trust others not to lie about sex.

In my own life, which at least in this particular way I do not see as atypical, trust such as the Planned Parenthood pamphlet recommends as the precondition for intercourse cannot develop in less than two or three years, and it only develops so rapidly at this stage of my life because I am finally mature enough to have some experientially based confidence in my judgment of others. Had I waited until I was able to trust another person to the extent the pamphlet recommends, I would not have lost my virginity until after the age of forty. And even then I might well have been deluded and made a mistake about my partner's past or intentions, which from the perspective of the abstinence philosophy would have been devastating. From this I conclude that attempting to follow the rules of abstinence is likely to produce a state of intense anxiety and self-doubt.

Finally, following the abstinence program has led many young people with whom I have spoken to see themselves as perverse to the point of mental illness. Told repeatedly that healthy sexual feeling can only be the product of complete trust and open communication, these young people are horrified to find themselves aroused by looking at or coming into casual physical contact with people they do not respect or could not imagine wanting to marry. Their inability to suppress such feelings results in excoriating self-hatred. Not only are their days bedeviled by terrible people whose flirtatious attentions they can only understand as arising from a desire to degrade them and give them diseases, they recognize in themselves similar impulses toward others. Perhaps this is one explanation for the propensity of young people who fall from abstinence-program grace to have unprotected sex. This trend and its tragic consequences have been extensively documented by Cindy Patton and Judith Levine, among others.[12]

These consequences are usually blamed on abstinence education's suppression of information about condoms; that abstinence programs are at fault is one of Lerner's central claims. However, we might recall that some moralistic people have always considered disease and unwanted pregnancy the wages of sexual sin. It does not, therefore, seem impossible that many of the formerly abstinent deliberately rush toward their doom as the damned. Certainly at various periods in history, sexuality has seemed more demonic than it does among abstinence education's true believers, but perhaps not so much so as we who are out of this particularly cruel game would like to think.

It is perhaps fortunate then that the majority of young people show little interest in maintaining true abstinence, as Lisa Collier Cool informs us in "an alarming report every parent should read" entitled "The Secret Sex Lives of Kids" in the *Ladies' Home Journal* (156). And we might pause to consider what confusing times we live in when this staid, conservative magazine sounds hipper than Planned Parenthood.

Although Cool considers sexual activity among "children barely past puberty" to be "a horrifying trend," she strongly and repeatedly makes the point that our current cultural emphasis on virginity is misguided because it only encourages young teens to try unprotected oral sex instead of engaging in vaginal intercourse with condoms. In Cool's estimate, based on a number of recent surveys, over half of middle school students have oral sex, and many young people begin this activity as early as fifth grade. The conservatism of her direct advice, for parents to censor outside information while encouraging questions from their children and then responding with admonitions to "resist acting on impulse," is somewhat tempered by her recommendation that schools provide information on "contraception and safe sex" to children entering puberty (158, 159). Still, the article's most important message is simply that whatever parents think or want, most young people are determined to have sex and more of them are having it earlier than teens did at the height of the sexual revolution (157).

I am proud to know many such young people and cannot overemphasize my respect for their strength in the face of societal disapproval. Still, I recognize that this disapproval exacts a high price in terms of their sense of self. McWhorter illuminates what is at stake in her autobiographical discussion of the concept of the "slut" as it was presented to her when she was in her teens. She tells us that "the condemnation of the proverbial 'slut' had nothing to do with the idea that a woman might want sex." Girls "were never given any advice on how to control or manage our own desires; the possibility that we might have them was never entertained." Thus, "a slut was not a girl who liked sex; a slut was a girl who craved men's attention so much that she would actually submit to physical risk, pain, and degradation to get it" (103). This discourse, still being replicated in thousands of advice columns, self-help books, and abstinence education materials, had a disastrous effect on the young lesbian McWhorter. She writes, "In the early stages of adolescence, I experienced my homosexual self as freakish first of all because I sometimes got sexually aroused and desired carnal intercourse. The fact that my arousal occurred in relation to females seemed less anomalous than that I had desires at all" (103). Crushing guilt, shame, a breakdown, and incarceration in a mental hospital at the age of eighteen were to follow. All in the service of "sexual normalization," as her defense of Foucault's sex radicalism brilliantly exposes.

It is hard to understand how adults who sincerely care about the young could really believe that the greatest dangers facing them are posed by sexual intercourse. Most adults who oppose sexual experience for teens refer to the risk of AIDS as their motivation. However, statistics do not support this privileging of AIDS as the greatest threat to a happy future for the young. Instead, suicide and automobile accidents account for the largest numbers of deaths and crippling injuries among youth.

Obviously teenagers kill themselves because they are depressed. Considering that the American Psychiatric Association continues to claim depression is at epidemic proportions among children and teens, we might want to rethink the ways our current public policies seem designed to induce sexual frustration, self-hatred, and the gloom that proceeds from feeling hopeless about ever achieving physical pleasure. During the early days of the sexual revolution many young people, myself included, risked unwanted pregnancies and even death from complications of illegal abortions. We risked assault by people who were confused or annoyed by the rapidity of changes in sexual mores, and who therefore refused to distinguish between possibly feigned resistance and real consent. And as numerous popular art products dramatically revealed, we even risked murder at the hands of our envious elders. But we were substantially less depressed.

As for car accidents involving teens, it is apparent that they occur because teen drivers are often too immature to make good decisions. This is another obvious truth that makes our current cultural insistence that, for safety's sake, youths attain full sexual maturity before engaging in sex play seem suspiciously like a sort of displacement. In *Club Cultures*, Sarah Thornton points out that "[t]he centrality of the car to American leisure is the main reason behind a strictly enforced legal drinking age of twenty-one" (17). Her comparison of the British club scene to the American "parking culture" as loci of sexual experimentation for young people leaves out, however, the increasing hysteria among American adults over adolescent sexual activity (16). Our mainstream culture is clearly more comfortable with sixteen-year-olds driving drunk than having sex, as is borne out by how much more strictly statutory rape laws are enforced than the laws against selling liquor to teenagers.[13]

Rather than worry that their children, like so many others who have become insurance company statistics, will die when they crash vehicles they were too young to control, parents transfer their concern to genitalia the young are deemed too immature to play with safely. Because it is common knowledge, reflected in hundreds of popular culture artifacts from cartoons to advertisements, that teenagers' eagerness to begin driving is a direct result of their desire to have a sex life outside parental surveillance, we might also rethink the advice generally given to parents to act as anti-sex police. Is it really preferable that kids die than that they have sex lives, or rather that their parents, and other concerned adults, know about those sex lives?

More and more frequently American adults evade this question by forcing upon the young their view that sexual experience outside marriage will inevitably prove fatal. Where once young people themselves formed groups like ACT UP and shouted out the truth, "silence equals death!" now would-be parental figures insist that sex is death and try to impose a deadly silence.

Fortunately for us all, that silence has being broken by rebellious voices from unexpected places, perhaps the most surprising of which is the heart of what I here call the Dark Empire, that place where the black, shining strands of Goth cultures converge. What Richard Davenport-Hines says of Poppy Z. Brite's marvelous Goth novels is equally true of this whole subculture. They reject "the punitiveness of bourgeois morality[, which] likes to impose a tragic fate on miscreants," and instead "make a virtue of abandonment; . . . they resist the tedious nullity of insipid convention with a nihilism that is anything but tedious" (362). And they embrace sex, that "very beautiful thing that can kill you," with all their strength.

2.◆

IN MEMORIAM
DARKWAVE HIPPIES
Angela Carter through a Goth Lens

American scholars of subcultures may be surprised to read, in ethnographic studies conducted in the United Kingdom, remarks like the following from a young woman whose appearance seems to mark her as Punk: "I started off, like, in the goth-hippy-type thing" (Muggleton, 121). While the category of hippie remains distinct from that of Punk in the U.S., as I shall discuss below, clearly in the U.K. Goth and hippie can overlap. And this overlap can serve as the launching point for a Deleuzian line of flight away from the mainstream concepts of youth currently dominating discourse on sexuality in America.

As many of us remember well, we did not always live in a society terrified of sexual contact due to its perceived potential to damage women, adolescents, and children more than anything else possibly could. Feminists demonstrated little concern over protecting teens from consensual sex. Nor did feminism always take as its one of its most pressing problems eliminating the production and distribution of pornography. Instead feminist activists concentrated on eliminating unambiguous instances of violence against women and nonconsensual sex, and promoting the empowerment of women through equal financial and political opportunities. Many feminist projects aimed to protect children from poverty.

Generally, whether they were feminists or not, most intelligent people considered the pollution that may yet destroy human life on Earth more of a threat to future generations than the possibility that children might see sexually explicit materials some might deem immoral, and acted accordingly, generally taking it upon themselves to instill in their offspring whatever values concerning sexuality they saw as necessary, but agitating for more public education about environmentalism. Moreover, people who cared about the immediate welfare of children did not always concentrate their energies on inflicting draconian punishments on adults who had consensual sexual relations with adolescents, but instead treated that issue with near indifference, preferring to focus on such problems as the United States' amazingly high infant mortality rate and other threats that poverty posed to children, such as lack of food and basic health care.

Likewise, for most feminists, sexual liberation of women did not always mean freeing women from pressure to engage in casual sex and helping them to enter into long-term monogamy. Nor did it mean convincing heterosexual men that all heterosexual women consider emotional intimacy an important component of every sexual relationship. Rather, feminists worked to make it possible for women to express their sexuality in a wide range of ways with the understanding that it is all right for us to want different things out of our sexual encounters.

Throughout the sixties and seventies American culture had increasingly been viewed as sexually repressive, and there was a general confidence, as I discussed in chapter 1, that sexuality was a good that could heal many of the wounds the culture had caused. The priority changes that took place after the onset of the AIDS pandemic displaced that confidence. In fact, we might see the last two decades as having reversed the values connected to the public treatment of sexuality in the sixties and seventies. Now many feminists and other political liberals actively solicit government regulation, through educational institutions, medicine, and the judiciary, of consensual sexual practices. In the earlier period we rejected this. The priorities of the seventies, epitomized by the flowering of the sexual revolution during this period, arose out of the much broader cultural revolution of the sixties. And it is to that fertilely chaotic landscape that I now turn in order to demonstrate how familiarity with the current Goth subculture can enhance our understanding of the art products of the sixties, removing the web of myths that currently obscures some of the most interesting features of the sixties' counterculture.

Because the scope of this book will not allow me to discuss the entire range of sixties counterculture art products that can be better understood through a knowledge of Goth, I will focus here on a group of texts in which that benefit is especially evident: the early novels of Angela Carter. My aim is to provide an approach to these texts that will help restore a lost piece of cultural history to the picture of the sixties, and that will also make possible an understanding of Carter's writing that does not relegate the pre-1977 work to the status of a sort of naïve juvenilia. The following two quotations may shed light on this chapter's project. The first comes from Guattari:

> The protest and counter-culture movements of the sixties must have ap-
> peared, for those most intensely involved, to be the first fruits of pro-
> found transformations that would gradually win over the entire social
> fabric. But nothing like this has happened, although history may still
> have some surprises in store for us. . . . Whatever were the hopes, the
> utopias, the innovative experiments of that period, only a hazy memory
> remains; touching to some, hateful and vengeful to others, and indiffer-
> ent to most. ("Four Truths for Psychiatry," 262)

The second is from a memoir of Angela Carter, written by Robert Coover for
the *Guardian* after her death in 1992. He says, "Gothic they called her, fan-
tastical, nightmarish" (10). My contention is that unless we penetrate the haze
of nostalgia and remember the sixties as a time in which such dark night-
mares occupied an important significatory place, we cannot understand
Carter within her cultural context.

Prior to the post-Columbine media frenzy of misrepresentation of Goth,
relatively few people in the U.S. familiar with young people who followed
Goth fashion clearly distinguished between this gloomy glam and the "dark"
styles that had been associated with Punk rock and Heavy Metal since the
mid-seventies. Goths did appear fairly regularly on television talk shows
throughout the mid-nineties, as the cross-over popularity of bands like Nine
Inch Nails and Marilyn Manson brought Goth some mainstream publicity,
and Goths, as well as the musicians who appealed to them, were occasionally
featured in rock and roll magazines such as *Rolling Stone* and *Spin*. However, Americans not involved in subcultural music scenes tended to see Goth
as a fad taste, like cigar smoking among young hipsters of the nineties, rather
than as a social movement or subcultural group. Goth was most clearly recognized as a subculture in Britain. It would be a mistake, however, to agree too
quickly with most commentaries on this subculture and conclude that just
because Goth directly followed Punk, drawing on many of its stylings, its
central values were the same. In *Hex Files: The Goth Bible*, Mick Mercer
explains that "[e]veryone knows that the original Goth spell came through
disenchantment with Punk" (7). From its onset, Punk has been associated
with aggressive masculinity,[1] while Goth is generally described as "non-sex-
ist" (*Hex Files*, 8). As Hodkinson points out, Goth has always been strongly
informed by a romanticized sense of "dark femininity" (36).

Fields of the Nephilim, a band many consider one of the early exemplars
of Goth, illustrate the prevailing attitude toward the feminine within this
subculture through their revision of a key figure from the work of one of
Goth's most beloved authors, H. P. Lovecraft (1890–1937).[2] Lovecraft's most
famous horror stories and poems are concerned with what is often called the

Cthulhu Mythos; they describe the god Cthulhu, ruler of the Great Old Ones whose return to power, through the book called the *Necronomicon*, threatens (or promises, depending on one's view of the status quo) to inaugurate a new regime of dark beings freed from the restraints of human morality. Fields of the Nephilim draw heavily on this mythology, but throughout their albums they identify Cthulhu, who is always referred to as male by Lovecraft, with Tiamet, the Sumerian Chaos-Mother. "The Watchman," on their 1988 album *The Nephilim*, features an invocation of Cthulhu with repeated references to "her" call. The masculine order of our dominant culture is equated with repression and ignorant fear, while the triumph of the feminine is posited as necessary to the wild freedom to realize and express their deepest selves.

Richard Davenport-Hines's discussion of Goth masochistic identifications also reveals differences between Punk and Goth. Whereas Punk can be read as a reaction against the hippies, whom Punk saw as maddeningly passive and often apolitically hedonistic, Goth might best be understood as a reaction against Punk's anti-romanticism, its anti-intellectualism, and, interestingly, its contempt for masochism, which Punks typically referenced in order to dramatize their contempt for social hierarchy. As Baddeley rather contemptuously puts it, "punk's self-appointed thought police . . . associated sexual dominance games with sexism and the hated middle classes" (186). Unlike the harsh, confrontational style most commonly recognized as Punk, Goth is deliberately decorative and yielding, with a decidedly "more submissive" style (Davenport-Hines, 364). Davenport-Hines cites James Hannahan's identification of "glorification of suffering" as "the defining characteristic of goth music" (363). As Lauraine Leblanc explains, Punk fashion characteristically appropriates the markers of S/M out of hostility to it as a mode of sexual expression, with Punks "adopting and displaying fetishized objects such as bondage collars and handcuffs in order to parody or subvert their original meanings" (204).

The mockery of S/M so common to Punk depends for its political impact as a critique of traditional gender roles on a construction of sexuality in which sadomasochism can only reinscribe male dominance and forced, involuntary female submission. Goth understandings of S/M interactions seem more sophisticated, including recognition that both dominance and submission can be free choices and that neither need be gendered along binary biological lines, or, indeed, in any way at all. Similarly, Punk's high valorization of spontaneity and earthy coarseness contrasts to Goth's investment in intricately detailed visual displays and multi-layered, carefully crafted (and increasingly electronically mixed) sounds. Thus, although both subcultures depart from the same point, complete rejection of mainstream values, they follow opposite lines of flight. In reaching back to the eighteenth and nineteenth centuries' Gothic, with its highly intellectual, grotesquely beautiful celebration of unreason and the unnatural, contemporary Goths depart from the deliberate crudeness of Punk, which was meant as a call to wake up from the psychedelic dreams of the sixties—which Punks misunderstood and totalized as unrealistically pretty fantasies.

The retrospective construction of the hippies by the Punks in some ways resembles the Modernists' similar imaginative re-creation of the Victorians. As numerous historians have observed, the Victorian period was far more diverse culturally than the Modernists and their cultural heirs understood. Obviously Victorian England could not have been characterized by fervent adherence to tradition in all matters, since a great number of changes, from the displacement of the arranged marriage by the love match as the most common way of forming a life-partnership to the development of a railway system that connected formerly isolated areas, transformed social life and customs markedly during Victoria's reign.

But how could Modernism be modern if the Victorians were not remembered as breathing, ambulatory emblems of the traditional and conservative? As Alex Zwerdling shows, Virginia Woolf's reduction of her mother into the comfortably domestic Mrs. Ramsay, who can read fairy tales to her children but cannot write them (as Woolf's mother in fact did), though gentler and more loving than most Modernist portraits of Victorians, is otherwise typical in representing the previous generation as deficient in understanding (to borrow a favorite Victorian insult) in relation to their children (188–91). Literary critics would, I think, all agree that Woolf was far more innovative a writer than her mother, Julia Stephen, and that Stephen's devotion to her chosen vocation, nursing, was less successfully expressed than her daughter's dedication to literature. In fact, the comparison seems faintly ridiculous and unfair to Stephen. But the portrayal of her as Mrs. Ramsay considerably increases the contrast between her feminine softness and her daughter's sharp professionalism. References by Punks to hippies have something of the same exaggerated flavor.

This passage lauding The Sex Pistols' performance at Winterland on January 14, 1978, from Greil Marcus's Punk masterpiece *Lipstick Traces*, provides an especially good example of how hippies were typically characterized by Punks:

> [Johnny Rotten] threw it all back on the crowd—which was, to him, no more than a representation of a representation, five thousand living symbols of Scott McKenzie's 1967 Love Generation hit, "San Francisco (Be Sure to Wear Flowers in Your Hair)," symbols of mindlessly benevolent hippies who knew nothing of negation—when he said, leaving the

stage, carefully gathering up any objects of value, "Ever get the feeling you've been cheated?" that was how I felt.

At Altamont in 1969, as the Rolling Stones played and a man was stabbed and kicked to death in the midst of the crowd in front of the stage, I had felt only loathing and distance: the peace symbols people flashed were almost as ugly as the violence itself. They affirmed nothing but symbolization. (88–89)

An empty rhetoric of peace and love chanted until it became meaningless, chanted until it engendered soulless commercial pop and made anyone with a grain of intelligence want to "smash" everything they encountered—that is what the hippie counterculture was in Punk's retrospective (Marcus, 90). The spectacularly horrible failure of the Altamont Speedway outdoor concert to duplicate Woodstock's "love-in" was read as an exposure of a secret truth that the hippies could no longer hide. They had dreamed their youth away on futile nonsense, and a cleansing explosion of nihilistic violence was the only sensible response to their silliness.

Well, maybe so. But which hippies had done this? Some of us were not at all surprised by Altamont. For one thing, as Shawn Levy recounts, by 1964 Rolling Stones concerts were "full-blown horror shows" complete with "fist-fights in the audiences, screaming mobs of hysterical fans outside hotels and stage doors, policemen attacking concertgoers in vain, angry efforts to stem the craziness" (169). By 1968 the band's interest in "the black arts" was infamous and frontman Mick Jagger's "satanic pose" defined their performances (297). The popularity of the Stones as an "anti-Beatles" group, whose filthy roughness and promise of particularly nasty violence offered an alternative to the Fab Four's clean image, should be understood as evidence that the opinions that sixties counterculture youth held on social relations were extremely diverse, and could hardly be encompassed by a few pronouncements about universal love. Nor could the enthusiasm for psychedelic drugs that was one of the sixties' most striking attributes be put down to a shared valuation of spiritual growth and seeking after deep connection to others. The primary reason some of us were not suddenly awakened by Punk to the realization that we had been cheated was that for us psychedelia had always been a bit more of a nightmare than a fantasy trip into a peaceable kingdom.

Some of the most perceptive analysts of Goth, like Baddeley, see it as the logical outcome of the sixties' experiments in altered states of consciousness, a theory that is lent strength by the concurrence of a resurgence in interest in LSD, psilocybin, and other hallucinogens at the end of the nineteen-eighties and the popularization of Goth during the same period. In addition to my own direct observation of Goth clubbing in New Orleans, San Francisco, Portland, and New York in the late eighties and early nineties, I have seen and heard much in music and films popular with Goths to corroborate Baddeley's opinion that psychedelic drugs fed into the development of Goth. Perhaps the most striking examples are provided by Rob Zombie's video *Dragula*,[3] which draws heavily on such techniques as flashing jump cuts and psychedelic color outlines, which are often used in film to represent hallucinogenic trips, and Marilyn Manson's video *Dope Hat*, a Goth-on-acid recreation of scenes from the 1971 film *Willy Wonka and the Chocolate Factory*. The latter is particularly interesting in its revisionist historicizing. (*Willy Wonka*, like *2001: A Space Odyssey* and *Fantasia*, was understood by hippies to be best experienced on acid.)

In Baddeley's view, Goth began in the sixties with Screamin' Jay Hawkins's ghoulish theatrics, the Rolling Stones' 1966 "Paint It Black," and above all, The Velvet Underground's 1965 "Black Angel's Death Song" (163–68). I would add to this list the Rotary Connection's marvelous 1967 rendition of "Ruby Tuesday," which, through the use of organ music and pseudo-religious chant, reincarnates the wayward girl as a dark saint of sexual freedom. The mystical echoing that follows the sepulchral intonation of the line "she would never say where she came from" is one of the most Gothic moments in sixties music.

Howard Brick perceptively comments,

> The sensed struggle of life against death gave the counterculture an apocalyptic tone, belying the impression of childlike innocence some of the "hippies" and their observers tried to convey. . . . Indeed, counterculture hedonism bespoke desperation, a feeling that life under the umbrella of the arms race might be too short or that life within the mainstream was doomed by deadening mechanistic routine. (116)

Songs like the Rotary Connection's "Ruby Tuesday" make this attitude explicit by positing a sexuality conscious of its unavoidable relation to death. Their Ruby Tuesday strolls through a musical landscape of cathedrals and tombs, reminding her audience to seize the day for we have nothing but now. Such songs might serve to remind us that all of the sixties' sexual liberation unfolded against a background stained red by the slaughterhouse that was Vietnam and black by the ever-more-evident death throes of poisoned Nature. All the pursuit of free love was at the same time a frantic fleeing from the discipline of technologies of governmental surveillance, which were growing exponentially, as were the suburbs. Suburbanization, and the paving over of previously open spaces that it brought, severely curtailed outdoor privacy. The erotic as it was approached through a Gothic imagination became a refuge from the blazing light of our increasingly panoptic therapy culture, the Liebestod more attractive because of its darkness.

What Baddeley calls "proto-Goth," a delirious wallowing in luscious, sensual darkness, a love affair with decadence, featured conspicuously in sixties cinema, too, from exploitation pictures such as Roger Corman's 1967 *The Trip*, which was marketed with the tagline "A Lovely Sort of Death," to art films like the works of Kenneth Anger—not only his best-known film, *Scorpio Rising* (1964), but also *Invocation of My Demon Brother* (1969) and *Lucifer Rising* (1973). Manson Family member Bobby Beausoleil wrote the score for the latter, which is exactly what makes the film important to the Goth students in my film classes.

When members of my generation are shocked by the enthusiasm the young often show for sixties nihilism, most notably demonstrated by the chosen name and the subsequent success of Goth shock rocker Marilyn Manson, what sometimes seems to hit hardest is being suddenly recalled to a version of the past that was smoothed over and sanitized. Brick reminds us that at the last open Weathermen convention, "leader Bernadine Dohrn lauded Charles Manson for 'offing the pigs,'" signaling the "conversion of radical sentiment . . . into what one movement veteran called a dark 'death trip'" (163). Brick argues that by this point violence was not simply regarded as the most effective means to specific political ends but had come to be invested "with meaning *beyond* strict utility, with value in its own right" (163, emphasis Brick's). It was seen by many as the dark gateway into social and cultural transformation.

As Guattari suggests in "Four Truths for Psychiatry," that famous time when the revolutionary counterculture seemed poised to change the world now seems to be slipping away from cultural memory, deep into myth. One of the most powerful indications that the era's signifiers are becoming incomprehensible is the current blurring together of the political designations "liberal" and "radical." As anyone who has recently been questioned by a political pollster no doubt knows, "radical" no longer exists as an official identity category. Once radicals regarded liberals as the enemy, people who were co-opted, who had sold out, so hopelessly bourgeois that they could imagine only working within the system. They were, in short, the older generation who had betrayed the principles of the Left for material security. Now liberals *are* the Left. So when we attempt to recall the sixties, we tend to do so through a rosy haze of memories of teach-ins on peace and love, flowers in the mouths of rifles, gentle people dreaming of butterflies. We forget the darkness of that other sixties in which the horrors of the Altamont concert debacle or the Manson Family, on their mission to violently dismantle bourgeois life as we knew it, were not all that discordant.

Carter's early evocations of the English counterculture make this apparent. Her 1966 first novel, *Shadow Dance*, depicts the life of an artist whose murderous best friend functions as a Jungian shadow as he grapples with two lovers, one a nice girl whose conventional behavior conceals the "destructive, mindless, vindictive machine" within (165) and the other physically divided into angel and demoness by the facial scar inflicted by his friend. *The Magic Toyshop* (1967) gives us "a dirty beatnik," obsessed with Satanism, who believes that "[i]n Hell all wrongs are righted" (153–54), and an adolescent girl who confers on those she loves "a Gothic kind of grace" (189). Together they strive to annihilate the patriarchal institution of the family, replacing it with a literally incestuous alliance of rebel angels. Because the protagonist of 1968's *Several Perceptions* believes that "this is the time of the barbarians" (4), he chooses to work "cleaning the dying and laying out the dead," in pursuit of "a black kind of innocence" (7). The following year's *Heroes and Villains* continues in this vein with its futuristic dystopia in which a girl destroys a modern primitive youth because she understands him as "nothing but the furious invention of my virgin nights" (137).[4] Carter's 1971 novel, *Love*, is an intermission from futurism that explores the youth culture's descent into despair through the relationship of a surrealistically deathlike mad girl with skin like "chilled rice paper" to her masochistic husband, whom she forces to have her name tattooed over his breast "in Gothic script," and his sadomasochistic, bisexual brother (93, 69).

Carter's work is usually understood in terms of progression away from male influence and toward a deliberately feminist imaginary. Her own published discussion of her processes feeds into ongoing confusion within literary studies about which attitudes about sex are proper to feminism. For instance, her retrospective epilogue to *Love*, written in 1987, to some extent justifies this interpretation by referring to the novel's "almost sinister feat of male impersonation" (113), suggesting that this is one reason so many critics see the work as masculinist. In seeing *The Passion of New Eve* (1977) as a turning point in Carter's work, Harriet Blodgett seems typical of those who read her from a majoritist feminism that valorizes mutuality of gentle affection and demonizes sadomasochism. Blodgett claims that the sex change undergone by the novel's protagonist represents Carter's own self-transformation "from a writer trained in male paradigms and reveling in male fantasies to a feminist who has learned to live and respond as a female" (51). What critics mean by this sort of progression narrative is clarified by Cornel Bonca's description of "male sexuality" as being nothing more than "the dead end of sexual domination," as opposed to female sexuality, a commitment to "cheerful, healthy sex" (61).

Carter criticism has always been troubled by her interest in S/M, which majoritist academic feminism continues to represent as antithetical to the goals of feminism and existing only in complicity with patriarchy.[5] So it has been convenient for critics to set aside the earlier work as interesting mainly for what it made possible later. They see it as a preliminary exploration of a dark alley that led nowhere, enabling Carter to turn aside to pursue avenues of cultural representation more clearly consistent with the wholesome sexual attitudes popularly associated with feminism by the majority of its spokes-women and by most male feminists. However, we might look at the early novels not as records of Carter's youthful false consciousness, but instead as a part of the archival record of those other hippies, the violent, intentionally crazy ones, the ones in love with darkness, who did not fit easily into the sunny, smiling, Summer of Love aesthetic.

A look at Fredric Jameson's current analysis of the postmodernist treat-ment of history helps reveal what might be gained by looking at Carter this way. As he observes, "[a]ny modification of the past, no matter how minute, will . . . inevitably determine a reorganization of the future" (704). His subse-quent attack on Deleuze and Guattari's *Anti-Oedipus* seems derived from a serious misreading of that text's engagement with this very idea. Jameson claims that the figure of the "ideal" schizophrenic, central to Deleuze and Guattari's anti-Freudianism, is a manifestation of the tendencies of contem-porary capitalism, rather than a node from whence we can generate "a radi-cally different order capable of replacing it" (711). He bases this reading on his view that by rejecting the Freudian account of subjectivity Deleuze and Guattari intend to reject the concept of history itself. This seems to me mis-taken.

Deleuze and Guattari's schizoanalysis is not intended to do away with history or negate its relevance to potential futures. As Claire Colebrook ex-plains, Deleuze and Guattari follow Foucault (and of course Nietzsche), in seeking a new relation to the past that can counter history's construction by dominant cultural discourses. Like these precursors they recognize that "[a] genealogy does not accept the current reason or understanding of the pres-ent; it looks to the past in order to unhinge the present, to show there is no justification for the present" (*Understanding Deleuze*, xxiv). They augment the Foucauldian genealogical approach with a model for the genealogist: their schizophrenic, a conscious being whose grounding in the body and focus on material interactions makes possible a relation to the past not determined by dominant cultural narratives. The relevance of this strategy to the study of history should be clear. As Jameson himself points out, the narratives that dominate our era's global communications system are continually informed by "new techniques of distortion by way of a suppression of history" (701).

Theoretical frameworks for the study of subcultures associated with youth seem in particular danger of becoming such techniques. For instance, compare two studies of rave culture, Sarah Thornton's 1995 *Club Cultures* and Simon Reynolds's 1998 *Generation Ecstasy*. Thornton's highly respected and much cited book argues that club culture can best be understood as a developmental stage in youth that holds little, if any, promise for political change. She attacks the very idea that a subculture can promote resistance to the mainstream, arguing that there is no such thing as a mainstream; it is merely the invention of young people who like to imagine themselves as rebels opposing a monolithic norm, just as subcultures themselves are the products of a sensationalistic media which creates moral panics in order to stimulate audience interest (114–15, 162). Because young people are "exempt from adult commitments to the accumulation of economic capital" and usually need not earn money to support themselves and others, they can devote their attention to the accumulation of what she calls "subcultural capital," which confers status on them within the subcultural worlds they inhabit in youth (102–103). In contrast, Reynolds's so far much less popular idea is that millennial club cultures are breeding grounds for lifelong resistance to societal norms and can be read as the harbingers of important "revolutions and reconfigurations" that are "yet to come" (390).

These distinct approaches represent competing visions of subcultures: the view of them as youthful expressions of rebellion which must perforce end with the responsibilities of maturity—and it is worth noting the affinity this view has with psychological theories of individuation—versus the Deleuzoguattarian view of subcultures as launching points for lines of flight that make possible ongoing revolution.

Must we always move toward a maturity defined as acceptance of the status quo? Be driven by the spirit of the times, as Jameson contends, to take an investment banker's view of temporality? Only if we forget the past so completely as to believe the cultural narrative (so obviously Freudian) that all our minoritarian relations to bodies and pleasures are simply reactions against parental authority which will end with our inevitable transformation into our parents—an account remarkably like the reading of Carter's early violent, transgressive, pornographically sexual fiction as a rebellion against being gendered female that had to end as she grew into a feminist woman and adopted all the attitudes majoritist feminism attributes to that identity.

But both Carter and Deleuze and Guattari can be seen otherwise. And it is in the continuities between Carter's Gothicism, Deleuze and Guattari's countercultural darkness, and contemporary Goth that evidence resides indicating that subcultures need not be mere stopping points on a developmental journey. Inspired by the political revolution of youth at the end of the sixties, *Anti-Oedipus* urgently poses questions of its times that remain relevant today, perhaps especially to Goths. The most important of these questions is probably, how can we maintain the energy of a Lawrencian demonic and celebrate the darkness of unreason without becoming fascists? It also asks, how can the minoritized resist rationality, as a discourse of the dominant power/ knowledge matrix, without being dismissed as the motiveless mad? And, which is especially relevant to Carter's early novels, how can we maintain the intensity of desire's flow through enactments of sexual dominance and submission without reinforcing raced and gendered social hierarchies? For Deleuze and Guattari, as for many Goths, the answer lies in reimagining a past uncontained by Oedipal narrative, rediscovering or re-creating a history in which the deliberate embrace of dark otherness was a political act. Carter's early texts can be read as artifacts of such a history: not as attempts to speak in the master's language—as many feminist critics would have it—but as attempts to chronicle purposefully dark gestures of a hippiedom even then being revised by the media and facing a premature burial that only resurrection in the gaudy graveyard of Goth could remedy.

Arthur Marwick ends his lengthy cultural history of the sixties with an indignant response to the contention of an unnamed academic with whom he spoke on a radio program that "'the sixties [were] a dry run for the nineties'" (802). Marwick insists the sixties did not in any significant sense fail. Instead, they began a "cultural revolution" with "continuous, uninterrupted, and lasting consequences" (802). I do not disagree. But I do take exception to his dismissive view of the sixties' projects that did fail, especially "the destruction of mainstream culture" (805). He mocks the counterculture idea, which he identifies as derived from Marcuse's adaptation of Marxist theory, that "since the mass of ordinary workers were so content with the boons of consumer society that they had no interest in revolution, the revolution would have to come from the outcast and deprived," immediately equating being an outsider with belonging to an economic "under-class" (805). This leads him to ask, "But why have a revolution? If the majority are already contented, would it not be better to concentrate in a systematic and pragmatic way on raising the living standards of the minority, and thus abolishing the under-class?" (805). Something seems off.

After all, Marwick endorses Lewis Yablonsky's estimate that "70 per cent of hippies . . . came from middle- or upper-middle-class families" (485). Yet he seems unable to recognize that the very fact that so many middle-class people turned to Marxism (or Maoism) during this period, and that so many more tried to do away with "the system," calls into question his assumption that prosperity brings contentment. The problem here seems to begin with the definition of "contentment." As a way of summing up Marcuse's vision of the emotions induced by prosperity under consumer capitalist regimes, "resignation," or even "stupefaction," might be more accurate. Certainly Marcuse's descriptions of the bourgeoisie in such texts as *Eros and Civilization* and *An Essay on Liberation* do not show them as enjoying a pleasant state of being that everyone should be happy to enter.

Counterculture young people clearly rejected the working world of their parents as a kind of living death, even when it brought prosperity. A nihilistic refusal of what was presented as adult reality is a salient feature of sixties fiction, poetry, film, and songs, and this is the same sort of refusal that Greil Marcus attributes to Punk. Marcus describes how Punk's "entry into negation," its dive into what he designates "the fire of nihilism," was both made possible by the unrestrained excess of the Free Speech Movement and fed by its suppression (442–45). He opens up for us again that day on the Berkeley campus in 1964 when "[t]here was only chaos. People who moments before [the arrest of Mario Savio] had been lulled into a lovely sleep screamed their lungs out" in pure negation (445). If the daylight side of the counterculture experience was the feeling of perfect spontaneous community with others, the dark side was the resounding and violent "no" it shouted to the "rules and regulations," to the imposition of a structure meant to bring "resolution" in the name of order (445).

Carter's *The Sadeian Woman* exemplifies this attitude. Majoritist feminist critics have come to terms with this difficult text, it seems to me, by stressing its valorization of mutuality, which is often didactically argued in the text, as when Carter criticizes the Sadeian libertine for whom "there is no question of reciprocity . . . because [in his view] to share is to be robbed" (142). Also in line with majoritist feminist condemnation of so-called "male identification" in women is Carter's judgment that because Sade's dominant heroine Juliette "attacks civilisation with its own weapons . . . her behavior reverts to the polymorphous perversity of the child, who has not yet learnt the human objections to cruelty" (148). Such passages can be read as endorsements of the gentle eroticism first advocated by cultural feminists as an antidote to phallocentric heterosex, and later promulgated by therapy culture as the only mature and healthy mode of sexuality. But Carter's vision of sexual pleasure is more complex, much darker and more radical than such liberal statements can fully express.

She praises Juliette's denial of the "use value" of her female body, as expressed through her determination to be infertile "because she has chosen sexuality as terrorism as a way of life" (106). Her "service . . . of the goddess in her demonic aspect, the goddess as antithesis" Carter deems necessary to the removal of the "repressive and authoritarian superstructure" that binds sexuality to reproduction (111). As a destructive force, Juliette begins a project of cultural renewal to be completed "with her own death" (111). Not only does Carter's phrasing privilege the violent, so does her discussion of the moment in his work when Sade comes closest to "transcendence," to making "room for hope" (129). Carter imagines this to be when, in *Philosophy in the Boudoir*, Eugénie rapes her mother Madame de Mistival, or, as Carter puts it, "opens her up for pleasure with the massive dildo" (128). What apparently

annoys Carter about Sade's depiction of this scene is that just as Eugénie
cries out that her mother is experiencing orgasm, Sade "censors her response"
by having the mother faint (128). She regrets that he cannot "allow himself to
violate the last taboo of all, and allow wretched and abused Madame de
Mistival to experience pleasure" (129). Consequently, when Carter writes
about "the holy terror of love that we find [to be], in both men and women
themselves, the source of all opposition to the emancipation of women"
(150), perhaps we should pay more attention to the terrifying circumstances
in which she most often envisions both pleasure and love occurring.[6] Certainly we would do so if we read Carter's Juliette in Goth mode as a female
Cthulhu (as imagined by Fields of the Nephilim), as the goddess of violent
breakthrough.

Carter's journalistic writings, collected in *Expletives Deleted* and *Noth-
ing Sacred*, illuminate her concept of the relation of the horrifically violent
to the erotic. She concludes a review of William Burroughs's *The Western
Lands*, in the former collection, with the claim, "He is also the only living
American writer of whom one can say with confidence he will be read with
the same shock of terror and pleasure in a hundred years' time" (40). *Nothing
Sacred* includes both an essay lavishly praising the dominant sexuality of
Marlene Dietrich as Lola-Lola in *The Blue Angel*, along with Ado Kyrou for
appreciating it, and a review of *Inside Linda Lovelace* harshly criticizing Lovelace's "reification" of desire, which "effectively antiseptises all the danger
from that most subversive and ambivalent aspect of our selves. No more terror, no more magic" (122–23) That last comment could hardly be more
closely connected in its spirit to the ethos of Goth, which evokes the terror
associated with dark, chaotic violence not only to wipe away a dominant culture to which it is antithetical, but also for the enchantment, the delight such
terror can bring. One of the biggest differences between Punk's nihilism and
Goth's is that Goth, like the literary Gothic from whence it came, revels in
the voluptuous possibilities of horror. Where Punk forcibly exposes the sadomasochistic underpinnings of proper society in order to de-eroticize them, as
in, for instance, Karen Finley's performance art,[7] Goth incorporates S/M into
its deliberately titillating performance of resistance to cultural and societal
norms.

The cover art of *The Whip*, a compilation CD produced by Cleopatra
Records, premier U.S. distributor of Goth and Industrial music, illustrates the
treatment of S/M typical within the scene. On the front of the CD we see an
androgynous boy in bondage, the words "The Whip" carved bloodily into his
bare chest, as a dominatrix stands by, her bullwhip entwined around his neck.
The back cover shows a male figure in a leather or vinyl punishment suit and
hood, chains around his neck and the shaft of a cat o' nine tails across his

chest. Inside the CD more pictures visually represent the erotic encounter suggested by the cover. The liner notes mark the CD as a project of historical reclamation. It is based on a compilation put together in 1983 "as a first testament to the then growing Batcave Generation" by Dave Roberts, bassist for the Goth group Sex Gang Children, who was inspired by the Comte de Lautréamont's Gothic/Decadent novel *Maldoror*. Cleopatra added to the compilation and rereleased it in 1993 as a reflection of what Goth had become: a celebration of the power of S/M to dissolve conventional sexualities and gender identities.

Which leads us back to Carter's early novels and their depictions of the performance of gender identifications. Her first, *Shadow Dance*, no doubt contributed to the critical view, now dominating feminist discussion of her oeuvre, that Carter began by ventriloquizing misogynist views of women. Misogyny characterizes the angry tone of her narrator, the artist Morris Gray, as he describes the manipulative behavior of his female nemesis, Ghislaine:

> She would want to weep and glitter with public tears and fatten her undernourished little self on them, her poor little vanity, all pale and thin with pinman Oxfam arms and legs. There would be an orgy of emotion, with blows and tears and violence, all about her and she would bulge fatly on it. (8)

Carter's use of Morris's voice goes further than mere parody. Body size plays a symbolic role both here and elsewhere, in the many descriptions of Ghislaine. Given that Ghislaine's appearance codes her as the female subject of mid-sixties art and the female object, par excellence, of its eroticism, her theatricality insistently reveals the hidden side of this aesthetic.

Prior to the beginning of the narrative, Ghislaine was "a beautiful girl" in the style of the times; Morris remembers that she was "so light and fragile and her bones so birdy fine and little and her skin was almost translucent" (2). Mutilated by Morris's best friend and shadow figure, Honeybuzzard, she becomes "a horror-movie woman," "the fiend woman from the monster magazines" (4, 167). One side of her face, hideously scarred, signifies "devastation," a grotesque ruin suggesting death and decay (153). Carter's description of the "raddled skin pitted with flaking makeup, like whitewash slapped on a crumbling wall" (153), strongly recalls Congreve's description in *The Way of the World* of the once beautiful Lady Wishfort, who has become a laughingstock to the young rakes because of her desire to continue having a sex life. Ghislaine's other profile is that of a girl "very beautiful and very young, perhaps only thirteen or fourteen" (152). Carter calls her face "the two sides of the moon juxtaposed" (153). It is also the two sides of a sixties ideal: the lovely starveling girl-child and the ravenous harpy skeleton.

Commentators on sixties culture often regard the fashions of the time as playful, fun for all involved. This is especially true of women's fashions and the fashion in women. In Marwick's view, for instance, "[t]he miniskirt was almost a logical response to sexual liberation and the new emphasis on the attractions of the natural physical attributes of youth, including neat bottoms and slim legs." He anticipates that women may disagree and cite facts about the postpubescent development of secondary sexual characteristics, like curved hips, but maintains that "[a]lthough feminists were shortly to speak darkly of it," the miniskirt "was very popular" with women (466). The same pattern occurs in his treatment of the rise of the supermodel mystique, initiated by Jean Shrimpton's success and the subsequent aggressive marketing of Twiggy. First he praises sixties beauty standards—including flat chests and straight hips on women—then defensively asserts their healthy naturalness. Since "throughout history slimness has always been highly regarded, fatness never praised," he claims, "it is absurd to argue that a new style of scrawniness was being created" (418).[8]

Despite the playful tone of his account, Levy sounds more reasonable when he quotes fashion entrepreneur Barbara Hulanicki: "The postwar babies had been deprived of nourishing protein in childhood and grew up into beautiful skinny people" (6). His discussion of Mary Quant, the designer who defined fashionable femininity in the sixties as the possession (or acquisition by any means necessary) of a body similar to that of a preteen and who denigrated visible breasts and hips as matronly, ugly, and out-of-date, is also instructive. He describes her "Peter Pan–ish idea about what constituted—or ought to constitute—women's fashions," quoting her statement "'I grew up not wanting to grow up'" (45). Since this attitude, an obsessive fear of attaining womanhood, is now treated as one of the first danger signs of anorexia nervosa, it is not hard to see why Carter depicts the physicality of the fashionably prepubescent-looking girl as a site of Gothic horror, the other side of which is not maturation, but rapid decay unto death. In the sixties, women had even more reason than men to echo The Who's "My Generation": "hope I die before I get old."

Carter's second novel, *The Magic Toyshop*, focuses more sympathetically on a girl trapped within a culture that demands female performances of immaturity. The book opens with the fifteen-year-old protagonist, Melanie, discovering "that she [is] made of flesh and blood," followed by masturbatory games in which she imitates famous female images in art and literature and her eager, anticipatory trying on of her mother's magnificent wedding dress (1). Melanie soon learns what her budding beauty will signify within the new world of sixties aesthetics and the social arrangements at the center of the emergent youth culture.

The sudden death of her parents forces her into the "dirty and common," but extremely unconventional, household of her dictatorial, eccentric toy-maker uncle Philip Flower, his mute wife Margaret, "struck dumb on her wedding day," and Margaret's younger brothers Francie and Finn (77, 197). Philip's creations are timely, "a unique fusion of folk-art and pop-art," in the words of a photo-journalist, whose camera Philip throws down the stairs because he despises the idea of producing art for a market (95). The family's life is organized around performances in Philip's private puppet theater. In symbolic terms Melanie's movement from one family to the other replicates the transformation of English popular culture during this period from one in which the young looked forward in excitement to maturity and adults provided models for identity to one that imprisoned them in a timeless toyshop of perverse pleasures and thrilling horrors.

Implicitly punning on Flower's power, Carter reveals a counterculture which is still firmly governed by patriarchs, grown-up "angry young men" who have dropped out of the bourgeois society against which they still rage, and who refuse to let women share their reign over the underworld. Philip chose his wife for her extreme poverty; she is an Irish orphan. Carter punningly depicts her as "frail as a pressed flower," and frequently mentions "her famine leanness" (73, 109). "She looked like an icon of Our Lady of Famine, pictured as a spare young girl" (113). Margaret's ability to gain sustenance, and weight, is restricted by the tight, high metal collar her husband bestowed on her as a wedding gift, which makes swallowing difficult, although it also makes her appear proud and beautiful. Unable to fully take in the cautionary aspects of her aunt's situation, Melanie is initially compliant when Philip decides to have her act with the puppets on stage because "[s]he's not too big, she won't be out of scale" (133). She even goes along with his choice of drama, Leda's rape by Zeus in the form of a swan, since, after all, the rapist will be a puppet. But Philip soon expresses resentment of her physical development, complaining, "I wanted my Leda to be a little girl. Your tits are too big" (143).

The only escape from this insane dollhouse in which she can never be more than a puppet is literal and figurative openness to Gothic darkness. Her self-confidence begins to trickle back when the beaten-down outcast Finn kisses her in the park and she has a sudden image of them together: "she thought they must have looked very striking, like a shot from a new-wave British film, locked together in an embrace beside the broken statue in this dead fun palace, with the November dusk swirling around them" (106). After accepting him as a lover and, even more momentously, accepting the knowledge that Margaret and Francie are an incestuous couple, Melanie realizes, "Now we have shared all this, we can never be like other people" (199). The novel ends with the house burning down and "everything" gone: "At night, in the garden, they faced each other in a wild surmise" (200). The garden of renewal, the paradise of mutual love, Carter suggests, cannot be attained through a determined adherence to girlhood because of the price girls must pay if they want eternally to forestall becoming women. Instead, they must enter the dark garden and "marr[y] the shadows," for only thus can the bourgeois world be rejected without something even more monstrous taking its place (77).

Several Perceptions descends more deeply into that monstrousness, through its older protagonist, the twenty-two-year-old proto-hippie nihilist Joseph. "Joseph had the chance of a fine education but threw it away; he had free choice on the self-service counter and voluntarily selected shit, old men dying, pus and, worst of all, most dreaded of encounters, the sweet blue gangrene" (4). His service as a hospital orderly in a ward of elderly male terminal patients addresses the guilt he feels as an unwilling but passive participant in the West's destruction of Vietnam, even as he recognizes that he inhabits "the world of no expiation" (13). He is unable to accept the potentially redemptive love his girlfriend Charlotte, a graduate student writing about Jane Austen, tries to give him. After he drives her away, he projects onto her the horror he feels at his own, inevitably privileged because "first world," existence. He dreams of her face as

> a Gothic mask, huge eyeballs hooded with lids of stone, cheekbones sharp as steel, lips of treacherous vampire redness and a wet red mouth which was a mantrap of ivory fangs. Witch woman. Incubus. Haunter of battlefields after the carnage in the image of a crow. After the bombs fell, in the ruins of the village, the rescue party surprised a woman gnawing gobs of flesh. His Madonna of the abattoir. (15)

Coleridge's nightmare life-in-death returns as a nice middle-class girl who can make your house a home, "since home is where the heart is and there is no place like it" (15–16). Still dicing with the devil for the sinner's soul, she has nothing to offer if she wins except life in "a pure bubble of whitewash" (14).

Joseph prefers Mrs. Boulder, the aging prostitute mother of his Mod best friend Viv, with her "startling and forlorn" eyes and "haunted silences" (34). As he tells her, the details of Charlotte's fresh beauty were often to him "kind of memento mori, reminders everyone was slowly dying everywhere" (113). In contrast, he is comforted by "the coarseness of [Mrs. Boulder's] skin and the melting ooze of her flesh [that] spelled in braille she was a ruin of time," remarking to himself that "all this palpable evidence of decay inspired no revulsion, instead, a savage passion of tenderness" (114). Unlike the self-assured and admonitory Charlotte, Mrs. Boulder has no words of wisdom to give him other than to share her cheerful recognition that "if death is the wages of sin, it's the wages of virtue too" (117). Their intensely pleasurable love-making symbolizes more than his acceptance of the inevitability of death. It also represents his acceptance that life can never be frozen into the idealized image of youth central to the sixties' aesthetic.

After adoring Mrs. Boulder's fat, flabby body and withered face, Joseph can make "friends with time again," and Carter, through this profoundly Gothic scene, rejects the Mary Quant concept of rebellion in favor of a form of transgression with more potential to endure (146). She rejects the sixties' aesthetic of eternal youth in favor of a Goth(ic) aestheticization of the grotesquely beautiful ruin. And in so doing, Carter is consistent with the movement of her times. Brick notes that as "[t]he impulse to strip away illusion, look behind appearances, and gauge the validity of long-held, oft-professed ideals or norms followed demands for social change," the early sixties' delight in decorative artifice gave way to a pursuit of "unhappy truths" in the name of "authenticity" (68). Carter's genius, and prefiguration of Goth, was to have this cake and eat it too by rendering those truths in luscious purple, just as Goth music and performance now strive to do. Her ornate playfulness makes a delicious meal, as it were, of Miss Havisham's decaying wedding cake.

Heroes and Villains is introduced with four epigraphs, including one from Leslie Fiedler's *Love and Death in the American Novel*: "The Gothic mode is essentially a form of parody, a way of assailing clichés by exaggerating them to the limit of grotesqueness." Carter returns, in this mode, to the problem she left at the conclusion of *The Enchanted Toyshop*, the fate of the young woman who seeks love outside the enclosure of bourgeois propriety. But whereas Melanie begins her story as a victim, cast out of the serene and proper upper middle class by her parents' untimely death, Marianne, the protagonist of the postapocalyptic *Heroes and Villains*, chooses life with the Barbarians over safety in an enclosure maintained and protected by a coalition of Professors and Soldiers.

The incendiary atmosphere of the student rebellions of 1968 and 1969 infuses Carter's dystopia, in which the Professors emerge from "the deep shelters" after a nuclear war that has left most of Britain in poisoned ruins. They hope "to resurrect the gone world in a gentler shape, and try to keep destruction outside this time," but quickly come to rely on the Soldiers to keep the Barbarians outside, even giving the Soldiers their first-born sons (8). The Barbarians, "[l]ike hobgoblins of nightmare, [with] flesh of many colors and great manes of hair [that] flew out behind them," led by Doctor Donally, who dispenses drugs and metaphysics, fuse the back-to-the-land hippie movement with urban modern primitivism (5). Marianne's first view of the Barbarian women evokes the residents of a commune or else "street people" of the period, although comparison to today's Goths would also be apropos:

> The women wore trousers or long cumbersome skirts made out of stolen blankets, or stolen cloth, or leather, or fur. They had blouses, some beautifully embroidered, and rough, sleeveless jackets usually of either fur or leather; some wore Soldiers' jackets though the black leather had been transformed by the application of beads, braiding, and feathers. They were all decorated with astonishing, tawdry jewellery, some of it plainly salvaged from the ruins and of great age, some weirdly fashioned from animal bones and feathers. Their hair was wound with ribbons and feathers; their faces were painted a little around the eyes or else tattooed with serpentine lines. . . . Most were barefoot, though some wore stolen boots or sandals made of straw. (13)

Marianne, "daughter of a Professor of History" after history has become meaningless and, as Donally paints on his wall, "MEMORY IS DEATH," goes into the Barbarians' forest to live with Jewell, a descendant of gypsies and a gender-bending "phallic and diabolic version of female beauties" (87, 141, 137). For a short time she is happy, but she soon discovers, as Melanie does, that the alternative world, the word in which mainstream culture is countered, still operates under a patriarchy that defines her by reproductive ability. Then "she want[s] to escape, as if somewhere there was still the idea of home" (52). But "[t]he roads were arteries which no longer sprang from a heart. Once the cities were gone, the roads reverted to an older function; they were used for the most existential kind of travelling, that nomadic peregrination which is an end in itself" (107). She must perforce accept nomadism because destinations no longer exist. As Donally tells her, "There's nowhere to go, dear" (95). She follows Donally's demand that she "[m]arry the Prince of Darkness" (Jewell), although, since "her ruling passion was always anger rather than fear," she cannot submit to him, only temporarily transform herself "into a mute, furious doll which allowed itself to be totally engulfed" (61, 69). Soon she is pregnant.

Is this the ultimate fate of the Swinging London dolly birds, Carter seems to be asking? To become bedraggled, always-breeding, commune hippie mamas? And to what end? Her Barbarians cannot make a new world because they depend on the one that excludes them and is still dominant to produce the goods they need to survive. And worse still, they cannot seem to imagine a world not founded on the gender inequalities of the previous ones. Not wanting to "accept the role of father" and join the patriarchs, Jewell hopes to join the Professors, who he believes have more visionary power because they have more education (122). But Marianne cautions him that among them he can never be more than "an icon of otherness," endlessly studied, "observed and judged . . . to see how you revealed your differences" (123–24). The novel ends inconclusively with Jewell's death and Marianne being told by Donally's idiot son, "there was nothing no more." Like the raven of Poe, one of Carter's favorite writers, he repeats, "No more" (151). This is the moment of exhausted hopes, when the world ends in the Gothic ruin where Barbarians are encamped because all the possibilities have already been dreamed and found incapable of fostering freedom. We are back at the moment, so movingly described by Greil Marcus, when community dissolves in chaos and there is nothing left except a resounding "NO."

After this, what could Carter's 1971 novel *Love* be but a roll in the ashes? Carter returns to depict, in "naturalist fiction," her own times, "those days of social mobility and sexual license," or rather, as she shows, their failure to inaugurate a new world (116, 113). The novel focuses on the disruption of the incestuous attraction between Lee and his brother Buzz by Lee's brief marriage to the mad girl Annabel. Patricia Juliana Smith calls it a "Gothic novel," because of its exposure of "the pleasurable terrors of the imagination lurking at the heart of romanticism" (25). But Smith seems to be misreading Carter's values when she argues that the novel also offers a Jane Austen–like critique of sensibility as "a lesson for us all," warning that we should not expect to maintain lives of intense sensation, since we shall inevitably become "the dreaded Establishment" for the subsequent generation (29). This conclusion seems undercut by the afterword Carter gave to the novel in 1987, in which we are told of the tremendous and lasting success achieved by Buzz, who in the sixties lists on a job application as his only interests "sex and death," and in the late seventies becomes "rich and famous" thanks to his ability to "[impart] the very quality of 'The Masque of the Red Death'" to the Goth clubs he manages (12, 116–17). If he suffers because of "his inability to feel as intensely in situations that were actual as he did in the events of his imagination" and because "[l]ife rarely rose to the demands he made on it," this is, as Carter explains, because in the sixties "he is still waiting for his historical moment," one in which the homosexuality he desperately tries to suppress can be expressed and his sadomasochistic passions can be unleashed (93, 116). Carter imagines his later, happier life immortalized in a "portrait by Robert Mapplethorpe" (117).

A sensible assessment of Carter's depiction of the sixties' sex ways should probably begin by recognizing the relationships she presents as romantic ideals in her later, more optimistic work, instead of by retrospectively imposing on her texts the values that took form in moral discourses on sexuality at the end of the twentieth century. One might look, for instance, at the most famous tale of her werewolf trilogy in *The Bloody Chamber* (1979), "The Company of Wolves," a coming-of-age myth in which Red Riding Hood meets and defeats a big bad werewolf.[9] "She has her knife and she is afraid of nothing" (114). But her defeat of him is not a destruction or even a rejection of this "carnivore incarnate" with "genitals, huge," who has devoured other women, including her own grandmother (116). Instead, she "freely" kisses him, makes love to him, joins him in a mystical union; she is, as Deleuze and Guattari say, "becoming-wolf." Or, as fantasy texts by Goth favorites like Poppy Z. Brite and Laurell K. Hamilton suggest, she is recovering the animalistic, very much including its violence and cruelty, as a means of escape from contemporary norms.

In *A Thousand Plateaus*, Deleuze and Guattari revisit Freud's account of the patient he called "the Wolf-Man" in order to explain "the dream of multiplicity," through which identity can escape the structure of arborescent hierarchy and become rhizomatic (30). For Deleuze and Guattari "the Wolf is the pack" (31). Carter says the girl and the werewolf join "in a savage marriage ceremony" that in no way excludes "[e]very wolf in the world" (118). Because for Deleuze and Guattari, "becoming and multiplicity are the same thing," so becoming-wolf means entering the intensity of the pack, returning to elemental community (250). This type of union is the antithesis of the sort of bourgeois monogamy, called in popular therapy discourse "a committed relationship," that the sexual revolution failed to help women achieve. Carter's early novels do critique the sexual revolution for breaking open suppressed hostilities between men and women and facilitating high levels of violent confrontation, but she also records a cultural history in which the intensity of that breaking open makes pleasure, and love, possible. For, as Deleuze and Guattari ask,

> What does it mean to love somebody? It is always to seize that person in a mass, extract him or her from a group, however small, in which he or she participates, whether it be through the family only or through something else; then to find that person's own packs, the multiplicities he or she encloses within himself or herself which may be of an entirely different nature. To join them to mine, to make them penetrate mine, and for me to penetrate the other person's. Heavenly nuptials, multiplicities of multiplicities. . . . We each go through so many bodies in each other. (35–36)

Carter's early novels show us young women as tough travelers trying to move toward such becomings. If they are killed along the way, she urges us to see them as fallen warriors, not as helpless victims. If they reach victory, she does not place that victory in the domestic sphere.

As feminism has become more domesticated, more invested in promulgating the myth that all women want to experience sexuality only as an expression of caring and only when it is deeply imbedded in structures meant to produce safety and stability, Carter's Gothic play with the gendered problems of the sixties has become less comprehensible. And the loss is doubled by the mystification that has obscured the dark well of the sixties' exploration into the eroticization of violence that was then forbidden on puritanical grounds and has since become taboo within majoritist feminism. Looking at Carter through the lens of later Goth's engagements with S/M allows us a clearer view of the nuances of Carter's resistance to the dominant culture and the toxic leakage of its sexism into the counterculture. As precursors to today's Goth fiction, her early novels are records of a long struggle to create a culture of terrifying pleasure not achieved at the expense of women or of the most vulnerable men.

3.

THAT OBSCURE OBJECT OF DESIRE REVISITED

Poppy Z. Brite and the Goth Hero as Masochist

Poppy Z. Brite's importance to the Goth subculture was best expressed for me through this response I received to an online questionnaire: "Do I read Poppy Z? I ALREADY TOLD YOU I WAS A GOTH!"[1] Anyone with more than a passing acquaintance with Goths should recognize as typical my respondent's astonishment that I would need to ask. Davenport-Hines calls her "the most impressive goth novelist to emerge in the USA in the 1990s" (345). And in case that seems faint praise, he also describes her novel *Exquisite Corpse* as "surpass[ing] even [her] *Lost Souls* as one of the century's finest gothic texts" (362). Although Brite has been and remains enormously popular with Goths of all sexual and gender identifications, my focus in this chapter will be on the appeal of her fiction to young women, both inside and outside that culture. This seems to me the approach most likely to reveal what it is about Goth's constructions of gender and sexuality that has made this subculture a major target of official discourses and policies that try to normalize the young. I focus on girls and young women here because in official regulation of the sexuality of the young, females are always the hardest hit.

If traditional binary gender identification is seen as essential to the proper socialization of the young into their roles as useful participants in our consumer culture, as seems strongly suggested by virtually any collection of abstinence education materials, then Goths constitute a problem. But if Goths follow the sixties' tradition in dark rebellion, so well represented by Angela Carter, of violently subverting sexual norms in order to free women from the tyranny of domestication, then they constitute a crisis. To explore the roots of that crisis, I will look at some of the major (counter)cultural contexts that determine the reception of Brite's novels within a reading community of young women, especially, but not only, those who identify themselves as Goths.

The late 1980s popularization of Goth and its influence on youth cultures has been crucial to the formation of a large number of young women's gender and sexual identities, as Lauraine Leblanc shows in her study of girls' resistance to cultural norms through involvement in music subcultures (81–83). We can understand Brite's novels better if we read their representations of sexuality and gender without imposing some of the most common interpretive frames used by critics working on youth cultures now, because those approaches make fundamental assumptions about sexuality that do not match concepts of sexual and gender identity in the Goth subculture from which the texts arise. Reading the sexual dynamics of the novels in ways suggested by the subculture that contains them can reveal much about the attraction of sadomasochism for postmillennial youth and the various meanings assigned to gender in the contemporary Goth(ic) aesthetic.

Brite's novels might initially seem a strange place to examine how the masochistic male body is displayed as an erotic object for women, since passionate attractions and affairs between males are central in her work, while females are peripheral at best. But consideration of some aspects of the Goth subculture that contextualize Brite's fiction helps explain the importance of the female spectators who sometimes figure as characters within the texts and who we can assume, for reasons I will discuss, make up a significant part of each novel's audience.

Goth social scenes, at least its public events and club nights, are filled with male masochistic spectacles explicitly staged for females' as well as males' enjoyment. If I wanted to comment on my local Goth scene in Portland, Oregon, I might discuss the 1997 Impulsive Theater production of *Titus Andronicus* reimagined as the story of Tamara, Queen of the Goths, dressed as the ruler of Fetish Night and topping a collection of eager male Goth club kids. Or perhaps the amazing show put on for a mainly Goth audience by performance artist Ron Athey, who hangs suspended by his body piercings. Or that, throughout the nineties and into the twenty-first century, the Paris Theater, painted black and decorated for S/M clubbing with, among other touches, a barred cage similar to the one featured in Nine Inch Nails' *Wish* video, served as the venue for most Goth bands. Or if I wanted to cover the national scene I might comment on Marilyn Manson, who continues to publicly identify himself with Goth, and I might focus on the implications of his "confession," in a *Rolling Stone* interview, that he fell in love with Rose McGowan after seeing her play the aggressive and adored girlfriend of a weak, vulnerable boy who is beaten to death in Gregg Araki's film *The Doom Gen-*

eration (Heath, 38). I might even discuss in some depth a number of the more than thirty thousand hits returned by a June 2004 Google search on the terms "goth club fetish night," which represent a stunning number of American and international spaces where those with an interest in Goth and/or fetishes can club together. However, the enthusiasm my young informants on Goth countercultural scenes showed for such developments was nearly negligible beside their passion for Brite, whom they dubbed the true Queen of the Goths.

If many of the young consider Brite essential to their Goth identities, she returns the favor in her first two novels, *Lost Souls* (1992) and *Drawing Blood* (1993). Both are set partly in a New Orleans populated almost entirely by Goth club kids, with a few disagreeable parental figures thrown in for dramatic effect, but most of their action takes place in Missing Mile, North Carolina, a small town in which the only major business seems to be a club called The Sacred Yew, refuge for "the forlorn, bewildered teenagers who had never asked to be born and now wished they were dead, the misfits, the rejects" (*Drawing*, 27). "Crowds of thin children in black," "omnipresent children in black" (*Lost Souls*, 310, 102), recognizable to readers as Goths, appear throughout Brite's work. *Lost Souls* shows us "kids with long dark hair and eyeliner, kids with razor scars on their wrists, kids already sick of life" in Missing Mile (193), and, thronging the streets of New Orleans, "kids wearing black clothes, black lipstick and eyeliner. Silver crosses, daggers, razor blades dangled from their wrists and earlobes. . . . Deathers: kids who loved the night, loved the bands whose music spoke of dark beauty and fragile mortality" (302). In *Exquisite Corpse* (1996), a prowling serial killer finds his favorite café "packed with a young Gothic crowd tonight, resplendent in their monochromatic regalia, the myriad textures of teased hair, torn lace, fishnet, and crushed velvet more fascinating to the eye than colour" (175). And in *The Crow: The Lazarus Heart* (1998), businesses, like the coffeehouse Pained Expression and the PaperCut gallery, are filled with Goth patrons: "androgynous bodies in latex and leather and fishnet stockings. Faces painted white as skulls, eyes as dark as empty sockets. Bits of metal and bone protruding from lips and eyebrows, jewelry like the debris of an industrial accident" (79).

Brite's novels are also always arranged around a central male figure who is above all else a Goth, whom we may see, at some point in the narrative, singing in front of a Goth band. He always has black hair, natural or dyed, a pale white face with heavily blackened eyes, and a body marked with scars, of his own and of others' making. The physical characteristics of these boys are described in lush detail, with great emphasis on their delicacy and vulnerability. True to the classic Gothic convention for heroines, they are always at risk, under threat of death from the forces of evil.

This evil is consistently connected to patriarchal figures who represent a masculine identification synonymous with real or spiritual death. In *Lost Souls*, Nothing is seduced by a band of vampires and in danger of being destroyed by their coldly vicious leader, Zillah, who happens to be the father who abandoned him before his birth. In *Drawing Blood*, Zach, a runaway from continual paternal abuse, joins Trevor in his struggle against his father's murderous ghost. In *Exquisite Corpse*, Tran, a boy cast out on the streets by his homophobic father, is targeted as the ideal victim by a pair of psycho killers, one of whom he hopes to bond with as a substitute for Luke, the older lover whom he lost to AIDS-induced emotional problems. In *The Crow*, Benny is killed by Stanley Hudson/Joseph Lethe/Jordan, a maniac with multiple personalities who believes he has a mission to eliminate boys who commit "gender transgression" (198), and Benny's transsexual twin, Lucrece, is under attack from the same man. While all four novels equate the policing of boys' and young men's gender identity with deathly danger from bad and powerful adult males, the connection is made most explicitly in *The Crow*, in which "the man named for rivers" tirelessly seeks to find and eradicate each "sexless creature that would hide itself in the world of men and women, the black and white world of opposites and opposition" (10). To him androgyny is "*alien*, viral," and he is "the foil who stands for order against Their chaos," a perspective that marks him as himself the sort of "monstrosity" he believes gay and transgendered males to be (10, 182, emphasis Brite's). In these horror novels forced gender conformity seems to be the ultimate horror. And the most powerful form of resistance to it is a male masochism to which refusal of conventional masculine identification is central.

Because Brite's work consistently valorizes gender fluidity, an optimistic reader could easily take her novels' popularity as a sign that gender is being radically revised by the young. Yet such optimism is not often found among prominent gender theorists discussing youth cultures, especially in instances in which male masochism is, as in Brite's novels, a major technology of change in gender identity construction. To discuss male masochism as useful and important to women's sexual liberation is a vexed project because as Linda S. Kaufman points out, "male heterosexual submissives . . . constitute a substantial subculture, unacknowledged, because their existence defies too many taboos" (21). She identifies among these taboos exposure of the fact not only that binary gender difference is "neither innate nor natural," but also that feminist theories founded on a concept of heterosexuality in which "man is [inevitably] the oppressor, woman the victim" still influence both academic and mainstream discourses (26).[2] Male masochistic performance, whether heterosexual or gay, Kaufman claims, expresses an "antiaesthetic" that threatens the "ideology of romantic love" that has been traditionally so disabling to women. Yet this very ideology, Kaufman demonstrates, ironically underlies feminist critiques of pornographic representations of sexuality as a violation of women's putatively different, less aggressive sense of the erotic (60). Within a schema that defines male sexuality as essentially objectifying and invasive and female sexuality as essentially nonviolent and anti-objectifying, women cannot be seen as benefiting from observing the enactment of men's masochism.

Angela McRobbie understands the code of mainstream romance as "the girl's reply to male sexuality"; in it aggression and penetration of the body are devalued in favor of warm emotional connection and gentle nurturing (86). If we adopt this perspective it seems apparent that, because they conflate sadomasochism with romance, Brite's novels offer young female readers a radical departure from what the dominant cultural ideology persistently identifies as their pleasure. The novels' consistent concern with the masochism of boys and men makes it seem even more unlikely that young women would be among their fans, if we follow tradition and understand girls as sweeter and gentler than males. In short, Kaufman's view of female dominant/male submissive erotics as subversive of gender norms importantly foregrounds the ways texts like Brite's challenge what Gilles Deleuze and Félix Guattari call majoritarian language, the language through which binary gender identities are conferred.

According to Deleuze and Guattari's theory of majoritarian languages and literatures, which is derived from Foucault's genealogies of dominant discourses, these forms express the identities that result from the coding of experience by cultural and societal power structures.[3] In its engagement with male masochism, Brite's fiction fits Deleuze and Guattari's definition of a minoritarian literature. Instead of affirming the universalized identities that best serve existent power structures, of which the binary gender system is the most familiar, minoritarian literatures create identities that resist bourgeois norms by insisting on the particularity of sexual experience (*Thousand Plateaus*, 105–106). As Claire Colebrook explains, "A minoritarian politics does not have a *pre-given* (or transcendent) measure or norm for inclusion or identity" (*Gilles Deleuze*, 117). I emphasize the word "pre-given" because it is important to recognize that minoritarian art does generate its own systems of meaning-making, otherwise it would be completely indecipherable. The full potential of female dominant/male submissive S/M to subvert gender binarity is unintelligible within majoritarian language, where masculinity invariably signifies the power to dominate and femininity inescapable vulnerability. Its practices confound majoritarian codes not by reversing or inverting them, but by suggesting the basic performativity of gender identity. Thus S/M is, as Deleuze and Guattari frequently assert, revolutionary in its opposition to the deployments of sexuality dictated by the dominant culture, for "no society can tolerate a position of real desire without its structures of exploitation, servitude, and hierarchy being compromised" (*Anti-Oedipus*, 116).

Interestingly Deleuze himself, so brilliant on the subversive power of male masochism, could be seen as having been, before his collaboration with Guattari, a bit under the sway of dominant discourses in his reading of the dominatrix figure as a sort of ventriloquist's dummy in *Masochism: An Interpretation of Coldness and Cruelty*, his study of Sacher-Masoch's *Venus in Furs*, the novel on which the clinical and popular definitions of masochism were based. If we see heterosexual interaction conventionally—that is, as inevitably determined by the male partner's desire—then it necessarily follows that the woman's place in the sadomasochistic scenario is that of duped tool, or puppet. Of literary representations of such S/M encounters, Deleuze writes, "the masochistic hero . . . dresses her for the part and prompts the harsh words she addresses to him. It is the victim who speaks through the mouth of his torturer" (22).

The irrepressibly playful Angela Carter picks up this image and spins a feminist fable out of it in her short story "The Loves of Lady Purple," in which a masochistic puppeteer "reveal[s] his passions" through "his didactic vedette, the puppet, Lady Purple" (27). His possession of the demonic marionette allows him to stage scenes of female sadism and male submission unto death. But one day she magically comes to life, tears out "the strings that moored her," and begins to enact "her own desire" (38). In Carter's tale, as in *The Sadeian Woman*, male desire is seen as the initial occasion for female sadism, but that sadism is recognized as a force in its own right, not merely a complementary response. Goth fiction takes recognition of female sadism further, as is evident in the writings of Thomas Ligotti, heralded by many Goths as the successor to H. P. Lovecraft.[4]

In "Eye of the Lynx," Ligotti's surreal tale of a confrontation in "The House of Chains" between "an enchanted puppet" and the dominatrix who manipulates him, the reversal of the puppet imagery culminates with the protagonist's plea that she recognize his importance to her own fantasy life so that together they can leave the brothel's "tinsellated sideshow" (77). Ligotti's vision of sadomasochism centers on the romantic, if also disquieting, union of those who quite simply "want the same things" (78). His masochist, unlike Carter's self-defeating puppeteer, is an artist/hero "doing away with gratuitous barriers" between, among other things, the two genders (78). This view of the dynamics between masochist and sadist is supported by Karmen MacKendrick's detailed description of the absence of fixed gender in contemporary S/M practice. While she cautions us that gender has not become "an irrelevant, socially discardable category," she maintains that within communities of S/M practitioners one sees "not only gender-bending but what masochist performance artist Bob Flanagan gleefully labeled 'gender demolition'" (100).

Images of sadomasochistic pleasure that escape traditional gender binarity are ubiquitous in Goth subcultures. And as their embrace of Ligotti's work shows, within Goth cultures one is likely to find an anti-binaristic dismantling of a masculinity that is often nearly, but not completely, unrecognizable as such. Baddeley observes that "no contemporary musical subculture can compete with Goth in presenting positive powerful roles for women —as embodied in the Gothic diva's aura of predatory femininity" (253). Goth fashion and personal style are consistently androgynous and playfully confound expectations about gender identity, as any visit to the photo gallery of a Goth website will show. Goth nights at most clubs include S/M and fetish performances, most of which involve some aspect of refusal of conventional sex/gender roles. And, unlike such performances in exclusively gay clubs, they are always viewed by audiences that include appreciative women. Brite identifies herself with such inclusive audiences when, in her foreword to his collection *The Nightmare Factory*, she explains that Ligotti's fiction affects her "as if the images have already appeared somewhere in the murk of my subconscious" (x).

Ligotti depicts S/M both as a collaboration between male masochist and female sadist and as a spectacle staged for the pleasure of an audience whose fluid identifications call into question an automatic equation of biological bodies and genders. And in so doing he gives us one useful framework for reading the complexities of the appeal of Brite's fiction to young women. Nine Inch Nails, which is often referenced in her novels, provides another. It is illuminating to view Brite's work in relation to both Ligotti's and Nine Inch Nails' representations of sadomasochism because of the differences in their emphases. Ligotti, like many Goth artists, helps us get away from the idea that sexual identity is about difference between male and female, while Nine Inch Nails helps us imagine male masochism as pleasure rather than defeat, a concept crucial to understanding how it is possible for some young women to receive these novels as romantic rather than as fantasies of revenge against the sex that oppresses them.

The musical tastes of Brite's characters tend toward what was popular and readily available at the time of each book's composition. So it is not surprising that Nine Inch Nails, a band whose status as Goth is debated among old-school Goths but who, nevertheless, defines Goth for many young people trapped within the suburban mainstream, is a strong presence in Brite's novels. Nine Inch Nails' debut album, *Pretty Hate Machine* (1989), was "the first rock & roll indie album to sell a million copies" (Gold, 54). Brite's characters—primarily uneducated rural and suburban youths who are disgusted by the American dream but lack exposure to sophisticated cultural alternatives, closely resemble the many teenagers to whom Reznor both introduced the independent rock scene and provided a glimpse of sexuality outside the strictures of heteronormativity.

Although several bands generally associated with Goth get an occasional mention in Brite's novels (especially Bauhaus and The Cure, which are referred to repeatedly in *Lost Souls*), Nine Inch Nails gets pride of place when Terry Bucket, the record store owner in *Drawing Blood*, tells the new boy in town that his store carries "[e]verything from Nine Inch Nails to Hank Williams" (62). And as the immediate clarification, "Hank Williams, *Senior*," lets us know, the stock consists of what the hippest townspeople consider important music (emphasis Brite's).

In *Exquisite Corpse*, Luke, the heroic DJ, plays Nine Inch Nails' "Something I Can Never Have," thinking, "It might as well be the theme song of this show, this radio station, everything he had ever written, his desperate love for Tran, his whole miserable life" (91). Tran seduces Jay partly by asking him, "You like Nine Inch Nails?" That Jay "hadn't a clue who Nine Inch Nails were" tells us that this psychotic murderer has "no discernment, no individual taste" (109). It is interesting that Trent Reznor's Nothing record label emerged in 1992, the same year as the publication of Brite's *Lost Souls*, one of whose protagonists is named Nothing. The talismanic power of the phrase he likes to repeat to himself, "*I am Nothing*" (73, emphasis Brite's), seems to echo the words emblazoned on the back of that year's Nine Inch Nails promotional tour t-shirts, "Now I'm Nothing."

A song functions as a parallel sort of emblem in *Drawing Blood*, in which Janis Joplin's rendition of "Me and Bobby McGee" is repeatedly invoked as one of the two central figures, Trevor McGee, attempts to understand why his subculture cartoonist father, Robert (Bobby) McGee, killed himself, and Trevor's mother and brother, but spared him. Bogged down by the responsibilities of family life, Robert McGee loses his art and subsequently his sanity. One can hardly avoid seeing that Brite is commenting on the way the song opposes freedom, which it equates with having "nothing left to lose," to the "home" Bobby leaves the singer to find. Similarly, Nine Inch Nails seems to symbolize for Brite the choice to resist bourgeois constructions of gender, sexuality, and love.

This reading of Nine Inch Nails makes sense because the most amazing aspect of the band's success was the way Trent Reznor presented himself as a heterosexual male masochist. Masochism is heavily represented in both Goth rock and Industrial music, two forms that Nine Inch Nails' sound brought together. However, Reznor's music differs from most well-known and readily available Goth rock in that the lyrics typically describe a craving for pain that seems to turn to anger only when the pain is withheld.[5] One might contrast Reznor to Robert Smith, creator of The Cure, or to Ian Curtis of Joy Division, both of whom sing about eroticized suffering. Reznor paid homage to Curtis's album *Closer* with his most famous song's title. Yet Reznor's song, and the widely aired video that promoted it, stress the pleasure to be had in pain—the "honey" he finds on his knees, the desire that overwhelms him in bondage. By contrast, the name Curtis chose for his band, which derives from the Nazi term for female death-camp prisoners forced into sexual service, suggests his mission to expose sexuality's potential to become horrific, as does the title of Joy Division's song "Atrocity Exhibit." Similarly, both Robert Smith and Morrissey, the singer-songwriter for the Smiths, whose influence on Goth is frequently acknowledged, are often labeled masochists, but their masochism is hardly expressed in the defiantly exuberant manner of a Bob Flanagan or Trent Reznor. (It seems worth noting that Reznor and "Supermasochist" performance artist Flanagan collaborated to produce the video *Happiness in Slavery*.) While Morrissey sings, "Oh, yes, you can kick me / and you can punch me / and you can break my face / but you won't change the way I feel / 'Cause I love you" ("Is It Really So Strange?"), there is no "but" about it in Reznor's songs. Instead he begs for "your kiss, your fist" ("Sin"). He is "sanctified," "purified," and ecstatic as the dominatrix of his dreams "walks [him] through the nicest parts of hell" ("Sanctified").

The first wave of Goth rock in the late seventies and early eighties was still close to its source in Punk, and it usually used sadomasochistic imagery and references to mourn a tainted and evil world in which the only pleasure left to the miserable subject was the eroticization of pain. As Davenport-Hines notes, Brite uses references to Robert Smith's "lyrics of mild sexual abasement" in *Lost Souls* to convey the half-heartedness with which Nothing eroticizes the rather dismal passive sexual relationship he tolerates with his friend Laine that precedes his much wilder and more satisfying life as a vampire (369). Nine Inch Nails shockingly demands that we recognize that some men unambivalently enjoy erotic suffering, and would not choose to have it any other way. We can even more clearly understand why Goths, such as Brite, believe that Reznor radically subverts gender when we consider the history of academic feminist work on the Gothic literary genre that informs contemporary Goth subcultures.

Feminist critics have shown interest in the Gothic since Ellen Moers's groundbreaking *Literary Women* (1977), a section of which deals with what she names "The Female Gothic." Demonstrating the ways women writers' Gothic fiction works to undermine patriarchal ideology is central to Sandra Gilbert and Susan Gubar's *The Madwoman in the Attic* (1979), and the list of feminist theorists who have devoted entire studies to this genre includes luminaries Eve Sedgwick and Julia Kristeva. However, as Anne Williams points out, the prevailing view has been that "the Gothic inculcated patriarchal standards in its readers while at the same time offering a kind of vicarious contemplation of patriarchal horrors" (123).[6]

One recent feminist academic study of Gothic literature, Michelle Massé's *In the Name of Love: Women, Masochism, and the Gothic,* illustrates the majoritarian position on gender and sexuality in this genre. Massé's politically invested approach, coupled with her apparent assumption that the masochism presented in Gothic texts is nearly exclusively female, predetermines her study's culmination in a chapter called "Resisting the Gothic." Massé concludes with the wish that all impulses toward sadomasochism be eradicated from our psyches so that women will no longer eroticize their own pain or that of other women, a time "when the spectator need not endlessly watch a woman being beaten" (274). Such a theory misses the potential of the Gothic to unsettle gender binarity, perhaps because it is not concerned with the Gothic stagings of youth culture at our century's end. Although I agree with Massé on several points, I could not read her reference to "the spectator" without thinking of a Goth student with whom I spoke for an article I was writing on the reception of Nine Inch Nails and Marilyn Manson (then both recording on the Nothing label).

I imagined this student saying indignantly that although she has no interest in watching women being beaten, she loves Gothic culture. In our conversation, she told me that, in her view, Gothic culture need not always replicate the traditional distribution of sadistic and masochistic impulses according to gender. Instead it allows for identifications that disrupt the idea that the victim must always be female and that sadistic pleasure must always involve thrilling to the spectacle of a woman's pain. This twenty-eight-year-old feminist found her Goth identity when she first saw Marilyn Manson on MTV in the video for his cover of the Annie Lennox/Eurythmics hit "Sweet Dreams," staggering around looking blissfully bloody in a pink tutu and Goth-inspired make-up, to the tune of his own voice enthusiastically growling, "Some of them want to use you . . . Some of them want to abuse you." While a number of Goths, especially those who belonged to this subculture before the late 1980s, reject Manson as a poseur who undermines the true meaning of Goth, for women like my student he embodies an attitude about sexuality that gives them hope. As she remarked to me about the battered character that Manson portrays in the video, "If there are men like that, then there's something to live for."

She, like most of my informants on youth culture, finds images of such men—who willingly and enthusiastically embrace the role of sacrificial victim—everywhere in Goth music and performances and in the writers favored by Goths, especially Brite. She described Brite as the heir of other pop vampire and supernatural story writers like Anne Rice, but also, without any prompting from me, connected Brite's work to *Dracula* and *Frankenstein*, and—a bit more surprisingly—to *Wuthering Heights*. All of these texts were, to her, about the excitement, romance, and eroticism of male pain and suffering, a suffering that she felt free to enjoy fully because of her assumption that men have choices women do not, and thus when they engage in eroticized suffering it is because they enjoy doing so. Many of my informants (both male and female), in giving such accounts of volition in S/M, solemnly quoted MTV: "it's all good." A comparison of this vision of Gothic culture to Massé's ("it's all bad"?) suggests that one fruitful way to understand the appeal of Brite's work to her young female readers is through the masochistic male's body, or rather its discursive translations and the symbolic systems in which it can signify.

In *Exquisite Corpse*, the serial killer Andrew Compton, upon contemplating the street boy Tran, thinks,

> He was pretty—very pretty—but so were loads of other boys. This one had something extra. How could a single person fulfill all the mannerisms, distill that vital blend of insecurity and insouciance, exude pheromones that so clearly begged *cut me, fuck me, lay me out cold and have your way with me?* (210, emphasis Brite's)

Such moments in which desire takes shape in relation to the all-too-vulnerable body and emotions of a beautiful boy abound in Brite's fiction and could even be considered its defining feature. Yet numerous details in the work suggest that it is aimed not only at adult men, who might enjoy fantasizing about taking such victims, and the beautiful youths who might feel a thrill of terror at imagining themselves as such victims, but also at women and girls, who, superficially at least, seem to have no role to play in such homoerotic dramas.

The most immediately apparent of these details is that, unlike the growing number of women who write sadomasochistic erotica for a gay male audience, Brite has not adopted a male or androgynous pseudonym. Even more striking is the pervasive romanticism of Brite's fiction, which is filled with depictions of lovelorn yearning—"again he wished that their hearts could be joined" (*Lost Souls*, 346)—and constructed around long-withheld scenes of deliriously passionate consummation, strongly reminiscent of the dramatic climaxes in women's genre romance. And crucially, unlike the relatively few genre romances now being produced for gay men, the stories often seem preoccupied with those conflicts over control of the female body traditionally called "women's issues."

For example, Brite's first collection of short stories was originally entitled

Swamp Foetus, a name that, together with its Louisiana settings, inevitably suggests illegal abortion and its aftermath.[7] The stories frequently refer to unwanted pregnancies and the conflicts surrounding them; for instance, "Angels" refers to a "crackpot doctor, the kind that uses coathangers to tear babies out of women's wombs in back alleys" (20). *Lost Souls* opens with a description of Nothing's vampire conception and the subsequent unnatural birth that kills his mother. Christian, a vampire, had reluctantly accepted the impregnated and abandoned girl as his lover, and when she dies Brite describes his mourning in these terms: "Then he knelt between Jessy's limp legs and looked at the poor torn passage that had given him so many nights of idle pleasure. Ruined now, bloody" (10). The plot is driven by the unsuccessful attempts of two friends and bandmates, Steve and Ghost, to rescue Steve's exgirlfriend Ann from a similar fate, "swell[ing] with a malignant child, a child that would eventually rip her open and bleed her dry" (241). Another character, Richelle, although herself a vampire, also dies horribly as the result of a pregnancy, which she knows will "mean the end of her" (272). Through the vampire experience, the novel codes pregnancy as alien invasion, absolutely incompatible with female survival. The book obsessively focuses on the darkest fears of heterosexual girls still young and inexperienced enough to view pregnancy exclusively as a terrifying threat. The theme of pregnancy as threat to survival returns in *Drawing Blood*, which early on introduces readers to the kindly club owner Kinsey Hummingbird, whose sympathetic personality is established when a dishonest employee asks him for money for an abortion and he "trie[s] to imagine that childish body swollen with pregnancy, [but] could not. The very idea was painful" (31).

Female sexuality is consistently represented, in Brite's fiction, as connected both to a reproductive process that is always either fatal or tragic and to continual exploitation by sexist men. Zach, one of the two protagonists of *Drawing Blood*, is the product of a tragically unwanted pregnancy, as his cruel parents often remind him. Brite describes the repercussions for his mother, whose resentful husband batters her ceaselessly. Another major character in the novel, Eddy, is a (female) stripper, through whose disaffected perspective Brite lingeringly explores how it feels to a young girl to be exploited by "crude and gross" misogynists (79). Because she is also a rape victim, Ann's introduction into *Lost Souls* brings with it detailed description of post-rape trauma and depression. Although men, both gay and heterosexual, can certainly find such topics engrossing, texts aimed exclusively at a male audience do not generally foreground women's reproductive problems, nor do gay male genre romances treat pregnancy as the most important possible consequence of unprotected sexual encounters. (AIDS is never mentioned in *Lost Souls* despite its themes of vampirism and tainted blood, and in *Drawing*

Blood, although Zach's refusal to use condoms is mentioned in connection with the possibility of HIV infection, pregnancy remains the only dramatized consequence of unprotected sex.) Because of the space these concerns occupy in each novel, it seems fairly obvious that Brite presents her lush spectacles of male masochism and suffering for the delectation of a readership meant to include women in substantial numbers.

However, despite this ample dramatization of gender-based oppression, Brite never puts female bodies at the center of her Goth(ic) horror shows. To do so would faithfully follow the Gothic tradition, in a way familiar to her readers from numerous popular cultural forms. As Chris Gallant argues in "Quoting the Raven," in a section called "Exquisite Corpses," contemporary horror genres often recall "the nineteenth-century obsession with idyllic depictions of death in the form of graceful, beautiful female corpses" (81). Outside the Goth subculture, contemporary horror generally adheres to the aesthetic that defines the writings of Edgar Allan Poe. Gallant describes how both Poe's work and twentieth-century horror films present the torture deaths of women as art, allowing males threatened by "aggressive female sexuality" not only to contain the horrors of potential female dominance but also to displace onto women, who become figures for death, their own inevitable relationship with death (81–83).

In contrast, Brite names one of the protagonists of *The Crow: The Lazarus Heart* Poe and structures the story around "The Raven." Poe's famous explication of his composition of this poem details the aesthetic on which Gallant's discussion is based. But Brite's Poe is a Mapplethorpe-inspired photographer whose lover and favorite subject, Benny, is a Goth masochist featured in an exhibition described as effecting "the complete deconstruction of gender and gender roles" (79). Lucrece, Benny's now transgendered but formerly identical twin, takes her place as the observer in his S/M play with Poe, saying, "Fortunately I like to watch" (62). By the conclusion of the novel she, and the readers, have watched some dauntingly terrible games.

In Brite's fiction, as in much of Goth, the gendering of classic Gothic iconography may seem reversed, for she presents her female readers with breaking and broken male bodies that fill the spaces of her prose as if it were the last act of *Hamlet.* What are we to make of this phenomenon? Should we take Brite's popularity with this segment of her audience to mean that her "pretty" and, in conventional terms, effeminate male victims—who often voluptuously surrender to their tormentors—symbolize girls' images of their own role in culture? The current majoritarian feminist position on the gender identifications of girls certainly involves a lot of hand wringing over their victimization. Popular psychology texts like Mary Pipher's *Reviving Ophelia,* whose title indicates the role adult feminists are called upon to play, tell us that girls' lives are in crisis because of a culture that poisons every aspect of their experience. In *The Body Project: An Intimate History of American Girls*, Joan Jacobs Brumberg cautions us that we should not take it as cause for celebration that "[t]eenagers today grow up in a world where rigid dichotomies between gay (homosexual) and straight (heterosexual) behavior are disappearing," since that change can result in girls' adoption of a sadomasochistic aesthetic, and, in Brumberg's view, interest in S/M can only increase girls' vulnerability to exploitation (132–33). If we read the male masochists in Brite's stories as figures who stand in for girls, rather than as objects of girls' desire, then works such as Brumberg's, which are predicated on majoritarian concepts of gender difference, would advise us to be very worried about what Brite is telling us about girls' self-perception. In such a reading Brite might be seen to express a new gender binarity with feminine victims (biologically male and female) on one side, and conventionally masculine predators (biologically male) on the other, and with the only sexual subjectivity open to girls being the tragic acceptance of their own painful destruction.

But even the briefest look at slash fiction, a very transgressive pop cultural form that has come into vogue among young people, disrupts this sort of gender symmetry. Initially consisting of texts in which fans of *Star Trek* and *Starsky and Hutch* expressed their fantasies about the television show, slash fiction is now mainly a form of pornography produced by and for women that features male celebrity heroes engaged in homosexual and sometimes sadomasochistic activities. *Star Trek* slash first started appearing in self-published fanzines around 1976 (Penley, 137).[8] Following Sarah Lefanu's analysis of feminist science fiction, Constance Penley argues that slash writing's "roots in the female Gothic novel" allow it to address women's "political concerns" while still leaving room for imaginative play and, of course, eroticism (138). Here, as in Brite's fiction, eroticism entails a breaking down of conventional male inhibition against intense feeling, often through the man's pain and suffering. The focus on male-male sexuality is essential to the eroticism because through it writers (and their readers) escape "the built-in inequality of the romance formula, in which dominance and submission are invariably the respective roles of male and female" (154). Penley recognizes that heterosexual women may identity with gay men because "gay men too inhabit bodies that are still a legal, moral, and religious battleground," but she attributes the primary pleasure fans take in the stories to "aggressive identification with the men and the taking of them as sexual objects" (157, 155). Perhaps most relevant to Brite's work is Penley's astute observation that slash's success with its target audience depends on "the tightest possible focus on . . . men undergoing [a] painful yet liberatory process of self-discovery and learning to communicate their feelings" (156).

Brite's interest in the slash genre was made evident by her chapbook *Plastic Jesus*, a fantasy about John Lennon and Paul McCartney being lovers. However, her Goth horror novels more clearly illustrate how Goth fiction now draws on the slash form. These books have clear affinities with the slash-like stories posted on E. L. Shawcross's Nine Inch Nails fan website, *Devils Speak of Bloody Angels*, on March 4, 1998. In the first one the narrator-protagonist encounters Trent Reznor in a record store shopping for a Cure CD. The rock star agrees to go to a hotel for sex because "You're a man. That's all I need to know." But the protagonist is not a man, s/he is a transman (a female-to-male transsexual, with female genitalia), and in the midst of forcefully dominating him sexually s/he discovers that Reznor is also a person of indeterminate biological sexual identity. What stands out in the story is not this imaginative unveiling so much as the loving depiction of the idol's submission to the fan, his literal opening (the transman takes his virginity), and his extreme vulnerability. Another passage on the site imagines Reznor as biologically male, but maintains the motif of the male (or "male") being forced open to the biological female's passionate gaze through a description of him as he appears in the *Closer* video as "this wet dream of a perfect slave who asks me to break him, hurt him, cut him, and hangs, masked and naked, from chains bound tightly round his leather-gloved wrists."

Like the protagonists of the slash discussed above, Brite's main characters have bodies whose biological sex is at odds with their sexuality or at least with the ways they might be gendered by conventional observers. Their bodies matter in every possible sense, but they resist traditional coding. Inside tales that are as Gothic as they are Goth, most of them inhabit spaces formerly reserved for women, the place of the vulnerable victim. Yet these characters remain heroic despite such feminization; they are not emasculated, not simply because their male sexuality is underlined by near pornographic descriptions of erections and phallic sex acts, but also because they act heroically, although almost never in traditionally masculine ways. Instead, they heroically submit and bravely allow themselves to be opened.

Brite's male protagonists almost always begin as closed-off people who fear emotional connection. A darkly comic element of *Lost Souls* is that the only lover whose affection the severely emotionally repressed Steve is able to return is Ghost, the psychic. Ghost gets inside because he is literally able to read Steve's mind. In *Drawing Blood*, Zach is so afraid of love that he refuses to have sex with anyone with whom he can imagine becoming friends. His ideal sex partner is one with whom coupling and parting take place "by some silent mutual consent" (97). His liaison with Trevor is the first love affair he has had, but Trevor's own emotional remoteness surpasses Zach's in that at age twenty-four he is still a virgin out of fear of letting another person get close. The affair of *Exquisite Corpse*'s central lovers, Luke and Tran, turns tragic because they cannot trust each other, and Tran is left so hurt by the way AIDS makes Luke retreat emotionally that he ends up giving himself to the psychotic murderer Jay, who "had never had a live friend before, and . . . wasn't sure what to do with one" (115). Jared Poe, in *The Crow*, is so chronically angry and disaffected that he is initially profoundly disconcerted to find himself attracted to Benny, whom he thinks of contemptuously as "this pretty, taunting Goth boy dressed up like some William Gibson version of 1890s London," while for his part, the coolly enigmatic Benny holds himself back from this man he suspects might be "just another poseur" (56, 61). Steve and Ghost have telepathy working for them, but in all the other cases only the violence of S/M sex can break through and allow connection to be made. Brite always depicts the young men's surrender to sexual invasion and pain as heroic. Thus, just as eighteenth- and nineteenth-century Gothic literary depictions of female heroes called both eras' gender conventions into question, these male, but not masculine, heroes call into question current concepts of the relation between S/M roles and gender identity.

They sacrifice themselves to protect others; they confront the evil creatures who embody their worst fears; they fight back, although usually only by forcing their tormentors to recognize the damage they do to others. But they are most effective when they gain the courage to distinguish between, and call by their right names, desired and undesired pains, despite their entrapment within a culture that, as Brite repeatedly shows us, fails to distinguish between consensual S/M and abuse. As Davenport-Hines observes, "The victims of her vampires and serial killers present themselves for destruction with entreating passivity, and rejoice in their acts of surrender, yet they have more free will than their killers and abusers who are *compelled* to submit to the rituals and appetites that excite and gratify them" (359–60, emphasis his). These are not, however, simply novels about adolescents attaining manhood by triumphing over their fears, teaching and learning what it is to choose; nor are they coded stories that offer young female readers a satisfying but necessarily transient identification with the boys they can never truly become short of undergoing sexual reassignment surgery. Instead the novels provide boy heroes so removed from conventional gender identities that identification with them allows female readers to imagine eventually taking on the power culturally reserved for men. But the novels do even more to combat the gender stereotypes that can imprison women because Brite's heroes, despite their heroism, remain sexual objects of an exterior gaze, the focal points of erotic drama.

For instance, Brite introduces a scene in which Zach will save his lover Trevor from demonic possession with a description of a masochistic abandon so extreme that it shocks Trevor into feeling responsibility and protectiveness:

> He looked down at Zach. Blood had run down over Zach's face in thick rivulets from a wound in his scalp. Blood leaked from his nostrils and from his torn mouth. He had a lurid purple knot on one shoulder, an encrusted bite mark on the other. His chest was crisscrossed with furious scratches. Where it wasn't cut or bruised, his skin was absolutely white. His eyes held Trevor's. His expression hovered somewhere between terrified and serene.
>
> "Whatever you want," said Zach, "It's up to you." (*Drawing*, 359)

Just as Trevor realizes that, as horribly wounded as Zach is, he still maintains the power to surrender, or not, and chooses to give in out of love, the reader is shown how a man can define himself as heroic through the achievement of masochistic equilibrium between terror and serenity. One may be reminded of Foucault's claim, in his introduction to Deleuze and Guattari's *Anti-Oedipus*, that the expression of outlawed and despised desire can be the strongest force against fascism (xxii–iii). For this, too, is a triumph of the will, but decidedly not in the sense of seizing power over others. Zach's self-possession teaches Trevor how to control himself, and his volitional opening up teaches Trevor how to love.

Brite's books are not about performing conventional masculinity heroically, but about the heroism of performing male masochism for a truly appreciative audience. Often Brite's accounts focus on the redemptive aspect of masochism, but the loving detail with which the valorized bodily injuries are chronicled can be troubling to anyone concerned about young people's physical well-being. She sometimes seems to be suggesting that only submission to nearly deadly beatings can make loving connection possible.

For this reason, *Exquisite Corpse*, even more than the earlier, softer, and more romantic novels, raises difficult questions. Baddeley calls it "breathtakingly perverse" (84).[9] It is a grossly transgressive, heavily eroticized account of men deliberately infecting with HIV, torturing, killing, and eating young boys. And to add to the shock effect, Tran, the ultimate victim, is Vietnamese American, and thus an obvious figure for the damage American racism and particularly Orientalism have wrought.[10] How can we read her romantic and sexy descriptions of Tran's submission to Jay, his tormentor, as anything but an invitation to the reader to be turned on sexually by what is most deathly, most ugly in our culture? Is the book's appeal to its female readers an indication that women now hatefully enjoy imagining the most extreme manifestations of male violence reversed from their usual female targets and turned against young men, and even worse, against young men from oppressed groups?

To read this novel otherwise, as many of its female fans seem to do, it helps to see it as referring to Goth not merely as a subculture but as a resistant counterculture. Gothic horror can point to transcendence of the gender roles that Brite's characters, and perhaps many of her readers as well, deem foundational to a mainstream culture that alienates them. Among such pointers are the repeated references, throughout Brite's books, to music that describes masochistic bliss through which bodily limitations are surpassed, including the cultural coding that links biological sex to binary gender identity. *Exquisite Corpse* inevitably calls to mind The Cure's song "Torture," with its central image of a masochistic hero who sings, "My body is cut and broken / It's shattered and sore / My body is cut wide open / I can't stand anymore" and then "screams for more," because "It's torture / But I'm almost there." Brite's reference to Trent Reznor as a major influence on Luke's life strongly suggests that Nine Inch Nails also provides an interpretive frame for the novel's troubling depictions of desire and its expression. The *Happiness in Slavery* video, which features the simulated torturing to death of Bob Flanagan; the infamous video collection *Broken*, in which the abduction, torture, and evisceration of a young man serves as a frame story for the musical numbers; and the images in the *Closer* video of Reznor dancing in an apparent ecstasy of agony in front of an open carcass on a meat hook all furnish ways to see Tran's fate as pleasure to which he consents in an astoundingly strange gesture of self-assertion. Like the videos, the novel presents the spectacle of male masochism as symbolic. In interviews, Reznor frequently explains the disturbing content of these videos as an expression of the pleasure to be found in giving in to vulnerability and letting go of control (Dunn, 29; Berger, 51; Gold, 53). Likewise, we might speculate that Brite's young female readers interpret the ultimate submission of masochistic heroes like Tran as a symbol of the self-transformation that can occur in much less extreme S/M practice.

As Foucault explained in the *Advocate* in 1984, the practitioners of S/M engage in "inventing new possibilities of pleasure with strange parts of their bodies," and by doing so actively resist sexual normalization ("An Interview," 27). McWhorter, who comments illuminatingly on this passage in Foucault's work (185–86), calls sadomasochistic sex one of the bodily "practices that transform who we are and who we take ourselves to be" (226). Goth culture's constant drawing upon S/M countercultural symbols and practices, referred to by Brite in all of her novels, can therefore be understood to prepare her readers to understand such theatrical set-piece torture scenes as Tran's death: to read them as a dramatization not of brutal sex murder so much as of the sometimes frightening erotic technologies of rebirth into a realm beyond gender binarity.

But while we may read the masochist as a self-transformative hero, the position of his observer remains problematic. Why, we may ask, does Brite include in her novels material that invites young women to consume these spectacles? Anne Williams says that women's productions of the Gothic are typically addressed to a female audience that "may contemplate both the horrors of the ways in which the culture at large regards the female, but also some alternative possibilities in imagining the world as it appears to a female I/eye" (122). Should we conclude that females are now pleased to regard males as potential torture objects? Perhaps, but we might also think of the torture as symbolic of a sort of consensual "play," as S/M practitioners often call their interactions.

Spectacles of male masochism offer girls options other than to struggle for an absolute sexual equality in which all power relations will disappear (the program recommended by many second-wave feminists) or to acquiesce to the traditional domesticity and family values that Brite's novels parody and ultimately dismiss as normalizing facades over systems of exploitation of women and the young. Brite's depiction of domesticity is consistent with the conventions of twentieth-century Gothic fiction by women. As Darryl Hattenhauer points out, in such texts, "[t]he Gothic exposes the home as a repressive location for the policing of gender roles" (94). This is particularly true in texts that contrast the urban and suburban, because these were actually created as separate spheres of American life by a movement in the 1950s to recontain women within domesticity, after the relative freedom afforded them by the chaotic work environments of World War II.

One of Brite's harshest condemnations of contemporary suburban family life comes through her depiction of Michael, a teenage runaway, who finds even the harrowing life of a street prostitute superior to "the gray shroud of suburban despair he escaped," as emblematized by his mother's denial of the repeated rapes to which his stepfather subjects him, a denial motivated by her refusal to accept her own aging and loss of sexual appeal (*The Crow*, 68).[11] In *Lost Souls* Nothing thinks of his adoptive parents as "out somewhere—a consciousness-raising group, a holistic health class, an expensive dinner with other people like themselves" (74–75). To feel as if he belonged to them, he would have to transform himself into "a normal son who would . . . bring home little fresh-faced girlfriends in clean skirts and pink blouses" (70). The idea nauseates him as a betrayal of everything he is. In *Drawing Blood*, Zach feels betrayed by a similar transformation in the film *Beetlejuice*: "The sight of Winona Ryder's character, formerly strange and beautiful in her ratted hairdo and smudged eyeliner, now combed out and squeaky clean, clad in a preppy skirt and kneesocks and a big shit-eating sickeningly *normal* grin" (39, emphasis Brite's). Instead of a male who will domesticate them, Brite's fiction offers young women images of males who recoil from the horror of proper femininity and the reproductive imperative at the heart of family values. *Exquisite Corpse's* Luke, speaking in the persona of Lush Rimbaud, host of a radio talk show, says of other, locally despised gay men, "At least the biological reproduction of our own DNA in the form of a slimy, squalling lump of meat isn't the greatest satisfaction most of us will ever know in life" (91).

The novels do show boys and girls in a deadlocked battle that is all too true to life, as when we are told that *Lost Souls'* Ann and Steve "both pretended to be so tough and cynical that there was no room left to give each other the gentleness they both really needed" (112). But, in addition, the novels offer a vision of boys giving in, giving, even if not to girls. In their swooning surrender, these boys who are always controlled by their passions, always giving wild, impractical and undomesticated love, figure the object, and perhaps even the consummation, of young women's least conventional desires. In *Blissed Out*, Simon Reynolds remarks that "the return of romanticism" in rock and roll valorizes passion rather than a politics whose "'radicalism' [is] barely distinguishable from the pragmatism and 'common sense' of therapists' and counsellors' discourse." He says the dream of a love in which nothing is held back may be "our last reservoir of spirituality in the face of those 'specialists of the soul' who would seek to reform relationships in accordance with their ghastly notions of 'negotiation,' 'support,' 'partnership'" (28). Certainly the dream of love—or, in her fiction, something more like the beautiful nightmare of love—serves as such a reservoir for Brite's readership, even if her romanticism is hardly the sort to which Reynolds refers. The romanticism he sees young people seeking reinscribes conventional roles; Brite's dark, perverse romanticism tears them to pieces.

In *Exquisite Corpse*, just before Tran is vivisected by the serial killer, he "imagine[s] how his father would feel when he found out about this: guilty and grief-stricken, yes, but also vindicated in his beliefs," maybe even seeing the murder as "a stroke of divine mercy" (225). At last Tran is freed from both the burden of adherence to Asian American model-minority behavior, as exemplified by his father, and from the imperative to enact conventional masculinity in order to prove white racists wrong in their supposition that Asian men are epicene.[12] He can finally, without shame, let others see him as he is. And he can be desired, no matter how terribly. Having recognized that he is absolutely incompatible with the world of suburban normalcy, he feels an odd, twisted love for his destroyer, who wants him as no one else ever has. In his voluptuous giving up we might see a Goth shadow of the scene from Kleist that Hélène Cixous claims, in *The Newly Born Woman*, saved her life by providing her with a "dream" of passions "unimaginable in conventional society": Achilles "gives himself" to Penthesileia so completely that "this is no longer the space of mastery. It is the ascent toward a new beauty, where, having exhausted all anguish. . . nothing will remain at stake between king and queen except knowing beauty over and over, no other law than body's insatiable desire" (119). Ronald Bogue's comments on a music form closely related to Goth also help us understand what horrors like the ones in Brite's fiction might mean to her Goth readers: "Death Metal, in short, is appropriately named. There is in its lyrics an obsession with death—not with nothingness and negation—but of the death at the heart of life, the desire/death of zero intensity, which is figured as life after death, the living death of zombies, vampires, ghouls, and devils, the undead, the already dead, the living dead: a becoming death" ("Becoming Metal, Becoming Death . . . ," 105) While in Death Metal such expression is "strongly coded as masculine" (83), within Goth it takes a more feminized form, or at least the line of flight reaches toward the feminine. In Brite's intensely transgressive romanticism not just the male body, but the worlds of meaning it anchors, are deconstructed.

These are stories for boys and girls who know the darkness too well to be able to go back to playing house as if they did not know what was outside, who cannot and do not even want to find love within the domestic enclosure, the survivors of the toppling of patriarchal order. Brite's stories provide a moment in which love appears like a white light in the darkness of a Gothic world. Or, to see otherwise, love appears like a white light *because* of the darkness of the Gothic world, and the one who wants so desperately to touch the other's sores, to lick his blood, appears not as villain(ess) but, as in *The Crow*, as a dark avenging angel.

Consequently, the novels provide Goths with a way to conceptualize the desire to see masculinity not as triumphantly invulnerable but, as in the lyrics of Trent Reznor, as most fulfilled by being "broken," "defaced," "disgraced," and, as a result, at last able to admit love. The broken-open bodies of young men in Brite's work literalize what her readers yearn to experience symbolically, the opening up of maleness to the ravages of passion. In *Exquisite Corpse*'s final image, in which the bones of the victim and his slayer merge in "an ivory sculpture-puzzle shining in the dark, waiting to tell their mute love story," Brite reimagines the male body as a site of reconciliation. Tran's skeletal embrace of his murderer's remains suggests the masochism that makes it possible for a man to be satisfied even by the sort of desire that destroys the integrity of the male body as it enjoys it. The terrible, lawlessly cruel hunger previously attributed in Brite's novels to vampires and ghosts and here figured as a serial killer's need to possess is seen in this final image as a means to a reciprocal experience of love. Since heterosexual women often also feel, as the result of men's traditional emotional remoteness, a desire to love by violently breaking into the male body that seems to prefer to keep them outside, for the female reader this conclusion suggests a kind of forgiveness. The male body opens willingly at last, and, surrounded by the corpses of those mystically defeated by this unexpected surrender, the cannibalistic reader feasts on what has always before been denied.

4.

B̶o̶y̶s̶ Don't Cry

Brandon Teena's Stories

As I hope is clear from the previous chapter, Goths are not merely the innocent victims of persecution by authorities who erroneously believe the Columbine shooters were motivated by a philosophy generated by this subculture. Yes, Goth has been misunderstood in that way. But it does, because of its
emphasis on demonized sexualities, disrupt abstinence education and other
official doctrines meant to regulate young people's sexual expression. Whatever else Goth has been as a youth subculture, it has not been innocent.

The novel *Narcissus in Chains*, by Laurell K. Hamilton, a best-selling
erotic horror fiction author popular with many Goths, offers a blackly comic
example of the sort of attitude prevalent in the subculture toward the values
promoted by the abstinence education regime. The novel's heroine Anita is
seen by most readers as a highly sexualized version of Buffy the Vampire
Slayer—the television character whose eponymous series Baddeley calls, "at
best, 'Goth-lite,'" despite its success with Goth audiences (104). In Hamilton's
fiction vampires and shapeshifters, including werewolves, belong to packs or
groups mentored by a dominant male, female, or couple. Under the tutelage
of these mentors, newly made supernatural beings learn to control their transformations, which otherwise occur spontaneously during moments of intense
emotion, and the outbursts of often deadly aggression that accompany the
changes.

In one scene, Anita discusses with her werewolf king lover, Richard, a
new member of his pack, Louisa. Richard is distressed because he "respected"
Louisa's religious "convictions" and thus allowed her to retain her virginity
until after her wedding. Her consequent ignorance of the power of sexuality
resulted in her transforming during her first intercourse and tearing her bride-
groom to pieces. Richard often functions in the novels as a foil for Anita,
establishing her authenticity and lack of hypocrisy. Their discussion of this
event serves in this way. At first Anita is confused about how the wedding

night tragedy could have occurred. She says, "if she could control herself during nonintercourse orgasm, then she should have been able to control herself during intercourse, too" (428–29). Richard must enlighten her. "Please tell me you don't mean she wanted to wait for *any* sexual contact until the honeymoon?" Anita asks, in amazement (429). When he tells her this is exactly what he does mean, she is unable to console him "[b]ecause it was a waste, a waste because Richard and the girl and her fiancé had been more worried about appearance than reality" (430).

For Goths reality, or authenticity, includes taking action to experience one's own bodily pleasures. Disciplining the body to conform to others' concepts of what desire should be or to some idea of consistent sexual identity is deemed not only dishonest but dangerous, because such discipline may create forces that can tear apart everyone they touch. Never has the central thesis of Foucault's histories of sexuality been more graphically illustrated than by this deadly proliferation of desires resulting from the imposition of taxonomies (such as virginity) and norms (such as chastity) on young bodies. The book virtually screams of the body, "let it bleed!"

To understand how this attitude is received by adults in authority over young Goths, once again a comparison to the Punk subculture is instructive. While, as Lauraine Leblanc notes, "American punks' construction of a deviant image became accepted at face value" by "sources of conventional socialization—families, peers, school authorities, and employers," resulting in "intolerance, ostracism, harassment, abuse, [and] threats of expulsion," Goth has been even more severely suppressed by school authorities and other regulatory agencies (58, 101). This seems illogical, since many Punks do value violent confrontation with members of mainstream society while most Goths eschew nonconsensual violence. However, the logic of the discrepancy becomes apparent when we compare the expressions of sexuality and gender identification that most typically characterize participants in each of the two subcultures.

Leblanc characterizes Punk as "a predominantly heterosexual subculture," including heavy emphasis on "norms and codes" that reinforce traditional masculinity (101, 125). Moreover, "punks rarely challenge the mainstream norms governing sex and romance" (125). Instead, "[s]exual relationships within the subculture tend to conform to the monogamous style of mainstream heterosexual relations" (127). Punk girls' attitudes toward sexual expression most often conform to mainstream concepts of virtue, including condemnation of female "promiscuity" and contempt for sex workers (207–208).[1] They often choose clothes that will discourage sexual attention from males; Punk women, like mainstream women, generally regard any expression of sexual interest from strangers negatively, even as tantamount to assault (202, 210–

11). Leblanc points out that "[g]irls pay a heavy price for becoming punks, for refusing to play the femininity game, for trying to change the rules" and shows us that part of that price is adherence to the conventional double standard still determining women's status in the mainstream (219). Like Leblanc, I understand "the femininity game" to be a combination of seductive behavior and denial of sexual desire used to manipulate a man into paying for sex with economic support and at least a pretense of monogamous commitment. Punk women's avoidance of this game makes sense because of Punk's opposition to the pursuit of material security by anyone, female or male. Also, many Punks censure women with a seductive appearance because it implies that they intend to engage in this sort of manipulation. Because men dominate all aspects of Punk, and women lose status by engaging in sexual activity except in response to a male lover's attentions within a committed relationship, and because few Punk men are willing or able to provide the sort of support that women in the mainstream seek, Punk women often adopt the strategy of becoming celibate virtual males. "They called this 'androgyny,' although it lacks the blending of characteristics that define the term. Rather, they were more likely to be unisex—masculine—and to pass as males" (151).

Since the publication of Leblanc's book, this situation has been somewhat complicated by the popular website SuicideGirls.com and subsequent magazine and photograph collection. The "suicide girls" present themselves as Punks and Goths who market their sexuality, primarily for male consumption, as "pin-ups," strippers, or porn stars in ways they see as a radical undermining of patriarchy through aggressive female self-determinacy.[2] Yet the very aggression required to make this sort of sexual self-assertion, as well as the name under which they have chosen to market their images, attests to the emotional costs of their project. These costs seem lower for Goth girls due to the differences that have developed between the two groups' concepts of heterosexuality.

In that most human beings are heterosexual, so far as we know from casual observation, clinical histories, and survey results, it seems safe to assume that heterosexuality also predominates in most, if not all, Goth subcultural groups. But, as I hope the previous chapters' discussions have demonstrated, not all expressions of heterosexuality are conventional, and sexuality of all kinds is differently expressed in Goth groups than in traditionally patriarchal cultures or subcultures. Whereas Punks, seemingly suspicious of pleasure and sensuality, attempt to discipline sexuality into recognizable male-dominant heterosexual forms, Goths most often express eroticism publicly and through subcultural artifacts as a flow of bodily pleasure that transgresses the bounds of normative sexuality. Goths disapprove of homophobia and misogyny, and even of fixed gender identity, and because of this they will often articulate even quite ordinary heterosexual relationships in ways that appear queered. For instance, a man and woman may be monogamously married to each other but also wear each other's make-up and clothing, including skirts, stockings, and corsets, in a serious attempt to look attractive. This is true of a number of Goths I know. In addition, they may practice small rituals of power exchange inflected with S/M, such as his kneeling in the street to lace her boots, thereby presenting themselves to the world as transgressive of hetero-sexuality as defined by the majority.

Ultimately, then, Punk threatens basic majoritist assumptions about sexuality and gender less than Goth, in which femininity dominates stylistic expression and through which foundational ideas about female purity and appropriate masculinity are called into question. Abstinence educators—and other extreme conservatives on matters of gender and sexuality among the young—are right to be even more concerned about Goth than they are about Punk. And Goths often structure their particular forms of rebellion and de-fiance in ways that amplify such concern.

One such form, which often troubles authority figures, is the much docu-mented overlap of Goth subcultures with vampire role-playing subcultures. As Davenport-Hines points out, some Goths "use vampirism as a way of sig-naling their reaction against family-centered pieties" (354). The openly erotic and inescapably violent vampire family structure serves to parody and expose the covert incestuousness and domestic violence that more and more seem to lie beneath the surface of American bourgeois life, while the literal blood drinking not only derisively mimics capitalist values, as described by Marx, but defies the precepts of safe sex. Another good example of Goth's extreme flouting of mainstream propriety is the tremendous popularity among Goths of Jhonen Vasquez's graphic novel series *Johnny the Homicidal Maniac*, which debuted in the Goth 'zine *Carpe Noctem*. Despite its parodic treat-ment of the character of Anne Gwish, a Goth poseur, *JTHM* remains a Goth favorite. Baddeley remarks that "[c]onsciously or otherwise, the lead charac-ter [Johnny] is a satire on the Goth revenge fantasy at the heart of *The Crow*," but achieved with the "disarming affection toward the Goth subculture that clearly informs [Vasquez's] work" (157). Numerous websites associated with Goth praise the series, identify it as appealing to Goths, and express affection for Nny (Johnny), its murderous, psychotic protagonist. A Deleuzian way to approach such fantasies is as nomadic "journeys in intensity" that serve not to establish justice but to "escap[e] the codes" of normative identities (*Desert Islands*, 259–60).

"I Hate My Parents," a special issue of the 'zine *While You Were Sleeping*, reminds us not to underestimate the wrath of Goths. In "A Girl's Guide to Getting Back at Your Parents," Lauren Cox advises teens to "listen to bad music" and directs them to Mike Weiss's article in the same issue (46). Weiss identifies Goth as particularly annoying to adults, and even to himself, remarking, "Goth kids. Can't live with 'em, can't kill 'em—they're already dead!" (77). Thus he pinpoints the consummate Goth strategy of resistance: absolute masochistic submission. Unlike the majority of Punks, who seemingly accept the identities gender and sexuality codes impose, wishing only to restyle them to reflect their rejection of consumer capitalism, Goths not only reject them all but express their rejection through a defiantly eroticized passive resistance. In effect, they fling themselves at the feet of their tormentors and say, do what you please to me, I will enjoy it and so transform punishment into triumph.

Kimberly Peirce used the title of a Cure song for her 1999 film *Boys Don't Cry*, about a female-to-male transsexual, a choice that initially confused many Cure fans, myself included. In light of the gender politics of Goth and their reception by the mainstream, however, Peirce's choice becomes understandable. For many young males, the song has expressed their alienation from a culture that denies their humanity. Through their typically Goth valorization of S/M, The Cure raise some questions similar to those brought into play by the very existence of transsexuals.

Both transsexuality and S/M constitute difficult epistemological problems for feminist gender theorists. S/M's troubling of feminist theory of gender has been extensively discussed by nearly all feminist theorists and metacritics since the mid-1980s. To summarize, feminisms that take as a primary goal bringing about sexual equality can hardly endorse a mode of expressing sexuality that depends on and eroticizes power imbalances between sex partners. Only feminisms that categorically oppose the regulation (either official or through disciplinary discourses) of consensual sexual acts and practices, of what Foucault refers to as bodily pleasures, can take the position that S/M can be compatible with feminism. Only feminisms that begin with the assumption that gender and sexuality are both constructs with no inherent connection to each other can regard S/M practices and identifications as matters with which feminist activism need not concern itself.

Transsexuality, although not nearly such a point of contention for feminists, raises similar questions. Should we who, as part of our political philosophy, do not believe that gender is binary and is intrinsically connected to biology support choices, such as sexual reassignment surgery, that could be read—just like S/M—as affirming gender binarity and complementarity? How can we avoid thinking that transsexuals should be supported by feminism only if they queer gender by performing sexual identities that confound mainstream expectations, and not if they pass as conventional men or women? Here we who would oppose such beliefs might take to heart Colebrook's comments on Deleuze's view of the opposition between art and the common-sense, everyday concepts of commonality that are at the core of capitalism: "Opinion will reduce love to its already known forms—bourgeois marriage—and then dismiss all other forms," claiming, "That's not love; it's perversion!" (*Gilles Deleuze*, 16–17).

Before love can be reduced to a form already known and agreed upon, gender must be correspondingly reduced to two such forms, which are at least imagined to occur naturally, so that one can see sexual reassignment only as the choice to be, as Leslie Feinberg puts it, "shunted into one of two deeply carved ruts" (6). Instead of making this mistake, one can choose to recognize that, as Feinberg asserts, the very existence of transgendered people is "proof that sex and gender are much more complex than a delivery room doctor's glance at genitals can determine," or than any performance of normality can represent, for part of that complexity involves the myriad, rhizomatic connections possible between any person's chosen gender(s) and that same person's body, however s/he may choose to modify it—or not.

In this chapter I will compare Peirce's film to Susan Muska and Gréta Olafsdóttir's 1998 documentary, *The Brandon Teena Story*, in order to show how presentations of sexuality and gender that trouble both majoritist feminist theories and conventional gender ideology, such as those effected by transsexualities and by Goth enactments of S/M, can be either judged and found morally deficient or else regarded without judgment, in the manner Deleuze attributes to great film. As Colebrook observes, Deleuze radicalizes phenomenology by arguing that "if we *really* want to accept the appearance of the world without judgement or presupposition then we will not refer to the appearances *of* some world; there will be nothing other than a 'swarm' of appearances—with no foundation of the experiencing mind or subject" (*Gilles Deleuze*, 6, emphasis Colebrook's). Cinematic montage can break down the visually perceptible formations that constitute everyday reality into components and thus allow us to see how majoritist meanings are made. Colebrook's synthesis of Deleuze's remarks in *Cinema 1* on the technique of Eisenstein could serve as a description of Muska and Olafsdóttir's documentary film as well: "It is the inhuman eye of the camera that liberates us from a fixed and moral notion of man, allowing us to assess the larger material forces that have constituted us" (48–49).

Through showing us photographs and other images open to multiple interpretations (such as the self-help book on transgender identity later found among Teena's possessions), through its often flat presentation of interview footage, and through its lingering long shots and tracking shots of the landscapes in which the tragedy unfolded, the documentary version of Teena's story asks us to contemplate how Teena was seen from multiple perspectives, and how, from all the subjectivities s/he inhabited, Teena saw the world.[3] In contrast, the fictionalized version of the story pushes us to see Brandon Teena in one specific way, suppressing ambiguity through a consistent narrative perspective and classic Hollywood-style cinematography.

Writing of Deleuze and Guattari's concept of such attempts to historicize through conventional narrative, Marco Abel rightly claims that for them "an event is not *of* history (i.e. a narrative or a plot), though it is born in and falls back into history through the inevitable appropriation of the event's becoming by narrative forces" (1245). Peirce turns Brandon Teena's life into one sort of history, while Muska and Olafsdóttir turn it into "pure becomings, pure events on a plane of immanence" in the type of act of creation that is also perforce, as Deleuze and Guattari assert, an act of resistance (*What Is Philosophy?* 110). Understanding how and why the narrative film overshadowed the documentary in the popular media's construction of Brandon Teena's life and death is crucial to understanding how and why institutions and discourses of sexual and gender normalization distort Goth, representing it as a dangerous source of outlaw male violence.

The tremendous success of *Boys Don't Cry* with critics and popular audiences was, for many reasons, predictable. First, it rode the 1990s wave of films and other cultural products that ostensibly argued for tolerance of sexual diversity. However, like most of those films, *Boys Don't Cry* did so only by representing lesbianism to the mainstream as soft-core eroticism through images of glamorous young women courting, kissing, and fondling each other, similar to those familiar to consumers of cable television pornography and drugstore men's magazines like *Playboy* and *Penthouse*.[4] Second, it cashed in on millennial America's ongoing love affairs with lurid true-crime stories and with exposés of sexual and gender transgressions within poverty cultures, an entertainment form brought to its apex (or nadir, depending on one's perspective) by television's *The Jerry Springer Show*. Third, the film is visually beautiful, and dramatically tells the sensationalistic story of Brandon Teena, a petty criminal transsexual from a trailer park in Lincoln, Nebraska, whose friendship with two Falls City ex-convicts, John Lotter and Marvin Thomas (Tom) Nissen, ended with their raping Teena, and then murdering him together with his friends Lisa Lambert and Philip DeVine, in a stupid and heartless effort to avoid being returned to prison for the rape. And finally, the film's romantic rendition of Teena's relationship with Lana Tisdel has been especially appealing to viewers.

Although heralded by many both as a classic story of doomed love along the lines of *Romeo and Juliet* and as an exemplary consciousness-raising experience, the film poses serious problems for cultural critics interested in discussing how gender-based legal inequities are institutionalized. In specific, the film's overt project of bringing belated justice to the case of rape and murder victim Brandon Teena, who was killed in response to law enforcement officials' exposure of his biological femaleness, is complicated by its apparently unintentional participation in our culture's current brutal denial that the civil rights of boys and young men matter. For that reason, I will begin my analysis of it with a brief discussion of the song the film appropriates for its title.

The most frequently reproduced image associated with The Cure is the famous black and white poster of frontman Robert Smith with his back to us, his long black hair loosely spiked, the neck of his guitar extending phallically from the front of his body in a gesture toward virility that his slumping, dejected posture belies. The words "THE CURE" appear in large print at the top left of the frame, with "BOYS DON'T CRY" written beneath. The Cure, an English band, began performing in 1977 and enjoyed moderate success in the U.K. two years later with their album *Three Imaginary Boys*. As the album title suggests, the band often concentrates on unhappiness associated with young men's failure to enact gender roles successfully, and this album was no exception. The album was retitled and rereleased later in 1979 as *Boys Don't Cry* due to the success of this song in the United States.

Typically, Cure songs open up the hidden depression and defeat traditional macho posturing attempts to hide. They convey a sense of the dark emptiness many young men feel as they perform culturally approved masculinity. Note, for example, these lyrics from the song "Boys Don't Cry":

> I try to laugh about it
> cover it all up with lies
> . . .
> hiding the tears in my eyes
> 'cause boys don't cry

Seen by many as a precursor to Goth music styles, which are always associated with (feminized) androgyny, The Cure remain extremely popular with young audiences today, especially those, like Goths, who reject conventional gender roles. The band floridly dramatizes the melancholy aspects of sex, love, and gender identity, making its appeal to such fans easily understandable. But the majority of Cure songs dealing with love or sexuality are explicitly heterosexual. Although Robert Smith, who represents the band to most fans, occasionally seems to invite listeners to think of him as bisexual (in songs like "Icing Sugar" and "Lullaby"), his public persona is far more often strongly coded as heterosexual, and he consistently presents himself as a biological male both in his songs themselves and in stage performances. Why, then, did a film about a female-to-male transsexual borrow his most famous song's title?

On the evidence of web-posted fan reactions to the gender-bending of Goth music celebrities, such as the fantasies about Trent Reznor (and by association Smith) discussed in the previous chapter, we might guess that the filmmakers see Goth as intrinsically concerned with transsexuality in its most Deleuzian modes of becoming. In other words, we might conclude that the film's title is intended to suggest to the audience not that transsexuality is a transition from one sexual identity to another that manifests one's inner truth, but that it is an indeterminacy to be inhabited and savored. But this tenuous connection between Goth play with sexual and gender identifications and the film's dour depiction of them seems strained to the snapping point by Brandon Teena's own strenuous resistance to the very concept of gender indeterminacy, which the film faithfully portrays. Therefore, the most likely explanation is that the filmmakers decided to appropriate the experience of young men as a metaphor for the experience of females, both lesbian and transsexual, who are rebelling against the genders assigned to them within a patriarchal system.

Such appropriation is unfortunate for an art work intended to effect political change, because it works by negating the importance of one group's suffering, considering it interesting only in its function as a symbol for the sufferings of another group. Over the past thirty years or so, feminist theory has had a great deal to say about cross-gender appropriation. Perhaps one example here will suffice. Male poets have traditionally compared their creative travails to the torments and joys of childbirth. Although, in the past, audiences apparently responded as the poets intended, most readers today find such comparisons odious, thanks to feminist theories, especially when they include the suggestion that the male poet's labor pains should be seen as more significant than the mother's. It is now the norm to read such texts as disrespectful of women, and belittling of female experience as a source of authority. To test whether it would be fair to assess the film's use of male experience this way, one might begin by thinking about differences in the ways the film and the song contextualize the prohibition against boys' crying.

As the lyrics indicate, in the context of the song "Boys Don't Cry," the prohibition represents a lie of culture that young men must enact in order to be understood as masculine. In order to have any hope of acceding to manhood, as defined by our culture, boys must not reveal that they can be reached emotionally. They must model a psychic impenetrability that complements the physical impenetrability our homophobic cultural definitions of manliness demand. Judith Levine persuasively argues that the general American understanding of masculine sexuality privileges performance over feeling in ways that young, inexperienced males often understand as absolutely prohibiting emotional response (170–71).

A passage from Dennis Cooper's novel *Period* may serve as evidence that it is not only heterosexual boys who desperately retreat from their emotional needs into a shell of affectless cool. Here Cooper describes a scene in which a boy who goes by the nickname Dagger surrenders his body to the sexual attentions of an older man, Walker, allowing their encounter to become the subject of a pornographic film.

> True to form, Dagger sulked, maintained his distance, and buried his face in a bong. He seemed mesmerizingly studied, a cute poseur doing whatever he could to remain one-dimensional. Then Walker opened the couch bed, screwed his old Betacam onto a towering tripod, and discovered Dagger's secret. He sobbed, shook, begged for any sign of affection and then reconstituted himself the moment he came. (51)

When one is determined to maintain the cold remoteness of traditional masculine affect because one sees it as essential to survival, sexual contact of any sort can be terrifying. Sex has the power to unleash tightly restrained desires to be caressed and comforted, to be given the signs, if not the reality, of love and caring.

But, as Dagger knows, within America's cultural construction of masculinity being vulnerable means one will be violated. The Cure's "Boys Don't Cry" tells us that living the lie of invulnerability doubles the emotional pain boys feel by adding pangs of repression, and triples it by requiring them to cover their anguish with false nonchalance. The song implicitly describes masculinity as agonizing, culturally enforced fakery. The lyrics of another Cure song very popular with Goths suggest the repercussions of such fakery:

> When I think of how you make me hate
>
> . . .
>
> I want to smash you helpless
> Down on the floor
> Smash you until you're not here anymore
> And I shiver and shake ("Shiver and Shake")

Boys, forced to deny their feelings, grow alienated and enraged.

One of the major ways the film departs from this vision of masculinity is in its depiction of a boy who does cry as both tragic and heroic. Brandon Teena differs most from the biological males in his environment not in that his genitalia do not match his gender identity, but in that he is far more emotive. While the other males in the film obey cultural prohibitions on expressing sadness, empathy, or other so-called soft emotions, and display only the anger and cold amusement culturally acceptable as part of masculinity, Teena shows a full range of emotions. Surprisingly, given how vulnerable and responsive to others Teena seems, those around him are convinced by his performance of masculinity throughout most of the film. He is only exposed as a "fake" male by a physical examination made by the police after an arrest and by his subsequent brief imprisonment in the women's facilities of the jail. In contrast, his unusual success with women is directly attributable to his gentle, highly emotional behavior with them.

Thus, one may conclude that the film treats the admonition against male tears as silly and ineffective. Biological boys may or may not cry; the film takes no interest in the matter, but it laments the fact that transsexuals are harshly punished for gender role deviation, and it suggests that they are also more severely punished than biological boys would be. In other words, it is as if the film replies to The Cure's song and to the male fans for whom it speaks, "What do you have to cry about? The situation of female-to-male transsexuals is far more tragic than anything you will ever experience." Such a message appropriates and dismisses the experience of others in almost exactly the same way as does a male poet's claim that writing a poem is more painful and consequently more of a labor than giving birth, since giving birth is, after all, natural to women due to our biology.

Feminists should know better. I borrow the strike-through of the word "Boys" in my essay's title from Lacan's *Séminaire livre XX: Encore,* in which he strikes through feminine pronouns to signify the function of the concept "woman" as the ultimate anti-universal, the one who is always other to universal man as the subject, always absence in relation to man's presence, the one whose signifier in language names only what can never be seen, spoken, or understood, even by women ourselves. Lacan asserts that, consequently, men's movement imaginatively and experientially into the feminine allows them to escape the demands of subjectivity under the regime of reason and to think otherwise, in every sense of the word. Alice Jardine astutely describes such theoretical moves, which she calls gynesis, as a sort of mystification of femininity as the unconscious in relation to male (self)consciousness. She attributes this twentieth-century philosophical and artistic trend to men's paranoia about women's increasing ability to direct a detached gaze toward men and articulate our own vision of them as seen from the outside. Of Lacan's theory, in specific, she remarks, "if 'woman' in his thought designates that which subverts Subject, Representation, and Truth, it is because 'she' does so in the history of Western thought. To make such an assertion is perhaps to continue it uncritically" (168–69). Similarly, we might well consider what we continue uncritically when we take "boys" to be the not-quite-men that women are not, can never be, but somehow essentially are, even more so than biological males themselves.

A charming image of this, in contrast to the problematic one offered by Brandon Teena (to whom I will return), is Mary Martin's famous and much repeated Broadway theatrical performance as Peter Pan, the boy who could never grow up. Part of the success of Martin's performance of sweetly heroic and yet vulnerable maleness no doubt derived from the poignancy of the sight of a boy who truly could not become a man—because he was really a woman. Martin's impersonation of a boy allowed audiences the fantasy of a love affair (between Peter and Wendy) that could never end with the subordination of the girl to a Victorian paterfamilias, a romance that would always be defined by a playful assumption of gender roles rather than an enforced enactment of them. And the price of that fantasy, gladly paid by most of us, was that the biological boy Peter Pan, as he appears in J. M. Barrie's novel, was erased.

A much less charming image of boys under erasure has been provided, for several years now, through media depictions of the "Scared Straight" program, in which young men who have committed minor crimes or seem at risk of doing so are taken by law enforcement officials into jails and prisons to be frightened by inmates who threaten them, primarily with rape and sexual torture. Here what is erased is not the possibility of maturation that depends on biological maleness, but instead the possibility of being accorded the respect due to a human being in a democracy, which depends on recognition of full citizenship and civil rights. Many criminologists have questioned the effectiveness of this approach to delinquency, with a number pointing out that the program seems to make young offenders more, not less, violent (Finckenauer, 140; Petrosino, Turpin-Petrosino, and Finckenauer, 364). In his conclusion to the most extensive study done of this program, James Finckenauer asserts what should be obvious: "We must recognize that a potential for either social or emotional injury to juvenile subjects exists. This is particularly true where aversive methods are used" (232). Nonetheless Americans not only accept the Scared Straight program as a legitimate means of crime prevention, but also accept the unconstitutionally cruel and unusual punishment within our system of incarceration that it exposes. This attitude says much about how we as a culture have come to understand both the legal system and the place of young males in relation to it.

Despite all the angry talk about the system's denial of victims' rights to which we are constantly subjected by news and entertainment media and by special interest groups, our justice system seems currently to exist mainly as a means of providing vengeance for victims and perhaps especially for those more numerous citizens who feel victimized by their proximity to crime and their anxiety that someday it may actually touch their lives. Not only is the U.S. unique among first world nations in its endorsement of the death penalty, which has repeatedly proven to have no deterrent value, we also seem to be unique in our enthusiasm for rape as a legally sanctioned mode of punishment. At least if the rape is inflicted on a biological male.

Countless mainstream and independent films about prison depict the rape of young men as business as usual behind bars, and many treat the topic as comical. Newspaper columnists regularly refer casually to rape as part of the culture of our jails and prisons. Many discussions of child molestation include, *as reassurance* to the morally outraged, references to the apparently inevitable rape and sexual torture of incarcerated pedophiles, despite the common belief that pedophilia can only be caused by the perpetrator's having been himself violated as a child. And everyone who is exposed to any form of popular media must be aware that rapists and sex offenders are far from being the only youthful prisoners tortured in this way. Boys who are arrested for property crimes or drug use can expect to be raped in jail, and we all know it.

Aside from Amnesty International and a small number of advocates for prisoners, some of whom are themselves imprisoned, no one seems to be speaking out publicly against this unconstitutional situation. While citizens' groups work tirelessly with legislators to make sure that more young men (who already constitute our main incarcerated population) are tried as adults and given longer sentences, unless they are executed outright, illegal assaults on these young men continue unabated and for the most part unaddressed except as a useful way of scaring youths into more socially acceptable behavior. In short, we are creating a culture that gives young men with low impulse control the message that rape is an appropriate form of discipline and a useful tool in maintaining conformity to the majority's values.

The results of this appalling message get an airing in *The Brandon Teena Story*, but this aspect of Teena's experience is edited out of the later, fictionalized film. Melissa Anderson points out in a review in *Cineaste* that "what is really in crisis, as Muska and Olafsdóttir suggest, is not Brandon's sexual identity but the male, heterosexual identity inhabited by people like John Lotter and Tom Nissen—an identity so fragile that, when threatened by Brandon's 'masquerade' of masculinity—it knows no other response than violence" (55). She notes that the sexual identity crises of men like this are inextricable from "the socioeconomic crisis gripping Falls City and thousands of other economically depressed American cities whose denizens can only move from one dead-end job to the next. Lotter and Nissen's rage, then, partly stems from a life in which hope has been extinguished" (55). However, Anderson does not discuss the documentary's persistent suggestion that Lotter and Nissen's rage may also have derived from their having been raped themselves during their past imprisonments. The film makes this argument explicitly through the interview with Leon Thompson, a prison inmate, who claims that he knows John Lotter was "sexually assaulted" repeatedly in prison and that, upon his release, Lotter wanted to "even up the odds," feeling that it was "my turn now."

Muska and Olafsdóttir contextualize this claim by cutting to a photograph of John Lotter at the time of his previous imprisonment. He is a slender boy with long hair and a delicate-looking face. More subtly, one of the interviews with the appropriately enraged U.S. marshal, Ron Shepherd, ends with his summation of his opinion of the murderers: "They're punks!" Presumably Shepherd, who clearly strongly disapproves of homophobic violence, does not intend this designation to suggest Lotter and Nissen were raped in prison and should be despised for that reason, but as a member of the law enforcement community he could hardly be unaware of the term's sexual connotations. And although Nissen's girlfriend, Melissa Wisdom, solemnly reports that he was taunted as a "faggot" after he sexually assaulted Teena, it seems unlikely that she is implying that this motivated him to attack Teena fatally the next time. Yet, as in the Columbine case, the presence of a cultural master narrative in which young male outcasts must be either victims or victimizers does much to explain why "Johnny" sometimes does become a homicidal maniac, as well as why school officials have become so obsessed with the possibility that Goths under their care will do likewise.

A few responses to Katz's "Voices from the Hellmouth" illustrate how deeply entrenched the cult of violent masculinity is in our schools and how much this causes them to resemble prisons to the nonconformist students trapped within them. "Pimpbot3k" answers a posting defending jocks and urging conformity:

> You just don't get it. We don't want to be the homecoming king/queen. We have never wanted that. All the geeks[5] want to do is be able to do their stuff in their group without being fucked with by the jocks, cheerleaders, yuppies, ect. I was less than a year into highschool when I quit and got my GED. I couldn't take it anymore. Every day I would get up, and feel sick. . . . I made myself feel sick just so I wouldn't have to go to that prison called high school. . . . When I was forced to go I was constantly tormented. . . . That's why these kids [Dylan Kleibold and Eric Harris] snapped, they were sick of it. They couldn't get up another day and be called names like "fuckup," "queer," "freak," ect. It was too much, trust me I know.

Another, who signs himself "Jesse," objects to the violent tone of many of the posts and advocates that others follow his example in learning "to be accepting." However, he notes that in high school, "everytime I did well, it was yet another 'beating', another time my books were stolen and burned, another time I was locked in a bathroom. Why?! I was different." "Derek" expresses pity for the Columbine victims, but says he understands the motivation of the shooters since "I was beaten daily. I'm not talked slammed into a locker or whatever, I am talking about being BEATEN! I was picked on, humiliated publicly . . . and people wonder why these kids hated others?" He advises, "Educators gets your heads out of your @$$3% start teaching kids, stop looking up to dumb jocks and little slut fashion queens, and start doing somethin about these kids who's lives are hell!" "BeanThere" testifies that "[i]n my school kids would beat up defenseless kids literally **right under the noses of teachers**. . . . Not once in all my years at school—despite kids with broken bones and stab wounds—did I ever see a single instance of this type of criminally violent behavior going punished at all" (emphasis BeanThere's). For me hundreds of such pages are summed up in a later contribution by "BeanThere," who says, "This whole thing reminded me of John Lennon's 'Working Class Hero,'" and then includes the lyrics to help us remember. This couplet seems particularly apropos:

> But first you must learn to smile as you kill
> If you want to be like the folks on the hill

Lotter and Nissen did learn this lesson. The logical response to the grotesque outbursts of violence that result from the lessons taught by both our schools and our society as a whole would be to enforce the laws of the land in schools and prisons so as to stop these illegitimate lessons. We might start with the Constitution's prohibition of cruel and unusual punishment. Instead, as was illustrated by the (temporary) removal of the film *Heathers* from video store shelves post-Columbine, the official guardians of safety in the U.S. seem determined to ignore the messages about masculinity continually delivered by our culture and instead place all the blame for violence on films and songs that dramatize the revenge of the marginalized or oppressed.

Through its explorations of the two murderers' pasts, the documentary makes clear that Lotter and Nissen were not simply promulgators of a culture of violence but immersed in it since childhood and subject to its mores, formally and informally enforced. In contrast, to the extent that *Boys Don't Cry* treats Lotter and Nissen as products of a particular society, rather than as emanations of evil, as Lisa Henderson observes, their crimes appear as "a new installment in a long history of popular images of working-class pathology" (301). Caricaturing its subjects as "white trash" and relying on a structure of contrast in which Teena's beauty and optimistic hopes of future financial success represent virtue while Nissen and Lotter's "scarred and mottled failures" represent badness, the film avoids considering the ways their fear of further victimization may have contributed to their ultimate, horrific crime (302).

A very different sense of what can happen to boys considered dangerous white trash is presented in Joe Berlinger and Bruce Sinofsky's HBO television documentaries, *Paradise Lost: The Child Murders at Robin Hood Hills* and *Paradise Lost II: Revelations*, which reveal the tale of the West Memphis

Three, whose case has become a favorite cause among Goths and Heavy Metal fans. In 1993 three eight-year-old boys were sexually assaulted and tortured to death in the Robin Hood Hills area. Shortly thereafter the West Memphis police charged three local teens, Jessie Misskelley, Jason Baldwin, and Damien Echols, with the crime. Because there were no witnesses, no obvious motive, and no physical evidence, the sole support for the case seems to be a confession the developmentally impaired Misskelley signed after being interrogated for many hours with neither his parents nor a lawyer present. The certainty of the court and community that the boys were guilty appeared to rest entirely on their interest in Wicca and their predilection for dressing in black and listening to "dark" rock and roll. Despite tremendous public support for the West Memphis Three, so far their appeals have failed, and their only real legal victory has come in the form of Echols's successful lawsuits against the prison system for allowing him to be sexually assaulted and tortured by other prisoners.

Andy Opel convincingly argues that, although the filmmakers obviously intended to help, the two documentary films' representation of Misskelley, Baldwin, and Echols codes them as "'monsters'" through its repeated aerial panning over "the 'scary' and 'dangerous' world of the trailer park" they inhabited (10). As his examination of the battle to free them shows, the West Memphis Three are victims not only of small-town ignorance and prejudice but of "the very gothic imaginary that is so carefully crafted in the cultural centers of the East and West Coasts [and that] takes root in the people and practices across the continent," which in this case renders up three young men as sacrifices to "a carefully constructed culture of fear" that serves as entertainment for those not imprisoned within it (11). Rural poverty has become a locus of gothic horror in ways that seem to short-circuit attempts to analyze the systems that determine the behavior of its inhabitants. Too often the rest of us watch them as if we were observers in a nineteenth-century madhouse, thrilling to a spectacular display of irrational and ultimately meaningless evil. The violence of this world is naturalized, as if it came out of the poisoned and exhausted earth itself instead of out of specific social circumstance.

As Melissa Anderson claims, *Boys Don't Cry* represents Lotter and Nissen as adhering to a "concept of masculinity . . . which assumes that committing acts of violence is their birthright" (56), but the film fails to recognize that this representation grows out of the actual situation of young men who learn through their experiences with our justice system that boys are born with no rights and must commit acts of violence in order to be awarded respect and an unmolested existence, which are culturally reserved only for brutally dominant males. The film sidesteps issues of hierarchy within masculinity when it virtually ignores the murder of Philip DeVine, and instead implicitly asserts that the only meaningful hierarchy in America is the gender binarity. Judith Halberstam, who sees the murder of Teena as a "chilling enforcement of normativity" perpetrated as a function of "the male gaze," remarks that the romantic relationship between DeVine, a disabled African American, and Leslie Lambert, the sister of murder victim Lisa Lambert, "could be read as a similarly outrageous threat to the supremacy and privilege of white manhood that the murderers rose to defend" ("The Transgendered Gaze," 295, 298). Perhaps their weak intellects did, indeed, perceive it this way, but should we?

The murder of eighteen-year-old Kelly Bullwinkle in Redlands, California, in September of 2003, by two of her high school friends who identified as Goths offers an instructive contrast, as well as providing sad evidence that some Goths are exceptions to the subculture's rule of nonviolence. At mainly affluent Redlands East Valley High, Goth became "a sort of catchall term" for anyone who could not fit into "a sea of blond, blue-eyed Abercrombie & Fitch clones" (Reitman, 64). The murderers, a Latino classmate and his girlfriend, acted out against their outcast status first by joining the school's large contingent of Goths, and finally by asserting dominance over the "vulnerable" and "trusting," and also more popular and successful, Bullwinkle with a scheme, that apparently went disastrously awry, to scare her with a gun (Reitman, 65). As in the Teena case, the murderers' perception that the crime was somehow "an accident" (Reitman, 67) is ironically more true than perhaps we would like to admit: such horrible violence is a side effect of teaching young people who cannot think reasonably that the only power worth having is power over others. Wherever hierarchies are created and institutionally enforced we, as a society, are most fortunate if all we see are fantasies of violence, such as those most characteristic of Goth culture, rather than acts of violence, such as those perpetrated in all of these deplorable cases.

Moreover, in light of the situation so many boys and men face, the dismantled males of Brite's fiction begin to seem the lucky ones. If, instead of seeing masochistic pleasure in gender dissolution as a possible path to righteousness for those who have the misfortune to be born male but are not endowed with patriarchal power, we see brutal dominance of others as the only acceptable avenue of male self-expression, then the only other way boys can respond to their existential situation is through absolute self-annihilation. As Deleuze points out, in a culture where all institutions for the young increasingly impose Benthamite discipline, "[y]oung people . . . walk a fine line indeed between a persistent temptation to commit suicide and the birth of a certain form of political consciousness peculiar to prison" (*Desert Islands*, 244).

Frighteningly, two films very popular with teen audiences offer the former solution. In *Donnie Darko* (2001) and *The Butterfly Effect* (2004) the premise of *It's a Wonderful Life* is reversed and the protagonists (whom we might dub suicide boys) face the hard lesson that their very existence is the central problem of their social worlds. They must choose to be wiped out in order to save those they love from destruction. That the later film insistently connects the hero's dilemma to his relation to Goth (through his college roommate Thumper, played by Ethan Suplee) explicitly says that young men must choose between suicidally giving up their identity or patriarchally and violently asserting it at the expense of the weak.

The story of Brandon Teena illustrates both the futility of such assertions for boys not born to privilege and its danger to the rest of us. The idea that Lotter and Nissen were actually enjoying any sense of supremacy, even in the depressed economy of Falls City, seems absurd, especially in light of the contemptuous assessments of them that their fellow citizens seem so eager to confide in Muska and Olafsdóttir. What the two young men seem to have experienced, instead, was a world not unlike the Vietnam era wryly memorialized in Johnny Cash's perennial Country music favorite "A Boy Named Sue," in which the boy begins life truly nominally feminized by a thoughtless patriarch who demands that his son "get tough or die." Not only did both the killers (and perhaps especially Lotter, whom the documentary describes as having the mental capacity "of a nine- or ten-year-old") lack the intelligence to understand their alienation with the sophisticated irony of Cure fans, they obviously could not achieve the countercultural perspective of a self-proclaimed outlaw like Cash, who exuberantly rejects the teachings of the fathers in the song's conclusion. But they were not left without guidance in a rape-or-be-raped world.

Unfortunately, our society conveys ideas about sexuality and gender identity so clearly that even the most simple-minded can grasp them. As James Messerschmidt argues, aggression, insensitivity to the feelings of others, and dominance of the weak universally connote masculinity in America across social classes, while lower-class youths are encouraged by violent example within their milieu to add contempt for education and for the respect for difference that it ideally brings (93). "A culture that lavishes gentle attention on its young also may encourage tolerance of the vulnerable and discourage physical power-mongering. People brought up to be aggressive and suspicious of intrusions against their own body's 'boundaries,' on the other hand, will be more self-protective and territorial and thus more belligerent, both socially and sexually" (Levine, 179). Once again the strange situation in our secondary schools, where intellectuals, geeks, nerds, and Goths are tortured by jocks while adults in power look the other way, comes to mind.

A *Teaching Tolerance* study of the alarmingly rising violence against homosexual students and those perceived to be gay in our middle and secondary schools suggests, just as does Brooks Brown's account of life at Columbine, that as school policies increasingly seek to enforce conformity in all aspects of the students' lives, the students become more like convicts, that is, more likely to establish a viciously maintained hierarchy among males according to masculine affect. One sixteen-year-old student who bravely decided to come out sums up his subsequent experience by saying, "I felt like I was in prison" (Walker, 25). If to be an effeminized male means to have no privileges, then to gain supremacy, or even safety, one must distinguish oneself as the opposite of effeminate, and the most obvious and emphatic way this can be done is by beating and penetrating the weaker male.

One of the most interesting omissions from both the films and the published reviews of them is any sustained attention to the possibility that Teena was raped anally as well as vaginally, although *Boys Don't Cry* does glancingly imply this, as does the transcript of the post-rape questioning in *The Brandon Teena Story*. One might chalk this up to the filmmakers' desire to avoid disrespectful sensationalism, but the choice should also be considered in light of both films' representation of Lotter and Nissen's sexual assault on Teena as motivated by their desire to restore a biologically determined coding of gender they find comfortable. Rachel Swan goes so far as to assert that the rape is meant to work according to a "cruel logic" that will "reposition everyone according to their 'god-given' gender. Brandon has a vagina, so Brandon is a woman. Tom and John penetrate his vagina, thereby reaffirming themselves as men" (50). Obviously the possibility of anal rape disrupts this neat logic.

However, the idea that the objective of Lotter and Nissen's attack on Teena was to restore gender binarity is more even seriously called into question by the sequence of events after the public disclosure of Teena's biological sex. Lotter and Nissen first forced Teena to expose himself to Tisdel, who disappointed them by responding with indifference to the revelation that Teena lacked a penis. In fact, in the documentary Lotter expresses frustration over Tisdel's adamant refusal to agree with his assertion that people without penises and with vaginas are not male. He complains that, even after Teena's multiple rape and subsequent murder, Tisdel persists in using the male pronoun to refer to Teena and to call Teena her boyfriend. The documentary establishes that it was only after Lotter and Nissen became aware that they could not force Tisdel to reject Teena as another female on biological grounds that they decided to rape Teena.

When we consider these facts another possible motivation appears, and it is that Lotter and Nissen were jealous of Teena's success with Tisdel, a woman both had dated, and with other attractive young women in Falls City. That Teena was not a man, whether because he was a biological woman or because his gentler, more vulnerable manner coded him as a boy instead, added insult to their rejection in his favor, and the sexual attack, like those we condone in American prisons every day, restored a familiar order among males in which the strongest and most aggressive dominate and make use of the weak.

The appropriative spirit of the fictionalized film *Boys Don't Cry* becomes clear when we compare it to the documentary; it blatantly manipulated factual material in order to prevent such a reading. Most striking is the casting choice of then twenty-nine-year-old Peter Sarsgaard to play John Lotter, who was twenty-two at the time of the murder. In the documentary Mary Anne Greene, a social worker assigned to Lotter, discusses his mental deficiency and his immaturity that made him unable to function away from his mother or outside of Falls City, where he was generally treated as an inferior and worthless person. "We as a culture haven't come to terms with our responsibility for helping kids like this," she laments. But in *Boys Don't Cry*, Lotter does not appear to be a "kid" at all. Dark and frightening, Sarsgaard looms ominously over delicate, pretty-faced Hilary Swank as Teena and Chloë Sevigny as an ultra-femme Tisdel (nineteen at the time of the murder). Like the real Teena, Swank in male drag looks more like sixteen than the nearly twenty-one she is supposed to be, while Sarsgaard, unlike the real John Lotter, looks closer to his mid-thirties. The idea that they could be in serious competition for the same girl thus seems morally wrong, especially given the current social atmosphere in which enforcement of statutory rape law is generally considered appropriate in cases where the "child" is sixteen or seventeen and the "adult" often only three or four years older. Every time Lotter makes an advance to the naïve and girlish Tisdel, it looks like an attempt at what we now consider child molestation, an interpretation reinforced by his flirtation with her mother, who is presented as his adult equal, and by the scene in which he erotically fondles his own four-year-old daughter. Thus Lotter's anger at Teena is coded as being as perversely twisted as his expression of it ultimately was.

Another seemingly deliberate misrepresentation in *Boys Don't Cry* concerns Teena's treatment of the women he courted. Swan and Anderson are typical of the film's reviewers in referring to the character Swank portrays as "chivalrous" (Swan, 47; M. Anderson, 55), but as Anderson's discussion of the documentary shows, this portrayal is a bit skewed. In the documentary's interviews "Brandon is remembered as . . . a skillful seducer of young women" (54). And rightly so. The documentary gives us a Teena who seduced one very young and inexperienced woman after another. We can get some concept of just how sexually inexperienced these girls were if we consider their easy acceptance of Teena as male despite his primitive attempts at concealing his breasts with elastic bandages and giving the impression of a penis by stuffing his crotch with socks. His former fiancée, Gina Bartu, repeatedly answers, "I have no idea!" to the question of whether he used a dildo to achieve intercourse with her. Looking at or touching a penis seems inconceivable to her. Obviously, Brandon's girlfriends were not women who thought of the male body as a pleasure source to be caressed and explored. Nor were they women who expressed their own sexuality in any way other than by submitting to male attention. In fact, the interviews reveal that most, if not all, of these girls considered romantic cards and presents of flowers and jewelry the primary way a boy could give pleasure to his girlfriend. It says a great deal that the girl Brandon pursued at the roller rink in his first public appearance as a boy—a magical, romantic scene in the fictionalized film, a simple snapshot in the documentary—was then thirteen years old.

More disturbingly, Teena seemed to specialize in stealing from desperate girls who regarded him as their only chance at escape from rural poverty. His collection of trophy-like photographs of these people, whom if he were biologically male we would probably refer to as his victims, sounds a sour note in *The Brandon Teena Story*, as does the reason Gina Bartu gives for breaking their engagement: because the ring was purchased with her own credit card, which he had stolen. *Boys Don't Cry*, in contrast, equates the murder with the death of Tisdel's hopes of a new life in a less brutishly backward environment. But would the real Teena have actually rescued Tisdel from poverty? He was certainly not above profiting from her financially, as his habitual forging of checks stolen from his girlfriends shows. Because I analyze cultural artifacts as a sex radical rather than a neo-puritan, I do not consider Teena an immoral person because he apparently seduced all the girls he could. Nor do I heavily condemn Teena for nonviolently taking what he could from these gullible people, as I understand that poverty often motivates property crimes. The documentary also avoids such moralization by simply showing us the artifacts without offering editorial commentary or imposing narrative form.

I point out these differences between the documentary and the fictional film not in order to blame the victim for his murder. A series of terrible crimes were committed against Brandon Teena and nothing he did could in any way be seen as justifying the behavior of John Lotter and Tom Nissen. Moreover, I do not intend to suggest that Lotter or Nissen should be excused from blame because each was raised in and inhabited a culture of violence in which he was taught that masculinity must be won through oppressing other males, as well as females. What I mean to argue, instead, is that the goal of combating vicious enforcement of gender norms is not furthered by disseminating misinformation. Like Sheila Wolf in her photo-journalistic piece on *Boys Don't Cry* for the self-described "Counterculture Chronicle" *Propaganda*, I applaud gender-benders and find it "good news" that so many of them are disturbing the binarity of rural America (25–26). However, I cannot share her enthusiastic assessment of John Lotter's condemnation to execution by lethal injection as "justice" (25). In the context of our current legal treatment of young men that word is meaningless. Nor can I share the almost universal enthusiasm among critics for the film *Boys Don't Cry*.

The film tells us that it is wrong to rape and murder transsexuals. True, but not very helpful in that the vast majority of people who are undecided on this issue are probably not going to be persuaded by the film. Very unhelpfully, the film also maintains the traditional gender binarity between men and women by creating a separate category "boy," or more accurately "~~boy~~," which is filled only by a biological female who refuses to act as either a woman (a group the film defines as hopelessly immature ultra-feminine beings) or a lesbian. Within this film, as within most of American culture, one is a boy if one lacks the power and authority of patriarchal manhood. But within the film there are no boys other than Brandon Teena. The biological males—Lotter, Nissen, and also Teena's gay cousin Lonny, as well as the other men with whom he comes in contact—wear the mantle of powerful, authoritative masculinity. They dictate throughout the film what it means to be a man, and in several cases they attempt to oversee Teena's performances of masculinity. The film de-emphasizes or simply obliterates from its story ways in which people in circumstances like theirs and the real people on whom the characters are based might have been forced into the position of boys in relation to more powerful males. Because we do not see the traumatic attacks on Lotter's and Nissen's own identities, including their gender identities, and how any possibility of adult power was stripped from them, we cannot read them within the film as boys, despite the fact that Lotter was only one year older than Teena and Nissen was the same age. The film's insistence that they struck out at Teena in a gesture of gender policing rather than as part of a perpetuation of the cycle of abuse within masculinity, in which they themselves were trapped, forecloses any useful examination of how and why masculinity in our times is so vexed.

The film erases the brutalization that characterizes biological boys' experience of gender identity in our culture, because it erases the boys themselves. Also erased are the strategies disruptive of gender binarity that some rebellious boys, such as many Goths, Cure fans and otherwise, have developed in order to cope with their subordinate roles within contemporary social structures that offer little hope of later manly power. Finally, and most disturbingly given its ostensible subject, the film erases transgendered females-to-males, by regarding what Halberstam calls "female masculinity" as a form of lesbianism ignorantly misrecognized by Teena as well as his associates. And "[b]y making female masculinity equivalent to lesbianism . . . by reading it as proto-lesbianism awaiting a coming community, we continue to hold female masculinity apart from the making of modern masculinity itself" (*Female Masculinity*, 7). This is sad because Teena's contribution to masculinity, like that of Goth boys and many others who choose to deviate from the path of American gender norms, seems fraught with political significance.

As Deleuze writes with Claire Parnet, "the binary gender machine is an important component of apparatuses of power," and we will misunderstand it if we believe it leaves no room for "the divergences of deviancy" (*Dialogues II*, 21). Those identities, too, will be fixed into taxonomies, so that what seems to be outside, what could have called the dichotomous structure into question, will be reduced to a pathological symptom. "So many dichotomies will be established that there will be enough for everyone to be pinned to the wall, sunk into a hole" (21).

At the millennium, as educational and employment opportunities dwindle for the lower classes, boys have increasingly seen their situation as fixed, since accession to patriarchal power in America has always largely depended on economic resources. Brandon Teena coped with this scary situation by drawing on his strengths, which happened to be a pretty face, an unthreatening manner, and a talent for manipulation. The other boys in his world did the same, but with more tragic results since the only advantages they had were brute strength, a knife, and a gun. If *Boys Don't Cry* had acknowledged these simple facts, if it had been less concerned with establishing dichotomies—men against girls, boys against men—its feminism would have been a help rather than a hindrance to the project of bringing down patriarchy.

5.
HETEROSEXUALIZING
THE FEMME BOY

From *Tea and Sympathy*
to *Crime and Punishment in Suburbia*

*We want to put an end once and for all to any rigid assigning of
sexual identity. We do not want to think of ourselves anymore as
men and women, homosexuals and heterosexuals, possessors and
possessed, older and younger, masters and slaves, but rather as
human beings who transcend such sexual categorization, who
are autonomous, in flux, and multifaceted.*

—Félix Guattari, "In Order to End the Massacre of the Body"

In the previous chapter Deleuzian theory helped me explain how the missed
connections between Goth subcultures and the film *Boys Don't Cry* could be
re-established, the erased rhizomatic lines retraced, to clarify problems in
America's current majoritist constructions of masculinity. This chapter will
examine how a feminist/Deleuzian approach to film narrative combined with
some awareness of current articulations of sexuality and gender identity in the
Goth subculture can lead to a new understanding of film depictions of biological boys coded femme.

I chose a title with problematic connotations in order to begin by recognizing the contending political discourses that are brought into play by the
topic of film representation of boys who fit cultural stereotypes of effeminacy.
Just as a foretaste of what is to come, readers may note that the title can
suggest, on the one hand, the conservative political majority's move to erase
male femme homosexualities by representing them as misguided identifica-

tions correctible through indoctrination into standard heterosexual gender affect. But please note also that the title can, on the other hand, suggest a radical move to break apart mainstream gender ideology's conflation of effeminate affect in males with homosexuality. I will begin by summarizing the plots of the two films I am using here as opposite poles, in order to sketch in possibilities in film representation of male effeminacy.

Robert Anderson's *Tea and Sympathy* began as a very popular Broadway play in 1951. In 1956 Vincente Minnelli directed a successful film adaptation featuring the Broadway star Deborah Kerr as Laura Reynolds, the unfulfilled newlywed wife of a bullying, closeted homosexual coach at a boarding school for boys. The film, like the play, concentrates on narrating the story of how her loving attention rescues Tom Robinson Lee, a sensitive and bookish student who is tormented by the others, including her husband, because they suspect him of being homosexual. Their relentless persecution drives Tom deep into self-hatred and toward suicide. Laura intervenes to save him not so much from the others as from the damage they have caused him to do to himself. Laura's maternal nurturing, her provision of the titular "tea and sympathy," takes a rather surprising turn when she seduces the seventeen-year-old and subsequently leaves her husband, although not in order to be with Tom, whom she also leaves, but in his case with the tender admonition to speak of their affair kindly in the future.[1]

Should we think of this plot as proto-feminist? That has not been the critical consensus. Feminist criticism frequently laments popular media's failure to represent as heterosexually successful women who do not fully conform to feminine stereotypes. But critics' own concepts of what constitutes heterosexual success often seem to prevent them from recognizing a narrative tradition in film in which women who defy gender codes win males who are not conventionally masculine. That most feminist critics do not see this film tradition as significant is understandable because of the history of such representations. In the past, stories about the wooing and winning of nontraditional males, as typified by *Tea and Sympathy*, usually reflected both society's homophobia and its misogyny.[2]

Critics' interpretations of *Tea and Sympathy* seem determined by one of two dominant cultural discourses through which gender ambiguity is accounted for. The first, which expressed psychotherapeutic approaches to homosexuality at the time when the film was made and has now migrated to the Religious Right, holds that homosexuality is natural to no one and therefore all homosexual identification is a misrecognition of one's true nature. This discourse offers an etiology in which young males perceived as androgynous (and so as effeminate by default) are recruited or corrupted into homosexuality by misguided men who themselves had previously been victimized in the same way. Homosexuality thus is understood in ways analogous to our current interpretation of pedophilia. A person who was abused by having attributed to him sexual desires that he could not really have had, because such desires cannot arise naturally and spontaneously, goes on to perpetuate this cycle of abuse with others.

If we read the film through this paradigm, Tom is rescued by the self-sacrificial love of Laura, whose intervention into his sex life breaks the chain of perverse misrecognition. Because he is able to respond sexually to Laura, Tom need not accept and internalize the homosexual identity attributed to him by the other males who surround him. In *The Celluloid Closet*, Vito Russo offers this interpretation of the film's message while persuasively arguing that the cultural climate of the times made it inevitable that the film avoid representing homosexuality as "a valid option for a real man" (113). Though the film does depict the persecution of effeminate boys as wrong, it justifies this position through the doubly homophobic move of suggesting not only that such persecution is wrong because all boys are born heterosexual but also that all adult males who bully the effeminate do so because they themselves are closeted gays.[3] Homosexuality can then be understood to be passed on not only through seduction but also through the persecution inflicted on effeminate or beautiful boys by those who would like to seduce them but are too conflicted or cowardly to do so. In this way, the sexual-orientation dichotomy of traditional film narrative in which straight is good and gay is bad remains in place.

The other dominant discourse, increasingly governing later interpretations of the film, is the naturalization of homosexuality not only as a genetically predetermined sexual orientation, but also as a determinant of behavior, tastes, and affect. According to this understanding of sexual orientation, Tom is clearly gay because he does not care for rough sports, relates to women as people rather than objects, enjoys reading, is sensitive, and shows emotion easily. Read through this discourse, the film becomes a rather horrific narrative of a young gay man's indoctrination into heterosexual behaviors, including sex with women, that he must adopt in order to survive.

But other readings are possible, including one in which we might see the young man as a victim of a system of simplistic gender binarism which codes any departure from normative masculinity as both effeminate and homosexual because these two conditions are considered inextricable from each other. The coach's deplorable behavior could then be read as a result of the same system's oppressive insistence that he be either femme or heterosexual, a similar violation of his own desires and sense of self. However, here the film's potential for radicalism is undercut by Laura's position in the film narrative. Laura is punished for her apparent taste for nontraditional males, first by a failed marriage to a man whose absurdly macho overcompensation for his attraction to boys makes their shared life miserable and second by reduction to a merely instrumental role in Tom's development. Her sexuality has importance only in that it prompts her to save him.

No matter what else was innovative about *Tea and Sympathy* at the time of its release, this plot detail marks the film's adherence to tradition. In discussing another very successful film of the era, the 1955 William Holden star vehicle *Picnic*, Brandon French notes the conventionality of its "subliminal message[, which] is that it takes *two* people to make a 'real man,' the man himself and the woman who sacrifices herself to his welfare" (119). As Amy Aronson and Michael Kimmel point out, romantic fantasies of redemption through one-sided sacrificial love have "been a Hollywood staple for decades," and the preferred format has always been the transformation of a bad man by an "innocent and virtuous" woman (44). Although, as John Clum observes, *Tea and Sympathy* draws on the Freudian concept of homosexuality as immature and perversely self-defeating in order to figure heterosexual seduction as redemption of a "bad" male, ultimately the female figure's lack of conventional feminine virtue (sexual innocence) demands that she suffer (51). Moreover, because to the extent that she wins at all, Laura wins only a male of dubious worth, one who is coded as flawed due to his incomplete achievement of masculinity, and because her winning of him is not permanent, the film urges us to read her own heterosexuality as unsuccessful.

The underlying assumptions that have made effeminate heterosexual males also nearly unreadable culturally are greatly illuminated by Eve Sedgwick's response to what she calls "the war on effeminate boys" in the late 1980s practice of psychology and its translation into both popular therapy culture and official policy for managing adolescents. She rightly contends that the 1980 "decision to remove 'homosexuality' from DSM-III," the third edition of the American Psychiatric Association's *Diagnostic and Statistical Manual of Mental Disorders*, was "accomplished only under intense pressure from gay activists outside the profession." Moreover, the hostility to homosexuality that still dominated (and continues to dominate) psychology dictated that the de-pathologization of adult homosexuality be compensated for, and to a large extent negated, by "the addition to DSM-III of 'Gender Identity Disorder of Childhood'" (Sedgwick, 157). "Nominally gender-neutral, this diagnosis is actually highly differential between boys and girls," as she shows by quoting the criteria applied to each (156).

In order to be diagnosed as suffering from gender identity disorder, girls must not only want to be boys so ardently as to perceive themselves as such, as Brandon Teena did, but must also believe that they possess or soon will grow penises. But boys are considered to be afflicted with gender identity disorder if they merely exhibit signs of identification with females (156). Further, Sedgwick observes that representative psychoanalytic theorists within professional practice in the eighties often maintained the traditional view that "effeminate boys turn out gay" because "other men don't validate them as masculine" (159). Due to "the therapists' disavowed desire for a nongay outcome," the commitment of the "helping professions" to "prevention of gay people" inevitably takes the form of treating all instances of effeminacy in boys as crisis-level pathology to be suppressed at all cost (161, 163).

This is, of course, very bad for gay youths, as Sedgwick shows, but it is also bad for all males who do not conform to gender stereotypes, as has been amply illustrated by the way that institutions governing the daily life of adolescents made opportunistic use of the Columbine massacre to justify suppressing Goth stylistic expression. Sedgwick asserts that oppression of homosexuals will continue "in the absence of a strong, explicit, *erotically invested* affirmation of some people's felt desire or need that there be gay people in the immediate world" (164, emphasis Sedgwick's). I concur, but would prefer to modify her statement somewhat to say that oppression of all boys and men who—like Brandon Teena, or the majority of Goth males—cannot or will not eschew the cultural markers of effeminacy will continue as long as we believe both that male effeminacy inexorably leads to homosexuality and that male homosexuality is an evil to be avoided. Therefore, although the heterosexualization of effeminate boys in film does not initially appear to support gay rights, it can have exactly that result.

There is hope for change in that new narrative conventions in film representation of heterosexual love and romance call for new interpretive paradigms. Films such as *Girl Fight* and *G.I. Jane,* which present aggressive, dominant women as heterosexually desirable and successful in love, are complemented by films that return to the previously denigrated figure of the so-called effeminate male and revalue him as a prize to be won (and cherished) by a strong woman. This change is particularly evident in films that reference Goth subcultures, such as *The Matrix, Sleepy Hollow,* and *Crime and Punishment in Suburbia,* which follow the Goth music and fashion scenes in drawing on standards of male desirability in circulation in gay subcultures to queer heterosexuality by reimagining it through what might be called new genders.

This sort of reimagination, or, as cybergoth might put it, reloading and refreshing of the cultural Imaginary, is necessary because majoritist discourses of the romantic are strongly flavored with that sexual normalcy that S/M practitioners often refer to as vanilla. As Ann Powers explains in *Weird Like Us: My Bohemian America,*

> The vanilla worldview encompasses more than an undue respect for the missionary position; it includes larger assumptions about how people should fulfill their destinies. . . . Gay men, historically damned as promiscuous monsters, are now threatened in their own ranks if they do not

'get married' like straight people do. . . . Bisexuals, older women involved
with younger men, aggressive women who aren't in it for love, gentle
men who don't want to take the lead . . . the vanilla myth condemns
them all to shame and secrecy. (107)

Powers posits as the diametric opposite of this mainstream delusion the "queer
club" scene of San Francisco, which in my own experience has for the last
forty years remained remarkably consistent in presenting us with "bulldykes
with major muscles, hairy Radical Faeries in chiffon drag, middle-aged rubber queens, teenage ravers—individuals spanning and blurring the categories
of race, size, sex, gender" (94).

I rediscovered that world in my Goth-hunting expeditions in the years
2001–2004. The scene at special club nights like "Assimilate," a collection of
all sorts of Goths occurring every Friday night at the Cat Club on Folsom
Street, reputedly the former locale of some of Foucault's forays into new
bodily pleasures, far exceeded anything academics usually seem to mean
when they exhort students to "celebrate diversity." One gay friend opined that
the weekly event's name reflected a response to the Radical Faeries' anti-
assimilation movement, which he called a sort of separatism for gay men.
Goth as interpreted at "Assimilate" includes some Punk and Heavy Metal as
well as more standard Goth and Industrial music. Club patrons included
very fat and very thin people and everybody between, people who were aggressively styling in elaborate fetish or "corpse"/vampire gear and generic dark
rockers in black jeans and concert t-shirts. Ages ranged from twenty-one to at
least the mid-fifties. There were identifiable lesbians and gay men, as well as
fairly easily recognizable transsexuals (m-to-f and f-to-m) of varied orienta-
tions, but the majority were of unidentifiable sexual preference. The only
unifying element was enthusiasm for erotic pleasures deemed deviant by the
American mainstream. Here as much as in the outer areas, the places of
exile, around and behind American middle and high schools without number, Goth opened up a welcoming space for those outlawed by majoritist sex
and gender mores.

It is within such a context that any sensible reading of Vincent, the hero
of Rob Schmidt's 2000 film *Crime and Punishment in Suburbia*, should begin, since he is coded by the film as a Goth.[4] He is also both some sort of
Christian, as his dialogue and t-shirt solemnly depicting Christ's crucifixion
make clear, and, in addition, recognizably masochistic. The film's titular reference to Fyodor Dostoyevsky's novel brings the masochism of Vincent in the
film into conjunction with that of the novel's prostitute Sonia, through what
Deleuze and Parnet might call "an encounter between two reigns, a short-
circuit, the picking up of a code where each is deterritorialized" (44). Sonia,
whom Dostoyevsky describes as "shy by nature" and "quite aware of her social

vulnerability," tries to "avoid trouble by being careful and meek and humble to everybody" (395), as does Vincent, whose characteristic pose includes hunched shoulders and bowed head. Like Sonia, he seeks the redemptive space opened by self-abasement, and asserts himself, to the extent that he ever does, through occupying it in quiet resignation. Vincent's courtship of his beloved, like Sonia's of Raskolnikov, is nearly indistinguishable from an attempt to religiously convert the other. In other words, the film draws on the novel to create a "becoming" that brings together the so-called moral masochism of Christianity with sexual masochism, unsettling the fixity of both, releasing each from predetermined signification. The film, thus, illuminates Goth masochism subtly, showing it forth through images rather than as part of a narrative that would fix its definition. We see what masochism does, at least in this instance, instead of being instructed in what it is.

As I have discussed in the preceding chapters, the view of S/M most prevalent in Goth differs from that of the mainstream, and the film adheres to the Goth vision. Davenport-Hines characterizes Goths as sexual submissives, noting that "their clothes, their décor, their manners [proclaim] them as people who [expect] to be abused. Fatality [is] at the center of their beliefs" (364). He also stresses the Goth investment in a sort of beautiful grotesquerie that seeks to make over the world's horrors as art products (365). And Davenport-Hines further comments that the Goth attitude toward death amounts to an "inverted religiosity" (366). Hodkinson's caution against interpreting the Goth predilection for styles associated with S/M as indicative of specific proclivities on the part of any given Goth is tempered by his assertion that Goths demonstrably value "transgression" of sex and gender norms, and seem particularly inclined to consider "non-hetero sexualities," especially female sexual dominance of males, "to be admired" (51–55). As Baddeley observes, within "Goth subculture . . . sexual fetishism and its trappings are widely accepted as the marks of an outlaw libido" (238).

On the less formal side, an English friend who was a Goth in her younger days responded with surprise when I told her about the American tendency to regard Goths as homosexual, but readily understood why Americans associate Goth with S/M. She answered an email message from me on the topic, "This makes more sense to me within the Goth world I knew. The leather thing fitted with overtones of bondage and sadism. The female Goth in her stiletto boots and leather jerkin could easily identify herself or be identified with a dominatrix." While the central figure in mainstream popular cultural depictions of S/M—from *Nine and a Half Weeks* to *Secretary*—is almost always either a dominant male or else a dominatrix who is obviously and often comically only in it for the money, the Goth scene opens space for the woman who dominates sexually for her own pleasure and that of her willing victim(s).

The venerable Goth band Christian Death's cover of Lou Reed's song "Venus in Furs" (which he recorded with the Velvet Underground), with its exhortation "Strike, dear mistress, and cure his heart," exemplifies Goth's frequent representation of S/M as its serious practitioners have known it, as a technology for creating intensities, a means of inhabiting what Deleuze and Guattari call "positive desire." In *A Thousand Plateaus*, they say, "the masochist's suffering is the price he must pay, not to achieve pleasure, but to untie the pseudobond between desire and pleasure as an extrinsic measure" (155). To the uninitiated the masochist's rituals of ordeal may look "dreary," but "in fact, [the masochist] uses suffering to bring forth . . . a plane of consistency of desire," and consequently experiences "a joy that is immanent to desire as though desire were filled by itself and its contemplations, a joy that implies no lack or impossibility and is not measured by pleasure, since it is what distributes intensities of pleasure and prevents them from being suffused by anxiety, shame and guilt" (150, 155).

Goth goes beyond even this radicalism to rewrite S/M as a minoritarian practice, not simply in that it is not treated as a pathology or, in the words of DSM-IV, a "self-defeating behavior," but is instead a technology for resisting gender binarity. When a woman takes the dominant role in S/M, according to the majoritist scripting of gender, she must do so through the culturally constructed feminine. She disciplines her own body with the usual tortures demanded by glamour to create the physical surfaces that signify female beauty in the moment she inhabits. She withholds herself from the man in order to punish him for desiring, herself occupying the female space of nullity in relation to desire. She remains object to his subject. As I have discussed in chapter 3, Goth fiction writers, like Poppy Z. Brite and Laurell K. Hamilton, re-envision female sadism and male masochism in ways that transgress gender norms. They create a minoritarian language of S/M focused on the aggressively desirous female's consumption of the beautiful male body.

All of the descriptive claims I have made about the function of masochism in Goth are amply illustrated by *Crime and Punishment in Suburbia*. In fact, one might say that by using a male Goth as protagonist, the film transforms the marks of Goth gender and sexual identities into what Deleuze calls "demarks." According to Deleuze, demarks in film are images that effect defamiliarization, but they do more. While a mark is "a term [that] refers back to other terms in a customary series such that each can be 'interpreted' by the others," a demark is a term that "leap[s] outside the web and suddenly appear[s] in conditions which take it out of its series or set it in contradiction with it" (*Cinema 1*, 203). Demarks unsettle conventional ways of understanding, forcing a reassessment of what is presented. Within the film Goth maleness and Goth masochism become demarks that interrupt the chains of thought that would otherwise structure our interpretation of the film, keeping us from assimilating it into a familiar narrative about the problems of sexuality for American suburban adolescents.

Loosely based on Dostoyevsky's novel, the film presents us with the dysfunctional Skolnik family, whose voluptuous teen daughter Roseanne (Monica Keena), is, as her name suggests, the Raskolnikov figure. Like Raskolnikov, she suffers from cynicism brought on by deep disillusionment with the shallow, hypocritical society that surrounds her. And also similarly, because she lacks the spiritual or philosophic knowledge that might guide her into more productive forms of rebellion, she strikes out murderously at the world's meaninglessness—although in her case with more motivation than Raskolnikov has. Her victims are her stepfather, whom she stabs to death after he drunkenly sexually assaults her, and her runaway mother, whom she heartlessly frames for the crime.

Her life is constantly observed, and rendered into film images, by her despised admirer Vincent (Vincent Kartheiser), who goes on to play the Sonia role as her spiritual and self-sacrificial lover, counseling her when she is in despair. He also models submission to the cruelty of the ignorant, including her unpleasant jock boyfriend and the other kids who read Vincent's alienation, sensitivity, and emotional depth as freakishly gender-inappropriate. That the section intertitled "Her Mother's a Whore" begins with Vincent's classmates deriding him as a "fucking faggot" and then shows us Roseanne's boyfriend attacking him suggests an affinity transcending biological sex between males and females who reject conventional gender roles.

The film overcodes this message through its depiction of the mother's sexual expression as misjudged. Audience members with conventional morals are nonetheless strongly nudged to sympathize with the adulterous mother by being told that her motivation for remarriage was to satisfy societal expectations of respectability by giving her daughter a father.[5] Her second husband's alcoholism and brutishness would certainly cause most contemporary viewers to excuse her decision to leave him for another man. But the film stacks the deck in her favor further by making the other man an obviously virtuous and even heroic African American, and emphasizing that the community's judgment that she is a whore is based in racism. Like Todd Haynes's *Far from Heaven* (2002), this film conflates rejection of the traditional wifely role and rejection of the pervasive racism of bourgeois society. But unlike Haynes's film, whose tone is far more parodic than melodramatic, *Crime and Punishment in Suburbia* stresses the old-fashioned message that sacrificial love redeems.

Crime and Punishment in Suburbia's plot is to some extent consistent with what Aronson and Kimmel describe as the postfeminist permutation of the film narrative of redemptive love. They claim the old version, with its emphasis on the love of the good woman, has failed in today's climate of "career women," and that, consequently, effeminate gay men have been assigned by Hollywood films the role of "good nurturing figures" whose attention redeems (47). "What gay men represent is priorities—relationships always come first, before commitment to work" (48), and before the desire for personal fulfillment or pleasure from any source other than loving submission and self-abnegation. But where *Crime and Punishment in Suburbia* departs from the currently popular formula is not just in the heterosexuality of its femme male redemptive figure, but in the focus of his erotic passion on the young woman he saves.

Aronson and Kimmel claim that "[i]n order for gay men to reorient heterosexual women's botched priorities, they must, themselves, be as virtuous as children, innocent and asexual" (49). This is particularly important, they rightly assert, because of the common understanding that it is "lust" that makes men bad (48). Yet the importation of the Goth sensibility into the film disrupts the usual pattern and creates room for a heterosexual masculinity that is neither butch nor "bad," that is neither invasive nor sadistic. In fact the film mixes conventional gender categories freely, presenting us with the spectacle of a black-clad, camera-wielding male loner with a motorcycle whose response to verbal and physical attack is absolute surrender, and with a pretty blonde female cheerleader with a propensity toward sadistic violence.

The film engages the question E. Ann Kaplan raises about contemporary film depictions of powerful, sexually aggressive women: "when women are in the dominant position, are they in the masculine position?" (128). Working from Freudian theory, Nancy Friday's published collections of sexual fantasy narratives, and analyses of pornography provided by the group Women Against Pornography, Kaplan reaches the conclusion that dominance/submission fantasies are pervasive in our culture, but that women lack the identificatory range of men, being "more consistently submissive, but not excessively abandoned," and thus, when women fantasize dominance, they usually prefer to identify with someone who dominates another woman (127). Cinematic examples of dominant females suggest to her that this is the case. Her conclusion is that "the gaze is not necessarily male (literally) but to own and activate the gaze, given our language and the structure of the unconscious, is to be in the masculine position" (130). For this reason, she concludes that feminism demands that we "move beyond long-held cultural and linguistic patterns of oppositions: male/female (as these terms currently signify), dominant/submissive," and so on (135). While the film certainly effects a movement beyond majoritist binary definitions of male and female, its interest in the erotics of dominance and submission—so typical of Goth culture—far from holding in place such binaries, works to dismantle them.

Most reviews of the film compare it to *American Beauty*, a comparison which seems valid and instructive, although not always in the ways the critics claim, since all are working from a standard of realism determined by *American Beauty*'s evocation of interiority, as it is commonly understood. Julia Levin, one of *Crime and Punishment in Suburbia*'s harshest detractors, sums it up: "Completed before *American Beauty*, this artificial little movie resembles it in every way possible, mainly because it examines the very same set of stereotypes about malfunctioning wealthy suburbanites." *American Beauty* exemplifies what she believes films should achieve: the indirect suggestion of psychological depth through visual representation of what are normally unobserved activities, seen as representative of inner life. She claims, "What Ricky was able to see with his lens in *American Beauty* revealed the hidden layers of human behavior." In contrast, *Crime and Punishment in Suburbia* fails to please her, because

> What attracted me the most in *American Beauty* was how punchy and derisive—yet humane—the film was. It carried a deep loss for the human connection, a charge that gave the film its integrity, the weight of reality. The humorless *Crime + Punishment* substitutes this depth with a slow motion camera, elaborate soundtrack, suggestive visual themes, and a stupid voice over.

A review by "MH" on the Political Film Society website takes the opposite position but remains under the same standard of realism: "The theme of angst of suburbia, from *Over the Edge* (1979) to *American Beauty* (1999), is replayed with far more raw intensity in *Crime and Punishment in Suburbia*." Interestingly, the reviewer notes that "Originally, the movie was to be called 'Crime and Punishment in High School,' but the title changed after the Columbine massacre so that the focus would be on the causes of violence rather than the violence itself."

Yet the reviewer does not, apparently, recognize that Vincent's obvious Goth identification would also have been problematic in the wake of the Columbine shootings, especially since, at the time of the film's release, parents and school officials were being urged to watch out for any signs of such identification because it might predict "at risk" behavior. The website review focuses on the pertinent question the film raises: "what can be done to prevent violence amid the material success of America's suburbs?" And the answer the film is understood as providing, to "deconstruct" the pervasive suburban "narcissistic individualism [as] the obvious source of the poisonous alienation" of the young, results in "the Political Film Society [nominating] the movie for an award as best film of 2000 advocating nonviolence and peaceful ways of solving human conflicts."

Roger Ebert is also enthusiastic, saying, "'Crime and Punishment in Suburbia' is no doubt 'flawed' . . . and it suffers from being released a year after the similar 'American Beauty,' even though it was made earlier. But it is the kind of movie that lives and breathes." In his view the film is "'American Beauty' told from the point of view of the cheerleader," whom he sees as devoid of any but an exteriorly imposed performative identity, "an actress— pretending to be a daughter, a girlfriend, a cheerleader, all the time screaming inside." The film is even more extraordinary in that it does not imagine the cause of this internal screaming to be, as is the current convention in representing active sex lives of teen girls, that poor Roseanne gets subjected to sex while really wanting only love.

Instead, the film remains true to bohemian values like Ann Powers's. Writing of her own coming of age, Powers says that when she "discovered the perverts' open universe, [she] began to see that the most damaging aspects of our erotic encounters stem not from too much scrutiny being given sex . . . but from not letting sex come into focus at all" (87). Roseanne is depicted as one of the teen girls Powers amusingly describes as "wear[ing] vinyl miniskirts to biology class, where they get a lecture on condoms if the parents' association hasn't barred it, but they won't hear much straight talk about how their own bodies have started to feel." The tragedy of these girls lives is not that they have become sexually active "too soon," but that, "given no other words for those sensations, they call them love. But their language of love is a lexicon of habits, wedding etiquette, and romance-novel scenes. And for sex, all they get is dirty jokes and a pamphlet about disease" (87). In other words, Roseanne's interior screaming expresses her horror at being forced into a relationship she does not want in order to get the sexual sensations she does, and at seeing her mother tormented first by an agonizing attempt to make domesticity satisfy her sexual desires and then by community condemnation because she gives up on that project and pursues sexual pleasure directly. Roseanne screams inside against the lies about female sexuality that define emotional health in the suburban mainstream culture she inhabits.

Jessica Winter observes that the film's shifts between Roseanne and Vincent reverse contemporary concepts of wholesomeness, first by insisting that erotic fixations can actually be healing for troubled teens and then by correcting the misconceptions about Goths that proliferated after the Columbine tragedy: "Much of the ongoing horror is viewed through Roseanne's eyes, but her perspective is tempered by co-narrator Vincent (Vincent Kartheiser), a pallid Goth wraith whose obsession with Roseanne is mostly healthy and potentially redemptive." In Winter's view the film shows us less about suburbia than about young people hip enough to escape its confines and worldview. "Roseanne's . . . shy, trauma-induced movements away from her dick-swingin' goofball Jimmy and toward the sweet, fucked-up, vaguely androgynous out-sider Vincent feel blisteringly true." Winter's unqualified approbation of *Crime and Punishment in Suburbia* and preference for it over *American Beauty* fit her audience at the *Village Voice*, whose readers tend to identify as outsiders to the mainstream.

American Beauty is majoritarian in its reliance on shared, common-sense codes and symbols which reaffirm the dominant majority discourse of family and sexuality. Its central question, "who will destroy the American male?" (figured by Kevin Spacey as Lester Burnham, a "baby boomer" suburbanite become a misfit due to his midlife crisis), is a variant on *Tea and Sympathy*'s central questioning of who can save a misfit boy by transforming him to meet normative standards of American masculinity. In fact, it would not take too much of a stretch to imagine the young, recently married, and apparently well adjusted Tom Robinson Lee gradually becoming *American Beauty*'s fran-tic Lester Burnham twenty years down the road, especially since Lester's mid-life crisis is precipitated by his lack of sexual passion for his wife and his fail-ure to achieve the amount of brute aggression apparently necessary to arouse any in her.[6]

As in *Tea and Sympathy*, in *American Beauty* the two candidates for the role of transformer of the weak male are a gay male bully who passes as straight (Lester's neighbor Colonel Frank Fitts) and a domestic woman (Lester's wife, Carolyn). This triangulation situates both protagonists within the Oedipal paradigm, between paternal and maternal imagoes, each with the potential either to destroy the protagonist or to reconstruct him as an acceptable male. Moreover, *American Beauty* surpasses *Tea and Sympathy*'s affirmation of the status quo by positing the American rebel's ultimate fate—at least until death frees him—as being caught up in the suburban mainstream. Everyone must sell out, the film suggests; there is no outside, all roads will lead to suburbia.

In contrast, *Crime and Punishment in Suburbia* is minoritarian in De-leuzian terms. Its perspective split between its dual protagonists, Roseanne and Vincent, is repeated within the characterization of each through demon-strations first of his and then of her ambivalent relation to the gender binarism of their society. The lyrics of the soundtrack song "Two Rivers," by the Meat Puppets, reinforce the impression that the two main characters are to be seen in terms of mutuality and transformative exchange: "Two waters side by side / Never touching, they remain / When they meet the waters change."

We can gain further insight into Roseanne and Vincent's mirroring func-tion in relation to each other through Deleuze's discussion of mirror images in *Cinema 2: The Time-Image*. Because Deleuze opposes the idea that pre-sentation and representation can be differentiated, since we can know "real-ity" only through images that effect its representation, "the actual and the virtual . . . are in continual exchange" (70). The actress or actor represented by the film image is also present, actual, within that image, with his or her diegetic role taking the form of a sort of ghostly virtual image. Cinematic mirroring heightens our awareness of the interchange between such images, and, as Bogue explains, "in Deleuze's analysis, when directors systematically play with the relationship between acting and being, stage world and real world, film and reality, they are not simply questioning art's function as a re-presentation of reality. They are seeing the world as a proliferation of *reflections*," and thus calling into question ideas such as natural unitary identity (*Deleuze on Cinema*, 122, emphasis Bogue's). In this case, Vincent as double/reflection for Roseanne (just like Roseanne as his reflection/double) serves to take us beyond Roger Ebert's astute observation that the film presents the character as an actress in her everyday life. The film also presents as reflections—or what Judith Butler famously called copies of copies with no original (141)—the binary gender identities that authoritative discourses of psychology affirm and that popular culture naturalizes, and that both of these urge us to impose upon the young.

The film's doubling of its protagonist(s) troubles gender binarity in another way as well. Through the casting of Kartheiser as the boy, the film doubles the actor's ordinary off-stage appearance with his appearance within the story, as is emphasized by the use of his real-life first name, Vincent, for the character. Blake Edwards's 1982 farce *Victor/Victoria* is typical of mainstream films about gender-bending in that the choice of the decidedly feminine Julie Andrews for the title role ensures audiences will not be troubled by the idea that gender truly is nothing but performance. As in the enormously successful *La Cage aux Folles* series, the failure of one sex to pass as the other both amuses and reassures audience members for whom it is necessary that gender binarity remain a basic fact of life.

For many viewers, myself included, Hilary Swank's effeminate appearance as Brandon Teena, not to mention her insistent conformity to Hollywood's female beauty standard at that year's Academy Awards ceremony, worked similarly to undercut the film's ostensible purpose of suggesting that gender is a construct. But even more compelling is *Boys Don't Cry*'s plot itself, which tells us that to question the linkage of gender to biology is liable to bring fatal consequences. Films in which cross-gender identification signifies tragedy, such as Neil Jordan's 1992 *The Crying Game*, simply show us the other side of the same reassuring piece of currency. (One side tells that passing is impossible; the other side tells us that passing is tragedy.) Moreover, the pairing of the gorgeously gender-indeterminate Jaye Davidson as transsexual hairdresser Dil with two big, traditionally masculine-looking men in masculine professions, the soldier Jody (Forest Whitaker) and the revo-

lutionary and construction worker Fergus (Stephen Rea), reinforces mainstream concepts of contrastively gendered complementarity as a necessary
component of sexuality.

In contrast, Kartheiser brings to his role as Vincent a genuinely fragile
androgynous appearance that contrasts with Keena's buxom, athletic build.
Their appearances are quintessentially Goth, with Keena's voluptuousness
suggesting the type of threatening sexiness first made Goth by Vampira (Maila
Nurmi), whom Baddeley identifies as "the first walking, talking pop-culture
version of the Decadent *femme fatale*" and thus "a powerful prototype for the
modern Goth babe," and then by her successor as television late-night horror
hostess, the "even more cartoonishly top-heavy" Elvira (Cassandra Peterson)
(95). By the nineties, he notes, definitive Goth goddesses made an "aesthetic
move away from the punk look toward [that of] a pulchritudinous heroine
from a period Gothic-horror movie" (219). As Hodkinson discusses, "an ample
chest" gives status to Goth women even when they are too large and fleshy to
fit mainstream beauty standards, which currently call for a very thin, "hard
body" with prominently jutting breastbones and hipbones and the sort of rig-
idly immobile breasts usually associated with implants (53). Meanwhile, for
Goth males a slender, "somewhat effeminate" appearance is preferred (53–
54). While some Goths obviously do adhere to mainstream beauty standards,
the subculture is distinguished from other currently popular youth cultures
by its generation, not mere tolerance, of another standard. Goth thus markedly departs from the mainstream concept of a physically well-matched pair,
in which, as is generally evident in Hollywood films, the man must be much
larger and heavier than the woman, and her femininity must manifest in ex-
aggeratedly contrastive relation to his masculinity.

The only other film I can think of to pair gender/sexual outlaws in such
an outrageous way is Alain Berliner's 1997 film about the early life of a transgendered boy, *Ma Vie en Rose*, which at its conclusion shows the cross-dressing protagonist happily befriending a tomboy. However, the fact that these
two characters are seven years old, clearly presexual, and that he, at least, has
already been identified as romantically oriented toward other males keeps
this film from challenging majoritist narratives of gender's relation to sexuality as deeply as the pairing of Kartheiser and Keena does. It is difficult to fit
their images as separate screen presences and even more so as doubles-with-a-
difference into any existent cultural narrative of successful, healthy heterosexuality, because we have never been presented with a screen couple quite
like them. Together the dual protagonists constitute a Deleuzian affective
cinematic event such as Bogue describes, "bypassing the brain and working
directly on the senses through images that defy assimilation in terms of standard visual codes" (*Deleuze on Cinema*, 189). Thus the film's central question

about each of the two protagonists, and about them as a couple, is Deleuzian: who will unblock their flows of desire from imprisonment within the Oedipal narrative so central to capitalism? Who will free them to take lines of flight outside the family and the familiar? And the film answers: each will do so for the other, for in the other they find that there is no "other," no opposite or same, only endless proliferation of possible identities.

According to Deleuze, one of the revolutionary ways images can function in cinema is to take us beyond the majoritist cultural narratives that reduce them to clichés, familiar signs in old symbolic systems, and open up infinite realms of potential meaning. Images do so by directly stimulating our emotions, without the intervention of language. They achieve this partly by inducing us to value observation more than the activity of assembling images into a coherent story, often through examples provided by characters within the story who "become seers, [who] cannot or will not react, so great is their need to 'see' properly what there is in the situation" (*Cinema* 2, 128). Vincent is such a character; his photographing and continual watching of Roseanne pre-empt action, and he inhabits what Deleuze aptly calls "the Dostoevskian condition" in which one treats seeing "the terms of a problem [as] more profound than the situation, and even more pressing" (*Cinema* 2, 128). Vincent seeks not an inner truth, but an insight into the mechanisms through which the real of his and Roseanne's world comes into being. His need to see Roseanne's reality as she constructs it is not the traditional mastering gaze attributed to men by feminist film theory, nor is his passion to record her image marked by the sadistic possessiveness usually attributed to males who film women within films.

As Chris Holmlund says, critics, "like Freud, often find it easier to associate activity with sadism and both with masculinity" (85). But her prescription for a more sensible approach to film representations of lesbians is also applicable to heterosexuals. If we are to get past get the limited and negative clichés governing their representation, "we need to insist on the diversity of [their] lives" (88). If we replicate the Freudian, and culturally dominant, equation of masculinity with sadism and submission with femininity, we will be unable to read any film images as challenges to this binary. Elayne Rapping's wonderful comments on the feminist anti-porn movement come to mind:

> That they behaved so irrationally and repressively speaks to the depth of the belief that sex is a dangerous, even fatal, subject for women. Even the hint that women might be someday free to have unfettered pleasure and the ability to create and be thrilled by erotic images conjures up for them the fear that women might instead reproduce existing power relations. (256)

In contrast to that fearful and repressive attitude, *Crime and Punishment in Suburbia* offers a boy who is much prettier, more delicate and yielding, than the big, brash young woman he loves. Also, in a break from traditions in love stories aimed at the young, although Vincent is from a lower social class than Roseanne, as the soundtrack's use of Modest Mouse's song "Trailer Trash" emphasizes for us, his lower class status means only that he is more beaten-down by the dominant powers than she is, less physically tough, and possessed of less confidence in the efficacy of aggressive resistance. The film explores without apparent fear the idea that perhaps reversing gender roles will not merely replicate the structures of unearned dominance and unwilling submission that have traditionally marked gender relations.

By the conclusion of the film, gender roles have not been so much reversed as they have been redistributed, with both characters engaged in "becoming girl" in Deleuzian terms. As well as describing the most characteristic sort of androgyny associated with Goth, Deleuze and Guattari's writing on girls brings to mind another offshoot of Punk, Riot Grrrl. This work anticipates in many ways the aspects of the recent, popular girl-power movement most concerned with breaking from gender binarism. Deleuze and Guattari claim that for the liberation of women from sexist systems of oppression,

> The question is not, or not only, that of the organism, history, and subject of enunciation that oppose masculine to feminine in the great dualism machines. The question is fundamentally that of the body—the body they *steal* from us in order to fabricate opposable organisms. This body is stolen first from the girl . . . [because] . . . [s]he is an abstract line, or a line of flight. . . . girls do not belong to an age group, sex, order, or kingdom: they slip in everywhere, between orders, ages, sexes: they produce *n* molecular sexes on the line of flight in relation to the dualism machines they cross right through. . . . The girl is like the block of becoming that remains contemporaneous to each opposable term, man, woman, child, adult. It is not the girl who becomes a woman; it is the becoming-woman that produces the universal girl. . . . [T]he girl is the becoming-woman of each sex." (*Thousand Plateaus*, 276–77, emphasis Deleuze and Guattari's)

For Deleuze and Guattari, as for those busily "Gothing up" in costume, "becoming-woman" means leaving the fixed identity of the traditional masculine subject or his feminine object and, instead, entering a state of constant psychic motion, never-ending response to perception, limitless discovery of the selves, sexes, and genders anyone can manifest. The universal girl, as the eternal prewoman, the being defined only by her motion in relation to that static thing she has not yet become, thus comes to represent becoming itself.

As Barbara Kennedy observes, the Deleuzoguattarian "'becoming-girl' is the means through which we can strive to resist . . . gendered categorisations of structured social processes" and attain "a vitalism and freshness, beyond any sense of gendered subjectivity" (160). By sharing his effeminacy with Roseanne, by modeling for her the state of being girl and so being nothing determinate, Vincent deflects her attempts to inhabit a position of social power, to be a (sexually alluring) woman, as defined by majoritist society and culture. Their departure from the prison house on a motorcycle, a line of flight through the winding hills that have signified "the road" in thousands of films, appropriately gives a sense of their entrance into becoming, unrestricted by the deadening gender roles of what our culture has been pleased to call maturity.

In its joyful tossing out the window of all the behavioral norms America currently holds dear and its subsequent suggestion that refusing fixed or culturally legible identities is bliss, *Crime and Punishment in Suburbia* is defiantly both a minoritarian and a Goth film. No wonder that audiences scarcely knew what to make of it. Despite the film's warm reception by many critics, as discussed above, and its nomination for the Grand Jury Prize at the 2000 Sundance Film Festival and for the Grand Special Prize at the 2000 Deauville Film Festival, it had only a limited theatrical run and has since descended into relative obscurity. As Timothy Shary argues, films made for and about youth at the turn of the millennium have generally been characterized by "increasing cynicism" and pessimism about romantic love, and by "an increasing vilification of young sexuality," as if overwhelmed by "anxieties about youth sexuality in society at large" (220, 212, 254). And this matters because, as he says,

> When a given social population is portrayed through existing and emerging genres, a consequential set of standards and expectations is developed over time by the film industry and the audience. The population in question is depicted as acting within a certain range of behaviors and having a limited number of concerns. In this way character paradigms are generated, easily identifiable figures who have a perceived—if not necessarily representative—connection to their real-life referents. Genres of human types are thereby formed. (255)

In addition to affirming the mainstream millennial vision of appropriate sexual behavior, that is, that sex is right only between people who love each other and want to make a lifetime commitment, *American Beauty* retells Hollywood's old story about human behavior and its consequences. Adults who cannot accept and conform to the norms of suburbia die. Teen girls deserve respectful treatment if they remain virginal until they can commit to their one true love. Teen boys whose behavior or appearance departs from the standards of butch masculinity should not be persecuted as "faggots" because they are probably not really gay. (With the implication, as always, that it might be all right for the closeted bully to torment the boy he assumes is gay, if the assumption were correct.) Within this paradigm, being saved and being normed are as indistinguishable as they are in *Tea and Sympathy*. *Crime and Punishment in Suburbia* imagines redemption otherwise.

In fact, a more appropriate, although unlikely, comparison for critics to have made might have been to cult horror director Stuart Gordon's film *Dagon* (2001). Derived from a short story by H. P. Lovecraft, the film dramatizes a bizarre romance between a conservative young man and a hideously mermaid-like creature, who he is alarmed to learn is his half-sister. Both are children of the eponymous legendary fish-god, although the young man is initially unaware of this paternity. Marooned, after a sailing mishap, in a remote village filled with other grotesque halfbloods, he must give up his normal, conventional life and accept his fated union with his half-sister.

As in Gordon's most famous Lovecraft adaptation, *Re-Animator* (1985), humor and horror mix together. This combination culminates in a final scene in which the protagonist, who has thrown himself into a fire and then into the sea to escape his doom and is as a result terribly mutilated, his previous clean-cut professional appearance effaced by floating rags of red and black flesh, finds not death but both immortality and peace as a monster swimming deep under the ocean beside his monstrous mate. This delightfully absurd and rebellious conclusion resonates with Deleuze and Claire Parnet's insight that humor is the masochistic mode and moreover a means through which the masochist "claims kinship with a minority, with a minority-becoming" (69).

To inhabit becoming, "one could also say, undo the face, unravel the face," says Parnet (23).[7] And this is what Gordon's film shows us, in a wildly over-the-top manner, as the crazed townspeople skin the faces of their conventional human victims and make masks of them to create ordinary appearances for themselves. When the protagonist is freed from his false self through a literal flaying, he falls into a becoming with no goal. This ending is consistent with what Deleuze and Parnet praise in Lovecraft's depictions of "the outsider," giving up his humanity, as defined by majoritist discourse, and so "becoming an entity, an infinitive . . . horrific and luminous" (42, 66). As Baddeley explains, Lovecraft was "the first important post-Christian Gothic writer, jettisoning the specters of the past in favor of something bewilderingly formless, and appallingly vast, that lurks at the threshold of tomorrow" (70). In other words, his writing evokes indeterminacy.

Deleuze and Parnet also admiringly quote D. H. Lawrence's apropos exhortation from *Studies in Classic American Literature*: "Let the merman turn away from his human wife and children. . . . Cross the seas, cross the seas, urges the heart. Leave love and home" (41). And so *Dagon* ends, with the young man who sailed out with his conventionally pretty little bride to celebrate his business success transformed into a monster who forgets her in unhuman bliss amidst the loosely flowing tentacles of his monster sister.

Certainly, *Crime and Punishment in Suburbia* is less grotesque, more animated by the spirit of the beautiful, if not the conventional. But what is truly lovely about the film is that like Raskolnikov, Roseanne is spiritually awakened by her lover's humility to a new vision of human possibilities. His voluntary masochistic self-abasement, his joyfully eager relinquishment of masculine privilege suggest to her the hollowness of the social power to which she had aspired. His contempt for the relative safety she sought in conformity allows her to recognize that we are not safe when we suppress our desires in order to take on the roles dictated by the suburban—or any other—milieu. His insistence on capturing and showing her the images that made up her false life pushes her to reinterpret the marks of her success at school, such as her football star boyfriend and her cheerleader status, as demarks that startle her into recognizing her own alienation. Under his patient guidance the events she had read as discordant signs, the demarks that represented her failures, such as her mother's love affair, become marks meaningful in a new narrative, one in which gender does not and should not determine how one feels or behaves because what matters is not sexual orientation but love. Sexuality continues to be meaningful to Roseanne, but not as a determinant of some ridiculously limited identity charted onto a majoritist graph of intersections between "the masculine" and "the feminine." Rather, together with Vincent, she enters the Foucauldian realm in which sexuality is displaced by bodies and pleasures, the Deleuzoguattarian realm where we are everything simultaneously through and in each other, and the Goth space in which, by willingly becoming Nothing, one discovers intense connection with everything. And finally, she is lifted out of the depression that her enactment of the cheerleader role always hid, by that defiant joy of those who move beyond the taxonomies that imprison us in "appropriate" genders and sexualities.

Vincent is, as the police call him, a "damaged little fucker," immature and pretentious, stuck, as his sympathetic mother says, in his "gloom stage." But through his obviously sexual love for her, Roseanne is not corrupted but instead inspired to connect to others. Her redemption comes not through dull domesticity and asexual servitude, but through pursuing the only justice available to us all—that which we ourselves provide through honest, equitable treatment of others—as aggressively as she previously pursued the gratifyingly sadistic sensations she achieved at the expense of others. "The established powers need our sadness to make us slaves" because depression paralyzes our ability to act. Therapy culture works to "administer and organize our intimate little fears," so as to make us into useful members of the

State, and nowhere more strongly than in the case of teenagers (Deleuze and Parnet, 61). Roseanne and Vincent's laughter as they escape the prison announces the end of all that. Because as they ride off together, they still look like a Goth couple who may well enjoy consensual S/M, and because the film has given us no reason to doubt their potential to live out that dream, we are given a final vision that separates this film decisively from most treatments of teenage problems with sexual and gender identity made since *Tea and Sympathy.*

6.

IDENTITY HUNTER A
Asian American Goths and New Masculinities

If Goth refreshes concepts of masculinity, allowing new ways of understanding previously demonized forms, this is especially evident in what might be called contemporary cinema's Goth-techno zone in which images of Asian American males[1] converge with images of so-called nerds, or the technologically invested and gifted. An examination of the connections between Asian American and Goth identities reveals, more than does any other focus in this study, why Goth has been a valuable force in the battle of nonconformist young people to attain social justice. In this chapter, I will consider how some of the conventions of the Gothic genre in film and literature have been changed by Asian American participation and also how that participation has broadened the field of intelligible gender identities for young Asian American men.

As I hope this book has shown thus far, officially promulgated lies about Goths often take the form of audacious inversions. We are told that Goths are violent when, as Hodkinson shows and Goths themselves consistently report, they are far more likely to be the victims of "prejudice and occasional violence" than its initiators (74–77). We are told that teenaged Goths are a threat to their schoolmates, while the personal accounts of hundreds of students quoted in and responding to Katz's "Voices from the Hellmouth" document the opposite situation. Not only do Goths seem to avoid conflict at school whenever possible, but the tendency of school authorities to consider Goths disruptive and noncompliant because of their appearance creates, in many schools, a situation of danger for Goths. We are told that Goths are sexually perverse, yet this definition can hold only if we understand perversity as attempting to achieve sexual self-determinacy, rather than following an official power-knowledge program in which all sexual expression is co-opted to serve consumer capitalism. And finally, we are told that Goths are racist. In this, my study's final chapter, I will address this most serious of the charges against Goth with the intention of showing that here, too, what is said about Goths by their persecutors is grotesquely opposite to the truth.[2]

Post-Columbine popular culture, as evidenced by such texts as Faye Kellerman's best-selling 2001 murder mystery *The Forgotten*, continues to view racism as a major motivation for participation in Goth youth cultures. Kellerman's beautifully crafted police procedural novels not only use Orthodox Jewish life to provide background color, they make a serious effort to educate readers through descriptions of Judaism meant to combat anti-Semitism. Therefore her conflation of the villainous new character Ruby Ranger's involvement in Goth with pedophilia (here defined as a twenty-two-year-old woman's interest in teenaged boys), nonconsensual S/M practice, white supremacist views aligned with those of the militia movement, a "fixation about the dark side," hero worship of Hitler and other mass murderers as "those who make an impact, albeit an evil one," and criminal computer hacking strongly reflects mainstream media images of Goth as essentially racist insanity threatening to destroy young people's decency in all possible ways (120–21).

Ranger's appearance is recognizably Goth to those familiar with the subculture's style. She dresses all in black and "[h]er hair was black and poker-straight. . . . Her complexion was chalk white, red lipstick outlined her mouth, and green eyes peered from black-lined sockets" (118). In case we lack the specific knowledge necessary to recognize Ranger's adherence to the subculture's standards from this description, another character explicitly identifies her as "Goth" (120). Although Kellerman's characters tend to be developed beyond the usual stereotypes of genre fiction, Ruby is presented as "[j]ust evil" (206). This depiction is understandable given that the novel focuses on the dangers posed to Jews by obsessive racism and that, at the time of the novel's composition, the Columbine shooters were generally understood to have been neo-Nazis on a mission to exterminate racially othered classmates.

The novel also reflects our current societal concern that the internet facilitates criminality and it connects web-based communication to Goth. This latter also seems reasonable enough. As Baddeley remarks about Poppy Z. Brite's *Drawing Blood*, "One particularly interesting theme introduced in the novel is that of hacking and cyberspace—which were becoming increasingly dominant in the Goth subculture, reflected in those who had already begun referring to themselves as 'cybergoths'" (86). It is easy enough to see why this fusion of Goth and cyberculture, evident in "Voices from the Hellmouth"'s treatment of Goths and computer nerds or "geeks" as synonymous, alarms many people. Powers seems right to claim that "[f]or bohemia to play a vital role in urban life, its devotees must claim space in the physical world, space in which to find the goods they need to work their private experiments, and then gather to debate its philosophies, flaunt its styles, and enact its spectacles" (281). Moreover, her identification of cyberspace as bohemia's new stronghold, where rebellion against and departure from the mainstream are "shared by spreading ideas and beliefs," seems accurate (282). To most Americans this phenomenon is probably not particularly threatening as long as the ideas and beliefs being spread are perceived as harmless manifestations of free choice, such as the information about health benefits of vegetarianism on various websites. But as Baddeley explains, Goth music not only expresses alienation, but is also scornfully and angrily abjected by Goths' more socially powerful peers (202). In addition, Goth music and style go beyond merely reflecting outcast status; Goth celebrates that status subversively. So young Goths' interest in using computers to build community becomes cause for concern since the internet is already associated in the popular imagination with pornography, sexual exploitation of children, and to a lesser extent— reflecting our current apparent societal consensus that looking at a picture of a child in underpants is worse than mass murder—recruitment of the mentally unstable and feeble-brained into racist terrorist organizations.

That Goths are out there in cyberspace is indisputable. But the type of raced and gendered place Goth cyberspace primarily represents remains, for the most part, misunderstood in the United States. In describing street life in the United Kingdom, Paul Watt and Kevin Stenson note that suburban youths, whose lack of "personal contacts across the ethnic divides" leaves them prey to "racialised anxieties," often express fear of geographic locations understood as "hang-out[s] for the 'Goths' and 'Indie' young people" (259–60). I suppose it is some cause for optimism that, in contrast, mainstream Americans seem to have assimilated the liberal message that racists are bad people. But in a rather darkly comic manner, this often translates syllogistically into the idea that all "bad" people are racists. And because in mainstream American discourse immorality always connotes participation in forbidden sexual practices and Goths are known to valorize and frequently to cultivate proscribed forms of sexual expression, Goth spaces are misunderstood as spaces in which racism flourishes.

One of the primary purposes of the "Voices from the Hellmouth" project was to allow Goths to talk back to mainstream media depictions of them as homicidal racists. This media depiction seems to have its source in some awareness of the traditional Gothic's preoccupation with otherness, especially racial otherness, so well explained by Judith Halberstam in Skin Shows. As Halberstam shows, the promulgation of racism has usually been a major component of the Gothic genre in literature, from which the contemporary Goth cultures have developed. She demonstrates that widely influential nineteenth-century Gothic texts, like Bram Stoker's *Dracula,* blatantly associate racial and cultural difference from the dominant Anglo-European group with both the unnatural and evil. Halberstam notes that "by linking [monstrosity] to sexual corruption, such fictions bind foreign aspects to perverse activities" (13). One of the reasons I am concentrating on Asian Americans in this chapter is that this linkage of racial otherness to sexual corruption is at least as prevalent in Orientalist representations of Asian Americans as it is in the traditional Gothic's representation of foreignness in general.

Numerous studies, of which Edward Said's *Orientalism* remains the most influential, document the representation of Asians as frighteningly and threateningly sexually perverse. Most typically, gender relations in Asia have been represented as viciously gynophobic and horrifically oppressive to women, since this representation has served to justify imperialist intervention into the affairs of sovereign nations. People of Asian heritage born in the West are often represented, as if by a kind of bleed-through of these attitudes, as hopelessly sexually corrupt. The conflation of Chinese (or, as is becoming more frequent, Japanese) identity with prostitution is a case in point, a striking example being provided by Ken Russell's 1984 film *Crimes of Passion,* starring Kathleen Turner as a fetish prostitute who goes by the name of China Blue. This choice of name seems explicable only if we translate the word "China" to mean "female pervert," since "blue" carries the connotation, as in the phrase "blue movie," of pornography or the sale of sexuality.

This concept of the essence of Oriental identity is elaborated in the lyrics of My Life with the Thrill Kill Kult's song "China de Sade":

> China de Sade, China lust . . .
> Deceiving and cold in her nocturnal mood,
> China grooves.
> Breed if you will your criminal style . . .
> Yeah China, you're so cruel.
> Bleed if you must your victims of trust,
> China lust . . .

Of course, like all Thrill Kill Kult songs, "China de Sade" is parodic and thus not to be taken at face value. However, the vision it conveys of the "China Girl" as the site of extreme corruption is such a commonplace of Western cultural iconography that David Bowie's release of a song with that title was initially received as evidence that he must be a National Front fascist (Dave Thompson, 21–22).[3]

No wonder the first literary anthology edited by Asian Americans is entitled *Aiiieeeee!* As editors Frank Chin, Jeffery Chan, Lawson Fusao Inada, and Shawn Wong note in their introduction, the situation of Asian American men in relation to the mainstream's gender systems is, if possible, even worse than that of Asian American women. While the women may still be seen nostalgically as victims to be rescued by righteous whites, the men are regarded by the mainstream, alternately, both as evilly active sexual corruptors and as passive, effeminate vessels of sexual corruption. The *Aiiieeeee!* project attempted to remediate what the editors saw as a uniquely poisonous image different from "the stereotypes of other races" in that "[t]he white stereotype of the acceptable and unacceptable Asian is utterly without masculinity. Good or bad, the stereotypical Asian is contemptible because he is womanly, effeminate, devoid of all the traditionally masculine qualities of originality, daring, physical courage, and creativity" (14–15). As I shall discuss, this project has largely structured criticism and theory concerned with the representation of Asian Americans according to internecine gender wars, with textual analyses primarily required to address the question of whether specific images could be seen as promoting Asian American women's feminism at the expense of men or as advancing the cause of recuperating Asian American masculinity at the price of agreement with the dominant culture's patriarchy. Goth has provided one avenue of escape from these dead-end roads of inquiry.

One of the strongest examples of what might be called a new Gothic that resignifies images of Asian men is Guy Maddin's film *Dracula: Pages from a Virgin's Diary*. Maddin cast Wei-Qiang Zhang as Dracula and through numerous techniques, including refocusing the narrative on Lucy's romance with the vampire, brings to the surface and critiques the novel's implicit Orientalism. This sort of new Gothic is closely allied to what young subculturists have made of Goth.

For anyone who thinks of American secondary school Goths as racist in their beliefs and common practices, there are many surprises among the thousands of responses to Katz's "Voices from the Hellmouth," one of which is that some Asian Americans experience Goth youth cultures as facilitating reinvention of their own gender and sexual identities in ways that fit their sense of self more closely than do either the stereotypes provided by the white mainstream or the models Asian and Asian American cultures have traditionally provided.

For example, a young Goth from West Chester, Pennsylvania, writes that the Goth community gave him a sense of belonging in a high school where he was one of a total of three Asian American students. A recurrent theme in the postings, and on other websites where Asian American youth discuss their interest in Goth, as well as in Goth music and fashion scenes as reflected in 'zines and other youth-oriented publications, is that in schools where whites are the majority, both nonwhite students and, what is often an overlapping group, students who like and are good with computers and other technology tend to be socially marginalized and sometimes seriously harassed by other students. Where athletics are especially valued, so-called nerds or computer geeks frequently perceive themselves to be despised and persecuted by their fellow students and school authorities alike. Because of the stereotyping of Asian and Asian American youths as naturally inclined to be scholastically advanced as well as good with computers, they seem especially likely to be outcast as nerds, and the nerd-friendly Goth community has become an attractive choice for positive identity formation.

Pedagogical theorist Athena Wang makes the important point that because of cultural differences in discourses of masculinity, we must study gender identity construction among young men and boys from Asian backgrounds before we can develop an understanding of gender that is neither entirely informed by nor purely reactive against dominant Western discourses of masculinity (121). As Wang notes, masculinity across diverse Asian cultures is "characterized primarily by a man's familial responsibility" (116). A survey of male and female, white, Asian, and Asian American college students by Peter Chua and Diane Fujino suggests some of the implications of this traditional Eastern view of masculinity as a component of Asian American youths' identity formation in response to the "model minority" stereotypes imposed upon them.[4] Chua and Fujino found not only that "Asian American men . . . are attempting to negotiate new forms of nonhegemonic masculinities," including a vision of caring, nurturing, and egalitarian behavior in relationships as an aspect of masculine power rather than effeminacy — and in this they radically depart from the more rigid concept of gender characteristic of college-aged white males — but also that neither Asian nor Asian American youths tended, as did whites, to regard masculine and feminine as mutually exclusive identifications (407–408). These findings are especially interesting because, as Peter Feng observes, American popular culture has followed imperialist tradition in typically representing Asian and Asian American men as patriarchal oppressors whom women must escape in order to achieve liberation (27). The imperialist vision of Asian and Asian American gender politics is increasingly contested by the young, and many studies support Wang's and Chua and Fujino's claim that Asian American men are, more than any other racial group, at the forefront of changes in American concepts of male identity.

Moreover, as Sau-ling Wong and Jeffrey Santa Ana point out in their overview of the representation of gender and sexuality issues in Asian American literature and criticism, "the cultural heterogeneity of mixed-race Asian Americans" — a group that has received a great deal of literary attention in the last twenty years — "challenges us to rethink and decenter [all] notions of fixed identities" (187). Jinqi Ling agrees that while Asian American literary studies in the seventies were structured by the battle between "a male defense of patriarchy and a feminist defense of women," later texts, focused on both Asian American homosexuality and racial hybridity, have broadened the discourse of gender identity in ways that challenge any simple equation of feminization and the "social and political 'emasculation'" that America's mainstream patriarchal capitalism has inflicted upon Asian men (313). In fact, these and other critics depict a trend in Asian American literature toward defiant expression of deviance from mainstream white norms that includes an ever larger presence of explicitly homoerotic texts and a new celebration of mixed heritage as an aspect of Pan-Asianism, all of which impact strongly on concepts of masculinity, opening it to radical reinventions.

One of the interesting features of the now defunct AZN Goth website (formerly at http://www.sevaan.com/krycek/azn), created for Asians and Asian Americans who identify as Goths, was that not only did almost all those posting suggest an at least somewhat androgynous self-image, in keeping with typical Goth sensibilities, but the majority of the members who identified their race in their profiles described themselves as being of mixed heritage. For these Asian Americans fluidity of race and gender seemed equally important, an attitude that may be seen as being determined as much by current concepts of Asian American masculinity as they are by Goth.

Strikingly, even relatively conservative treatments of gender by Asian American writers, such as David Mura's memoirs of his struggle to conform to bourgeois marital norms, adhere less to mainstream American heterosexuality's sharp divisions between male and female identities and more to what Alan Sinfield identifies as the mode most common in gay identity formation, a sense of oneself as "embodying an element of the alternate gender" (129). The most notable depiction of such gender fluidity is no doubt the character Song Liling in David Henry Hwang's brilliant play *M. Butterfly*, which, incidentally, uses a line from David Bowie's "China Girl" as an epigraph: "I could escape this feeling with my China girl." The play is based on the true story of a French diplomat recruited as a spy by his Chinese lover, with whom he carried on a passionate love affair for twenty years without realizing, he claimed, that the lover was male, not female. In the play, when that lover, Song, must account for his deception in court, he explains that in the Western imagination "the East is feminine—weak, delicate, poor . . . but good at art, and full of inscrutable wisdom—the feminine mystique. . . . Being an Oriental, I could never be completely a man" (83). So he takes advantage of his situation between two gender stereotypes in order to gain what power is possible to him. Notably, Song uses Orientalism to justify opportunistically drawing on a mix of associations Westerners have with both Japanese and

Chinese people. If the dominant culture refuses to distinguish among those they dominate, Song shows that this, too, can be a source of strength.

While sexuality and gender identity remain relatively fixed and determined by mutually exclusive binaries in mainstream popular culture, Asian American contributions to the fringes of popular culture are becoming more and more sophisticated in their problematization of gender, in ways similar to those of queer culture. Gender identification among Asian American young men, regardless of their politics, seems to be growing closer to the flexible near-androgyny that culture critics attribute to participants in various rebellious youth subcultures and countercultures, including Goth. Theorists offer varied accounts of the greater sophistication of Asian American concepts of masculinity. Some, notably Frank Chin, have argued that the flexibility of Asian American masculinity is to be understood negatively as a pathological response to the particular, emasculating policies and attitudes directed at Asian immigrants and Asian Americans by the U.S. government and the dominant, white, racist culture. Chin lambastes Hwang and Maxine Hong Kingston, among others, for selling out to white concepts of Asian American men as effeminized. As David Eng notes, with the 1975 publication of *Aiiieeeee!* "feminization—and resistance to feminization—became one of Asian American studies' motivating and central debates" (210).

However, almost all accounts of what masculinity is becoming for Asian Americans have some similar features. As Xueping Zhong argues in her study of male subjectivity in contemporary Chinese literature, intellectualism has traditionally been, and remains, an important marker of successful masculinity for the Chinese in China (152), whereas mainstream America views intellectuals as effeminate. In America, this heritage has translated into the stereotype of the brainy Asian American, good with math and technology, financially successful, but nearly asexual. But, as Allan Luke explains, this need not be entirely negatively understood, for, if it is true that "[w]ithin white dominated public culture" Asian heritage serves as "a marker of your vulnerability and invisibility—as a cultural and political being, but also as a sexual being," it is also the case that the lack of appropriate masculine models within the dominant culture opens a gap within which Asian males living in the diaspora "can explore new kinds of masculinities that run counter to traditional male power and sexism" (33–34).

While Eng decries the *Aiiieeeee!* editors' valorization of "a 'pure' Asian martial tradition" (21) and Viet Nguyen goes so far as to claim that authors like Chin and Gus Lee exemplify how "Asian American masculinity Americanized itself in the most ironic fashion, by affirming patriarchy through violence that had previously been directed at Asian Americans en masse" (132), others see, even in literary recuperation of the martial arts tradition, hope of a new model for nonsexist masculinity. King-Kok Cheung praises Shawn Wong's novel *American Knees* for "overturn[ing] American stereotypes about Asian men," through the protagonist's embodiment of the Chinese classical ideal of the poet-scholar (266). This beloved literary figure "breaks down the putative dichotomy of gay and straight behavior" and the Western division between masculinity and femininity, seen as mutually exclusive, through his "seductive" erudition and gentleness, his wisdom and wit, and his attractive "artistic sensibility" (264). Rather than seeking power through dominance, he pursues relations with other people of both genders "who are his equals in intelligence and integrity" (264). A similar argument could be made about Wong's first novel, *Homebase*, in that the protagonist, Rainsford Chan, experiences no conflict between his athleticism and heterosexuality (two qualities the dominant culture marks as masculine) and his empathy and intellectualism. Wandering in search of truth, a motif that also structures Garrett Hongo's memoir *Volcano* with its lovely discussions of his nurturance of his small children and his sensitivity to the beauty of nature, these scholar-poets exemplify successful and positive gender flexibility.

Less admirable but much more Goth, Tran, the Vietnamese American protagonist of Brite's *Exquisite Corpse*, queers concepts of sexuality and gender, as well as traditional Asian American propriety, through his simultaneous insistence on rebelling against mainstream masculinity, including heterosexuality, and on asserting himself as a desiring and beautifully desirable man. While the most discouraging aspect of Chua and Fujino's study is that few college-age people of either gender or of any race surveyed saw sexual attractiveness as a major feature of Asian or Asian American men, Goth culture, which emphasizes that androgynous bone structure, black hair, and dark eyes are essential to beauty, offers a different assessment. This Goth assessment is picked up in the Japanese animated films, called anime, that have crossed over into popularity with Goths in the United States. In the interest of brevity, I will limit my discussion to one of these, the cult favorite *Vampire Hunter D: Bloodlust*, released in 2000, and directed by Yoshiaki Kawajiri, who also wrote the screenplay in collaboration with Hideyuki Kikuchi, on whose popular Japanese novel series (*Kyūketsuki Hantā*) the film is based.

An earlier film entitled *Kyûketsuki Hunter D* (*Vampire Hunter D*) was released in the United States in 1985, on video only. Directed by Toyoo Ashida and Carl Macek, *Kyûketsuki Hunter D* draws on another novel in Kikuchi's series. This eighty-minute video is generally criticized for its more primitive animation and lack of character development. It is notable, though, for helping develop the American market for anime and for introducing the character of D, an alienated and disaffected bounty hunter whom most critics recognize as a version of Clint Eastwood's "Man with No Name" in Sergio

Leone's spaghetti Westerns, beginning with *A Fistful of Dollars* (1964). East-wood's role was developed in turn from Toshiro Mifune's ronin samurai in Akira Kurosawa's *Yojimbo* (1961).[5]

Goth fascination with dark, cynical, revisionist Westerns is attested to by the name of one the bands that has defined Goth for two generations of participants in the subculture, The Sisters of Mercy. The name is taken from Leonard Cohen's song by the same title, which is perhaps best known as the theme song of Robert Altman's revisionist Western *McCabe and Mrs. Miller* (1971). The film depicts the frontier as a place of capitalist exploitation reduced to its most dismal level, where human subjectivity can only take the forms, dictated by gender, of pimp or prostitute. As is so often the case with Goth, the band turns this depressing vision into a spectacle of shimmering black delight. The same sort of contrarian energy, always on the edge of eroticism if not fully within it, surges through the Leone Westerns, so that at the same time that we perceive his characters as corrupt we also take pleasure in their refusal to docilely accept capitalist discourses of virtue. They are Deleuzian nomads in a world ruled by gold, openly contemptuous of all the rhetoric that obscures the simple truth that money determines everything in American social life. *Vampire Hunter D* is doubly marked as Goth, not only by telling a vampire tale but also by the particular postmodern pastiche style in which it is told. The dress and style of the vastly influential Goth band Fields of the Nephilim, who released their first record (the 1985 EP *Returning to Gehenna*) the same year that the first Vampire Hunter film was released, also derive from Leone's Westerns. Japanese renditions of Goth often appear to Americans, as did Leone's very Italian Westerns, as flights of fantasy into terrains opened, but not exhausted, by classic Occidental genres.

There is a vast area deterritorialized of nationalist overcoding by stories of frontiersmen whose classic heroism translates freely from one culture and locale to another. Consider, for example, the Chinese Water Margin tales that have been such a rich source of film drama, and in particular, Cheh Chang and Hsueh Li Poa's 1972 Water Margin kung fu hit, *Sui Woo Juen* (*Seven Blows of the Dragon*), which was followed in 1975 by *Dong Kai Ji* (*Seven Soldiers of Kung Fu*, directed by Cheh Chang and Ma Wu). These tales follow Akira Kurosawa's *Shichinin no Samurai* (*The Seven Samurai*, 1954) as well as its Western remake, John Sturges's *The Magnificent Seven* (1960), chronologically, but the legends that seem to have inspired all four films are far older than Kurosawa's masterpiece.

Another sort of fantasy fusion of Western and Eastern popular cultural icons so interesting that it merits a brief digression is the Goth Lolita phenomenon. In the late nineties, so-called perkygoths (also known as perkigoths) began to appear in clubs on Goth nights. Commentators on the scene, like Baddeley, interpreted "this futuristic mutation of the Gothic aesthetic," with its neon brightness of clothing and often of hair dye and its science-fictional metallic or deliberately childish accessories, as reflecting "the playful influence of Japanese cartoons" (Baddeley, 283). Playfulness certainly defines this movement, not so much in the form of the, often sinisterly battered, toys many of its adherents carry, or their own deliberately doll-like appearance, but in the way they make into jokes many aspects of Goth previously taken seriously. My own favorite is on the Encyclopedia Gothica website, where the "Perkygoff [sic] Manifesto" concludes, "let *this* be our rallying cry! 'DO NOT STAND IN OUR WAY! WE WILL WALK AROUND YOU!'"

Goth Lolitas emerged as among the perkiest of the perkygoths. Mostly biological women, these cos-players (costumed role players), follow the stylistic example of Mana, the cross-dressing frontman of the Japanese Punk/Goth band Malice Mizer, which broke up in 2001. Like their transvestite model, Goth Lolitas undermine the concept of essential gender identity through their emphasis on the performative. A semi-annual, glossy, fashion-oriented Japanese magazine, *Gothic Lolita Bible*, provides instruction in dress and some behavioral advice. The Goth Lolita look is recognizably Victorian—or at least fantasy Victorian—modeled on Lewis Carroll's Alice as she appears in John Tenniel's famous illustrations, but with ample disquietingly morbid touches and plenty of cybergoth trimming. Most Goth Lolitas make themselves look as if they have been exhumed in a science fiction future from nineteenth-century interment and then given a cursory updating. Almost everything published in print or online about this subculture insists that, in defiance of the name they have given themselves and their very provocative style of dress, the Goth Lolitas are not interested in attracting sexual attention. Instead, the subculture emphasizes the sort of investment in innocence and purity contradicted by Humbert Humbert's concept of "the lolita" nymphet as a type of very sexually aware and manipulative preadolescent. And this despite the presence in Tokyo, documented on various websites, of a Goth Lolita S/M club scene.

While both using sexuality to sell commodities to children and marketing the sexual allure of eleven-year-olds are standard practices in American advertising, official government policy strongly encourages public expression of outrage if anyone over the age of eighteen regards a teenager as a legitimate object of sexual attraction or anyone under the age of eighteen dares claim the right to erotic pleasure. The Japanese Goth Lolitas have mirrored this new take on adolescence through a schizophrenic representation of young teens as feminized innocents always tottering on the verge of unspeakable corruption. Goth Lolita suggests that if we demand that teens be understood as presexual virgins in distress, always besieged by perverts and always in need of our rescue, then young people, male and female, will present themselves as ridiculous Alices lost in a wonderland of erotic fetishes who endlessly pose provocatively while never recognizing that they are being lustfully observed. Like the translation of Sergio Leone's "Man with No Name" into a sci-fi half-vampire, the Goth Lolita figure parodies American cool through freewheeling exaggeration of its pretensions.

Made for world-wide distribution, and thus with special attention to the lucrative American market, the second *Vampire Hunter D* film, *Bloodlust*, has a look and to some extent a theme consistent with the Gothic Lolita movement. The settings mix a mythologized American West with postapocalyptic forestscapes and fancifully Victorian Gothic architecture. They are peopled by Darkwave cowboys and cowgirls, sadomasochistic space soldiers of both genders, nineteenth-century vampires in swirling capes or blood-colored gowns, and doll-faced women in enormous hoop skirts and capes. Luscious color and exceptionally fine detailing create dream visions of great beauty, impressions of wide-eyed childlike innocence, and moments of grotesque horror.

D's character interestingly mixes quintessentially American frontiersman individualism with aspects of what might be called the new literary Asian American masculinity, as discussed by the critics whose work I touched on in the beginning of this chapter. His half-human half-vampire heritage places him between cultural worlds and gives him a superior understanding of both, at the price of a vexing lack of stable identity. D also has an affinity for women and girls, as do many of the most popular Asian American male writers working today—Chang-Rae Lee stands out as an example—and the most beloved Asian American male characters in contemporary fiction. He seems to like women and girls and not to view their sexuality as a trap or evil.

Lee's novel *A Gesture Life* traces the psychic journey away from self-destructive despair of a Korean American who goes by the name Franklin Hata. He has passed for Japanese most of his life, including a stint as a medical officer for the Japanese army in Burma during World War II, when he unwillingly participated in the exploitation of the wretched young girls, then known as "comfort women," who were enslaved into prostitution to the Japanese army. Hata, who has always taken the path of least resistance, continues in the postwar United States as he did during the war, publicly identifying with the dominant group while secretly empathizing with the racially othered women that they brutally oppress and destroy. Just as he failed Khuteah, the comfort woman with whom he fell in love, he fails Sunny, the mixed-race Korean and African American girl he adopts under the mistaken belief that he has contracted to receive an orphaned Japanese child. Yet in the end he awakens from his near-amnesiac state of depression and is at least partially redeemed in his own eyes by his recognition of why he failed.

He sees that his failure to rescue these women occurred because could not believe that he, or by extension anyone who could be considered inferior by the dominant powers, deserved better than what he was given. His ineffectual attempts to shield Sunny and Khuteah from violence are undermined by his inability to offer them a vision of minoritized difference as anything but a source of shame to be disavowed. The best he can offer himself or them is to take on the model minority role so strongly pressed on Asians outside their homelands, a life of never-ending self-effacement, humility, and deference. At last he realizes "how much sense it made years ago, when perhaps without exactly knowing it herself, Sunny was doing all she could do to escape my too-grateful, too-satisfied umbra, to get out from its steadily infecting shade and accept any difficult and even detrimental path so long as it led far from me" (333). He then decides that he will also travel away from that compliant, conformist, suburban self, his only goal being to embrace the alien identity he has always previously resisted, to fully and willfully inhabit the "outside looking in" (356).

Vampire Hunter D: Bloodlust engages such ideas while remaining within the conventions of a science fiction vampire tale. The story also has as part of its premise the sort of vexed hybridity typical not only of Asian American identities but of the concept of "the Oriental" seen through Western eyes, a figure compounded of a mixture of traits associated with various Asian cultures undifferentiated by Occidentals. Because D had a human mother and a vampire father he is called a "Dunpeal" ("Dhampire" in the earlier film). He is ostracized by the human beings as a half-vampire, except when they need his aid to destroy a vampire. An early scene in the film mimics the classic Western moment when a racist saloon-keeper refuses service to a "half-breed."

Perhaps more than the filmmakers recognize, this scene shows a part of the history of Asians in America that is ripe for reclamation. As many Asian American writers remind us, the participation of Asians, and especially Chinese, was intrinsic to the development of the frontier as a place of railroads, gold mines, and cattle and horse ranches. Shawn Wong's Rainsford Chan has a "Chinese *vaquero*" grandfather and consequently chooses the undeveloped wilderness areas and ghost towns of the West, "my grandfather's America, to give me some meaning and place here, to build something around me, to establish my tradition" (47–48). It is, however, perforce a tradition that includes the attempts of racists to deny him his place, his chosen identity. Although Rainsford comes from Jackson Hole, Wyoming, and was "[r]aised by a song about buffalo and antelope, by a song about home on the range," he is also very aware of the Exclusion Acts and the enforced removal of Chinese Americans from the open plains to ghetto confinement in San Francisco's Chinatown in the nineteenth century (65). Asked by classmates to account for his origins, Rainsford is haunted by his great-grandfather who "lost his faith in the land" after being compelled to leave the Sierras (13). Such histories seem recapped in miniature in *Vampire Hunter D*, when Leila, a bounty hunter who partners D, tells him, "We have that much in common, that we're both hunters and both alone," and he replies bitterly, "Because I'm a Dunpeal, I don't get to have a life, not like you." While the film avoids any sort of preachy message about racial otherness, it suggests that willing identification with outcasts and the oppressed, very much including women, is as essential to the preservation of D's sanity as it is to that of someone like Franklin Hata.

While D preserves the silent power of the Western hero, he also exemplifies the sensitive male. His tremendous physical prowess is balanced by an androgynous appearance. D relies on a combination of wisdom, knowledge, martial arts skill, and near-psychic empathy to fight the vampires. Hired to rescue Charlotte Elbourne (a young woman whose appearance defines Goth Lolita) by killing the vampire Meier Link, who is believed by her family to have abducted her, D must come to understand not only that she left her family willingly because she loves Link but that she, like everyone else, deserves the freedom to exercise sexual self-determinacy. The retreat of the lovers to "The City of Night," allowed by D, evokes another sort of frontier, one in which race no longer impedes belonging. Somewhere outside the shrinking, ever-diminishing possibilities of our dying world, there is a place of imagination, sexuality, and romanticism. It seems fitting that the rocket ship that takes them there looks uncannily like a Gothic cathedral.

This film is an obvious influence on the *Blade* film series, a vampire action vehicle for Wesley Snipes, also inspired by a graphic novel. In the first *Blade* film (1998), Snipes's character is hyper-aggressive, cold, cynical, and stereotypically masculine in every way. In the 2002 sequel he is almost a clone of D except for his traditionally masculine, muscular body. The plot also parallels many details of the Japanese film. But in it the Asian American male does not learn masculinity from the most masculinist models of the Black Power movement, as Chin advocated. Rather, this film is part of a growing body of work in which Asian Americans model a more flexible masculinity for both whites and Blacks.

I end this chapter by discussing a film series popular with all the Goths I know that is not generally considered relevant to Asian American studies but that I hope to show, in light of the discussion above, is truly representative of where Goth is taking Asian American masculinities, and also where Asian Americans are taking Goth. The series began with the 1999 blockbuster *The Matrix*. As the humble corporate computer nerd Thomas Anderson by day and the code-cracking Goth computer hacker and clubber Neo by night,[6] superstar Keanu Reeves is not explicitly described as Asian American, as is typically the case in his films. However, the majority of Reeves's fans do recognize his racial make-up as Eurasian (half Chinese-Polynesian), as website discussions attest.

In an essay on race in *The Matrix*, Douglas Cunningham asks whether "the extra-diegetic racial heritage of Reeves" is pertinent to "his role as Neo within the diegesis." And Cunningham concludes that "Anderson's/Neo's reification of such Asian American stereotypes [as Goth and computer nerd] alludes to the film's anime and manga source material and lends even more weight to his status as an invisible 'other' in a world populated by representatives of white authority." Cunningham argues that Neo "represents difference on both the diegetic and extra-diegetic levels. As Neo, Reeves personifies a type of 'neo'-multiculturalism that stands as a threat to the stark whiteness of authority and normalcy within the Matrix."

The narrative, in which a rebel band discovers that Earth has been colonized by aliens who use humans as power cells and that life on Earth has become nothing more than an interactive video dream, draws heavily on a mixture of Eastern religious concepts, such as the Buddhist vision of material existence as mere *maya*, and staples of Western religion, such as the self-sacrificial redemptive Christ-figure Reeves portrays. One might pause to consider that not only was one of the first Goth heroes portrayed in film played by another Eurasian, Brandon Lee in *The Crow*, but that Lee's famous father, Bruce, rose to fame in a film (*Enter the Dragon*, 1973) in which the hero's martial arts master conveys a message very similar to that of the Matrix series: "the enemy has only images and illusions behind which he hides his real motives. Destroy his illusions and he will be powerless." Thus we can look back over a cinematic history of countercultural breakthroughs initiated by Asian American figures who bring with them concepts of reality that challenge those central to the Western status quo.

The theme of altered consciousness is crucial to *The Matrix*, in which, as with The Sisters of Mercy and the *Vampire Hunter D* series, there is a nod to the Darkwave of the sixties in Neo's following the white rabbit, who was forever redefined as the purveyor of LSD by the Jefferson Airplane's song "White Rabbit." When Neo chooses to take the red pill and awaken from his profound physical investment in the system, the color seems to symbolize sixties Leftism and collectivism, his conversion to which is effected, as it was for many hippies, by ingestion of a consciousness-altering drug. But the tone of the film is most in keeping with the new Asian American masculinity, especially in the conclusion when Trinity (Carrie-Anne Moss), the most faithful of Neo's disciples, resurrects him with a kiss. Man enough to save humanity, gentle and nonmacho enough to be himself saved by a woman, and easily sexually attractive enough to inspire her devotion, Neo models the new masculinity born out of the meeting of Goth with Asian American traditions of representation.

In *The Matrix Reloaded* (2003), an inferior film in terms of plot innovations, the subtextual concerns about race are developed further, even to the point that Cornell West appears as Councilor West in Zion, the stronghold of the unplugged rebels. What is only visually hinted in the first film is made much more explicit in the sequel, that racially othered subjects are more likely than whites to realize that they are being used as batteries to run a machine that exists not for their own benefit but for its own, and so they are also more likely to choose to "take the red pill" and disconnect. As Jane Dark says, in a *Village Voice* review essay, what the film gets right is "that the masters of reality don't want to destroy us. They want us jacked directly into the economy" (36). Logically, those who would be most likely to awaken and reject the system are those whose place is lowest in the economy of the Matrix itself, that dark mirror of the human world that was most familiar at the end of the twentieth century, with all its racial hierarchy intact.[7] Cunningham points out that all the figures who have official power within the Matrix are apparently white in the first film. The sequel makes it obvious that in Zion almost all the rebels are people of color.

In the second film's most striking action sequence, Neo engages in a kung fu battle with a large number of replicas of Agent Smith (Hugo Weaving), the evil computer-program-in-human-form. The scene can easily be read as a vision of the embattled outsider fighting for his life against the world of "white" conformity, where humanity as well as specific ethnicity dissolve in sameness. This point is hammered home visually by the presence of bleached-looking twins (Adrian and Neil Rayment) as enforcers for the villainous Merovingian. The twins' hair is dressed in dead white corn-row braids and their faces are horribly pale, to match their powder-white suits. But their magical ability to become frighteningly corpse-like or skeletal ghosts when threatened—that is, to fade into a "pure" and purely grotesque whiteness—suggests the deathliness of the manifestation of white power. It also suggests the "white ghosts" familiar to readers of Asian American literature, especially Maxine Hong Kingston's *The Woman Warrior.*

For contrast we have the inflection of Neo's character by both Hong Kong action and Japanese samurai films. His cassock-like robes make him look amazingly like the wandering monk figure central to so many of those dramas, especially when he is kick-boxing and punching white ghosts. As Kristin Thompson observes in an analysis of the ways images from Asian action films inform the character of Gandalf the White in the Lord of the Rings films, the expectations of youthful audiences are increasingly met by the conflation of the images of the samurai and the white-bearded monk (or white-eyebrowed *sifu*) with the man of virtue (50–53). The result seems to me an adoption in Western films of an aesthetic friendly to the depiction of Asian masculinities as heroic, which is realized in Neo, despite his anglicized name within the Matrix.

Contemplative, spiritual, non-egotistical, committed to truth and protection of the weak, Neo is the very image of Eastern philosophy as it is articulated through hundreds of Asian martial arts films concerned with martial arts masters or samurai. The idea that ancient Asian wisdom translates into power to fight the system is reinforced by the character called the Keymaker (Randall Duk Kim), a small, stereotypical Asian "nerd" type, who has the key to every lock and, showing remarkable courage under fire, saves the day. Both characters would be at home in the "White Tigers" segment of *The Woman Warrior*, which combines motifs from Chinatown action film matinees with material from the legends from which they came—most strikingly the story of Fa-Mu Lan—as a commentary on Kingston's own "girlhood among ghosts" (the novel's subtitle).

The result of the film's pastiche approach to mythologies is not revisionist mythologizing, but rather a postmodern decoding. About two-thirds of the way into *Anti-Oedipus*, Deleuze and Guattari pause to ask, "So what is the solution? Which is the revolutionary path?" They then answer, "Psychoanalysis is of little help, entertaining as it does the most intimate of relations with money and recording—while refusing to recognize it—an entire system of economic-monetary dependences at the heart of every subject it treats." The answer cannot be, in their view, withdrawal "from the world market," as this move would be a "revival of the fascist 'economic solution.'" It would be better, they say, "[t]o go still further, that is, in the movement of the market, of decoding and deterritorialization" (239). Thus a very commercial series of films that freely appropriate myths in order to better market themselves empties out the myths' traditional meanings by doing so, decodes them, and pushes them into the nomadic zone of unlimited becomings.

The Matrix series's deterritorialization of myth is painted over with the somber and beautiful red, black, and gold tones of Goth during the sequence depicting the party in Zion. As Neo and Trinity make love, their bodies intertwining like an Indian temple relief, we see the rebels leaping and gyrating in celebration of their continued existence in the face of the inhuman world that would destroy them or force them back into mindlessly compliant sleep. Sexual, sensual, spiritual, but in none of the ways the currently dominant cultures prescribe, the inhabitants of Zion have more than a passing resemblance to perkygoth dancers at a rave. This aspect of the imagery is far from incidental.

In her 1985 screenplay, *Ecstasy Unlimited: The Interpenetrations of Sex and Capital*,[8] Laura Kipnis laments, through the voice of the narrator, American sex ways of the times, and focuses on the belief, then prevalent, that S/M and other forms of sexual experimentation could be liberatory. She insists that, because under the regime of "advanced capitalism our lives are subordinated to the laws of the market . . . in consumption, in recreation, culture, art, education, and personal relations," all that remains for us is "the dream of escape — through sex and drugs, which are in their turn, promptly industrialized" (43). She concludes that "we can say of sex what was once said of religion: that our pleasure is the sigh of the oppressed creature, the heart of a heartless world, and the soul of soulless conditions. It is the opium of the people" (99). The Matrix series, as if in response to this sort of critique, asks, what if the dream is not the escape from capitalism *per se*; what if, instead, the dream — from which we can still be awakened through a careful choice of sex and drugs — is that tightly bounded form of capitalism that serves the hegemony of the bourgeoisie?

Kipnis herself recognizes that

> [a] class becomes hegemonic not through its capacity for sheer domination, but through its ability to appropriate visions of the world and diverse cultural elements of its subordinated classes, but in forms that carefully neutralize any inherent or potential antagonism and transform these antagonisms into simple *difference*. Classes exist as hegemonic forces to the extent that they can absorb the popular into their own discourse, but in such a way that "the people" as an oppositional force are neutralized. (30, emphasis Kipnis's)

But what happens when, as has been the case at the millennium's end, the bourgeoisie begins an aggressive campaign against the vision of rebellion most cherished by the nearly socially powerless?

The rave cultures so demonized by the Right began in African American ghettos. Their appeal to more privileged youth is clearly connected to a desire to dismantle social hierarchy, as commentators on these cultures, such as Simon Reynolds and Sarah Thornton, note. Thus they have proven inimical to appropriation by commercial interests. They continue to take place under official prohibition outside socially legitimized venues (in fields and warehouses rather than clubs or stadiums), and their participants continue to value artifacts produced outside corporate culture (recycled disco clothing and ornamentation, mix tapes of illegally reproduced music). But above all else, rave participants, like Goths, seem to value the group experience itself, those Foucauldian bodies and pleasures, Deleuzian intensities. Far from demonstrating that everything eventually will become grist for the mill of consumer capitalism, the end of the twentieth century and the beginning of the twenty-first, with the renewed fervor of their official anti-drug and anti-sex wars, demonstrate that majoritist power-knowledge will continue to oppose any pleasure that might distract Americans from the acquisition of objects. Unbounded intensities are not being promoted by consumer capitalism; ownership is. The choice to have nonmarital sex or to use recreational drugs has been more, not less, politicized within medico-judicial discourses that stridently reject the idea that these choices represent simple differences in individual tastes. The last twenty years have been marked by continuous moral panics over the increasingly early involvement of young people in sexual activity and the growing refusal of young people to adhere to traditional forms of proper sexual expression, as well as over the rise in use of psychedelic drugs and MDMA (ecstasy) to raise political consciousness and encourage the questioning of authority. If such activities constitute a new religion, it is not one that fosters quietism.

For some young people who grew up under the regime of the Christian Right, spiritual experience, which a great many of us find necessary to maintaining the will to live, can no longer be felt within traditional Western religious institutions because they seem hopelessly contaminated by the leading role they have taken in the war on sexual expression. Forced to choose between accepting abstinence-program Christianity or else adopting an image of themselves as subhuman evil-doers, young people often turn to subcultures that allow them to integrate physical pleasure and spiritual awareness. The overlap between the initially opposed Goth and rave cultures might usefully be understood in this way. Simon Reynolds notes in his provocatively entitled book *Generation Ecstasy*, "rave culture provides 'the youth of today' with an experience of collective communion and transcendence" (233). This experience, he explains, is not without parallels to some manifestations of Christian mysticism, "[b]ut the rave experience probably has more in common with the goals and techniques of Zen Buddhism: the emptying out of meaning via mantric repetition; nirvana as the paradox of the full void" (243). For the young rave participants, as well as the audience for *The Matrix Reloaded*'s staging of rave, the connection to Eastern religions is reassuring; these religions are idealized and imperfectly understood among counterculture groups in the West, where the sexism and anti-sexuality that often come into play in the actual daily practice of religions such as Buddhism and Hinduism in the countries where these religions developed are muted or erased. To Reynolds rave culture is specifically Deleuzoguattarian. He argues that the rave

> corresponds to Deleuze and Guattari's model of the 'desiring machine';
> a decentered, nonhierarchical assemblage of people and technology
> characterized by flow-without-goal and expression-without-meaning. The

> rave works as an intensification machine, generating a series of height-
> ened here-and-nows—sonically, by the music's repetitive loops, and vi-
> sually, by lights, lasers, and above all the strobe (whose freeze frame cre-
> ates a concatenated sequence of ultravivid tableaux). (246)[9]

All of this is evident in the images the film provides of the party in Zion.

Writing of how the Deleuzian perspective enhances apprehension of the futuristic dystopia film *Strange Days* (made in 1995 and set in 1999), Barbara Kennedy sums up its spectacular presentation of uninhibited clubbing in a way that could also describe *The Matrix Reloaded*'s party scene:

> psychoanalysis might well provide some exploration of the erotic and
> the exotic in the movie. But the aesthetics at work in the mind/brain,
> whilst 'felt' at a level beyond subjectivity, at the point of the microtubu-
> lar, can also invoke, prosthetically, mechanisms which lure the emo-
> tions into play—the space 'between' the subjective encounter and the
> non-subjective space of pre-verbal singularities, the 'depth' of that pri-
> mordial sense of aliveness—autopoiesis. (191)

No matter that *The Matrix Revolutions*, the final film in the sequence, leaves still unanswered the philosophical questions the narrative of *The Matrix* raised.

This film, like *The Matrix Reloaded*, works visually to give audiences a sense of existence as becoming rather than being, to endorse the importance of openness and lines of flight in ways that not only are the opposite of the values fostered by American consumer capitalism, but are specifically coded here as racially other, and frequently as Asian American. Such coding in-cludes expansion of the role of Seraph (Collin Chou), the Oracle's protector, who we learn was himself The One in a previous Matrix. Since both of the avatars to whom the film series introduces us are Asian American, this revela-tion hints that the Eastern perspective is necessary if humanity is to be saved from the Western world's deadening tendency to reduce us to batteries for its consumption machines.

One has to look hard at the Matrix series to recognize its advocacy of understandings derived from Asian cultures, just as one has to look hard to see serious resistance to consumer capitalism ever so paradoxically portrayed in this series of big-budget blockbusters. Similarly, Goth lurks in the film as a sort of haunting presence, rising to the surface at the moments when the black trench coats swirl or those perkygoth-appearing dancers emerge from the shadows of Zion's cybergoth cityscape. But consistently throughout, those acquainted with the cultures and subcultures the series references can tell that, thanks to the Asian American influence, Goth has met gender identity in one of its most interesting and enduring crises and shown us another way to break free.

CONCLUSION
Goth's Come Undone

And I say, "I'm dead," and I move.

—*The Crow*

Around 1982, when the club called the Batcave opened in London, Goth had achieved as coherent an identity as it would ever have. No longer merely a catch-all term for various bands and fashions considered Gothic or influenced by Gothic rock, Goth had come to signify specific types of music and styles of dress. By the mid-eighties the originally British Goth had already both expanded and diffused, through its importation into European and American rock scenes with different, culturally determined, concepts of the Gothic and through its adoption by young teenagers ignorant of both the music scene's history and historical concepts of the Gothic. While major Goth bands continued to perform to large audiences throughout the eighties, as a scene providing subcultural identity for its adherents Goth entered a period of doldrums toward the end of the decade, according to commentators on the scene like Mercer, Baddeley, and Thompson. Goth came to be mainly regarded as a type of music rather than as a style of personal identification. Then the American scene, which had incorporated Industrial music, grew wildly from the surprising success of Nine Inch Nails in 1989, when *Pretty Hate Machine* went platinum. Kids in the know thrilled to Goth-savvy films, such as Tim Burton's *Beetlejuice* (1988), *Edward Scissorhands* (1990), and *The Nightmare before Christmas* (1993). As had been the case in the early eighties, at the height of adolescent interest in Punk, boutiques sprang up in malls and gentrified downtown areas to make sure protected suburban youngsters could find clothing and accessories with the requisite look, without venturing into sex fetish supply shops.

If Goths, as a subculture, never achieved the name recognition with mainstream Americans that the Star Trek fans who call themselves Trekkers did, they were regarded by most of the popular press with a similar condescending amusement. As I have discussed throughout this book, all of that ended with the Columbine school tragedy, since which Goth has been fairly consistently treated by those in authority as a major threat to the wellbeing of the young. These authorities have their own accounts of why Goth constitutes a threat. My explanation comes from *Anti-Oedipus:* "desire can never be deceived. Interests can be deceived, unrecognized, or betrayed but not desire" (257). And because Goth demands that the darkest desires not only be acknowledged but be served, it provides young people with a mode of resisting mainstream America's culture of denial. The persistence of Goth's popularity with many young people, attested to by such phenomena as the success of the Goth band Evanescence, which sold 3.3 million CDs in 2003, makes plain how important this particular mode of resistance remains.

In *Anti-Oedipus* Deleuze and Guattari identify "two poles of delirium" operating in the formation of identity. The fascistic type "invests the formation of central sovereignty," binds desire in the name of hierarchy and order, says, in effect, "yes, I am your kind, and I belong to the superior race and class." The other type they call "schizorevolutionary," because it exemplifies their nomadic ideal. It "follows the *lines of escape* of desire; breaches the wall and causes flows to move," says, in effect, "I am not your kind, I belong eternally to the inferior race, I am a beast, a black." They then comment, "Good people say that we must not flee, that escape is not good, that it isn't effective, and that one must work for reforms. But the revolutionary knows that escape is revolutionary—*withdrawal, freaks*—provided one sweeps away the social order on leaving, or causes a piece to get lost in the shuffle" (277, emphasis theirs).

In their passionate embrace of the status of the defeated and destroyed, their defiant styling of themselves as those already dead, Goths effect such an escape. And now, as they are pushed further and further underground, as their gathering places outside the internet close and the style choices that identify them to other Goths are forbidden on secondary school campuses, Goths come undone as a subculture that can offer a fixed, consistent sense of identity to participants, only to pass into a state of continual becoming. The meaning of Goth becomes something not easily codified, as I have tried to show here. Instead it becomes a grouping of styles of resistance, a series of dark archways through which one can be always entering resistance, always departing from the officially known. "Becomings—they are the thing which is the most imperceptible, they are acts which can only be contained in a life and expressed in a style" (Deleuze and Parnet, 3). So although there can be no summing up of Goth, no postmortem of this living dead culture, I will take one last look at what Goth is up against and what sort of responses to mainstream madness we might extract from yet another film text apparently in harmony with Goth's dark chords.

John Keats was right to say in his "Ode on a Grecian Urn" that unheard melodies are sweeter than those we can hear. And Goth has taught me to perceive them darkly. Here, as with my interpretation of the Matrix series, I will look down below the film's surface to the darkness within it, most often unrecognized by critics, where the visuals unravel the culturally privileged discourses through which the film might otherwise seem to speak. To understand film in this particularly Deleuzian way allows one to see the lines of flight opened by films commercially successful enough to be considered majoritarian.[1]

Once upon a time in America, which just happens to be the title of another film about poisonous aspects of our culture, a chilling ghost story like M. Night Shyamalan's millennial *The Sixth Sense* seemed almost superfluous, because in 1999 those with eyes to see could horrify themselves with the sight of the following spectacles: Record numbers of drivers killed and injured in accidents obviously caused in large part by the sheer number of people crowding the roads and highways; children slaughtered in crashes and crushed by airbags designed for adults as more and more parents adopted a schedule of activities for them that involved hours of transportation time, all to be spent in cars or the increasingly popular sport utility vehicles; and, as SUV accidents increased to the level of a national scandal, the daily release of terrifying statistics about their unsafe tires matched by reports that their sales to families with children remained strong.

But what else could the parents do? Urban and suburban car culture emptied sidewalks of just about everyone except the homeless, making all non-enclosed, public spaces seem alien and dangerous. Unorganized outdoor activities appeared more and more hazardous as the ozone shield thinned and air quality worsened daily, and an alarming number of children developed life-threatening respiratory problems, while melanoma, once almost exclusively a disease of the elderly, began attacking increasingly younger Americans. By the beginning of the year 2000, global warming was a fact undisputed by any reputable scientist, but televised news reports lamenting this situation were interspersed with commercials for cars, trucks, and SUVs that strongly suggested that ownership of one of these vehicles was the only available, legitimate means to self-assertion, identity, privacy, or happiness. The outdoors as most adults had once known it (a place of fresh air and healthy sunshine) was disappearing fast, and the only answer people seemed capable of finding for their children was to keep them inside cars as much as possible.

Motor vehicle deaths and injuries emerged as a huge threat to the survival of teenage drivers, as studies showed that one of the most frequent causes of these accidents (just like those where adults were the drivers) was simple physical exhaustion. As the gasoline price crisis of the summer of 2000 escalated, news commentators took to ending reports with the rhetorical question, "But what can these people do, since they have to get to work?" Apparently all Americans over the age of sixteen considered driving everywhere to be their birthright, no matter if they had to work exhaustingly long hours to afford to own and operate a car of their own. A major parental gauge of the beginning of maturity was that teens could take over some of the family's driving duty—even if it killed them. During this period, even more than during the Vietnam War, Americans could be described as destroying their own children while vehemently denying that they were doing any such thing. But who is there left to do the describing, one might ask, since, of course, this abominable situation does not exist in some scary past but right here, right now?

Meanwhile two films with dead protagonists rose to enormous popularity. In *American Beauty*, which dominated the Academy Awards in 2000, the main messages seem to be that the typical American suburban life is so alienating and thus so agonizingly unfulfilling that the only way to survive it is on drugs (as the American pharmaceutical industry, as well as the DEA, can attest to) and that it is impossible to see anything worthwhile in this life until we have lost it. The less successful, but still very popular film *The Sixth Sense* conveys the latter message more subtly, but, also, as I will argue here, in a way that takes more fully into account how deeply children are hurt by our current culture of environmental destruction and denial. What makes *The Sixth Sense* Goth-like, if not simply Goth outright (like such films as Tim Burton's *Sleepy Hollow*), is its predication of horror as a place of escape for children, not a place they must escape from.[2]

Depressing as it is, the destruction of the environment is not the only area where adult Americans' pervasive state of denial poses deadly threats to their children, and *The Sixth Sense* explores these other danger zones as well. I have discussed the effects of car culture at such length because this is probably the danger to children ignored by the largest number of Americans. *The Sixth Sense*, however, goes almost immediately to the heart of our national disgrace by beginning with a scene of psychiatric self-congratulation violently interrupted by a retribution that will prove perfectly suited to the crime.

We first meet the protagonist, Malcolm Crowe (Bruce Willis), as he and his wife Anna (Olivia Williams) return from a dinner at which he was honored for his contributions to child psychiatry. The sudden appearance of one of the recipients of this contribution, now a furious young man who shoots the good doctor and himself, is so blatantly ironic that it may obscure for some viewers other less dramatic, but perhaps just as telling ironies of the situation. For instance, we are shown that the great benefactor of children is himself not only childless, but in a parental relation to his own wife, a deferential younger woman whose final conversation with her husband reveals that she has always been his patronized subordinate, spending her life waiting for him to give her some playful attention. When we meet the film's other protagonist, the eight-year old Cole Sear (Haley Joel Osment), and his mother, we shall see that this pair actually show each other more mutual respect than the husband and wife do. The question of how such a man could respect the perceptions of people less socially powerful than himself is answered by his assailant's anguished accusation that his doctor never really listened and, thus, never really understood anything about his patient's situation.

The film quickly develops into a ghost story that is as at least as darkly comical as it is creepy in retrospect, as we rethink the action subsequent to the shooting in light of the revelation near the conclusion that Crowe has been, since that night, a ghost unaware that he is dead. This is not just a Twilight Zone twist. It is vital to the film's symbology, which plays brilliantly with prior texts as diverse as James Joyce's "The Dead," T. S. Eliot's "The Waste Land," and the 1994 cult film *The Crow*. The film's allusion to the last of these is the most obvious because Crowe, like the main character of *The Crow*, is a walking dead man, and also because, like Brandon Lee (the actor playing the protagonist of *The Crow*, who was killed during filming), he moves on the scene necessarily unconscious that he exists now only as an image of what once lived, and now and forever more can have no existence outside that spectral presence. Presumably part of the enormous appeal of *The Crow* to young people in the Goth scene was that like them, although not by his own choice, Brandon Lee appeared as a dead man walking, one of the revenant sacrificial children of whose consumption our culture makes a spectacle. Like the hero of *The Crow*, Crowe comes back to help a child in peril and is also tormented by guilt about how his wife was affected by his overconfidence in his ability to protect others.

Thinking about Crowe's existential situation may lead us to recall his similarities to another lonely and regretful man walking through his world oblivious to his own truly lifeless condition: Gabriel, the protagonist of Joyce's "The Dead." *The Sixth Sense* begins where Joyce's story concludes, with the protagonist and his wife returning from a party, he preoccupied with a vague feeling that he has neglected her and that, consequently, they have lived a life of forms without content, of domestic rituals, without passion. But Crowe takes the entire film to see what Gabriel understands in a flash, that he should have paid more attention to the insights of those people who are so simple and meek as to have nothing to lose by honesty, because such people can be visionaries providing the key to meaningful experiences. And because they can hope for nothing better than what they find themselves with at any moment, they can resist bourgeois deferment of gratification and live in the now. From the amorous, teenage Michael Furey who rapturously gives his life for one last look at his beloved to happily self-sacrificial Aunt Julia, Joyce's most humble characters see into life's mysteries in ways that elude Gabriel until his story's end, a theme repeated by Crowe's relation to the equally symbolically named Cole Sear, the "disturbed" child whose treatment Crowe takes on to expiate his guilt for failing the patient who shot him.

In all three stories, the protagonists' failure to grasp what should be of premier importance is attributed in part to their social milieu. As in the opening to Eliot's poem, when the office workers entering the financial district are compared to the lost souls in Dante's *Inferno*, each of these men inhabits an "Unreal City" where value is generally determined exclusively in material terms. But while almost all of Joyce's characters and all of the virtuous characters in *The Crow* believe life has a mysterious and wonderful spiritual dimension, even if they themselves cannot gain access to it, for the sane characters of *The Sixth Sense* the only nonmaterial aspects of life worth attention are assumed to reside in the mappable terrain of the Freudian unconscious.

When the child actor Haley Joel Osment delivers his most memorable line, "I see dead people," and then chillingly explains in terms that suggest a metaphoric level to the film, "They look like ordinary people. They are everywhere. They don't know they are dead. They can't see each other," what the psychiatrist hears is not a cry of existential horror like Eliot's or Joyce's but instead a simple revelation that this little boy suffers from a mental illness. This nearly farcical misunderstanding (blackly hilarious because Crowe is, all unknowingly, one of the dead people whom the boy sees) is examined throughout the rest of the film as events slowly reveal that psychiatric theory, no matter how well-intentioned, like Horatio's philosophy, cannot account for everything in heaven and earth. But the point isn't just that psychiatric theory is flawed by a failure to give any credence to the occult; that idea has been mined for horror film plots almost since the beginning of cinema. What is extraordinary here is the way the film turns the psychoanalytic concept of denial back upon itself, asking us repeatedly to think about exactly what aspects of contemporary life are apparent to sensitive children but uniformly denied by adults whose interests the denial serves.

The ghostly apparitions of *The Sixth Sense* insistently remind us that while educated Americans generally have faith in psychology to explain how and why things are so bad in our world and, more importantly, to help us fix personal problems, what is at work undermining our efforts is not what we are unconscious of in the Freudian sense but rather what we subconsciously know but cannot acknowledge, because to do so would mean abandoning the project of the American Dream as we now understand it: continual reconstruction of gender binarity, channeling sexual expression into life commitment, maintenance of a suburban domesticity based on accumulation of material goods to substitute for experiences in the larger world, fetishization of male aggression through emotional investment in violent sports and war, fetishization of feminine narcissism, relegation of spirituality to the enclosure of organized (Judeo-Christian) religion, and promulgation of car culture to which denial of dangers is intrinsic. Crowe has to learn that by adhering to this code he not only caused his own death but added to America's storehouse of officially sanctioned harmful disinformation. As he looks over his old case notes he becomes increasingly aware that he let his little patients down by insisting that their communication with the dead must be delusional, but he let them down even more profoundly by failing to recognize why the dead might want to communicate with us, to let us know where we are headed.

Freed by death of his own investment in the materialist culture that makes walking corpses of us all, Crowe is finally able to concentrate in an open-minded way on a child patient and get beyond his old habit of writing mundane little diagnoses based on taxonomies in psychiatry's *Diagnostic and Statistical Manual.* He finally begins to listen. Thus he learns that Cole does not just see dead people. He sees people who died because of what the people who should have protected them felt compelled to believe, even against what should have been common sense. Among the ghosts that appear to him is a housewife who was apparently, judging from the style of her clothes, battered to death back in those not very distant days when the police just took physically abusive husbands for a walk around the block because to arrest them would trouble the domestic ideal. Another importunate ghost is a little boy who asks if Cole wants to see where the boy's father "hides his gun" and then turns around to reveal, terrifyingly, the gaping red exit wound in the back of his head. At Cole's school, where the teachers present him with expurgated history lessons designed to convey the importance of obedience to authority and to promote a vision of America as just and egalitarian, Cole sees the ghosts of revolutionaries lynched a hundred years earlier, on one of those many historic occasions when the law was looking the other way. The incident that forms a turning point involves a vomiting girl ghost who begs Cole to help her little sister. When Crowe travels out to the suburb where the girl lived in order to check out the story, he finds a family where what is only a small exaggeration of ordinary tensions results in a fatal syndrome familiar to all true crime aficionados.

The family's departure from normal behavior consists of the mother's slow, cumulative poisoning of her small daughters in order to draw attention to herself. The scary ordinariness of the situation resides in the roles the family members play. Rivalry between the mother and daughters seems virtually guaranteed by their shared investment in traditional femininity. The mother is a pretty, girlish narcissist in a frilly red satin party dress and ringlet hairdo. We see that even at her daughter's funeral gathering she spends most of her energy courting male attention. Her daughters, dressed in lacy pink and white costumes and hair ribbons, seemed groomed for a similar future, at least until the sacrifice of the elder one. The younger one shows her vocation for parasitic femininity in her obvious preference for men over women. The business-suited father's stiff pomposity constitutes a near parody of Willis's usual overdone traditional masculinity.

Naturally, in every sense of the word, mothers should protect their daughters, not treat them as rivals. They should see their daughters as vulnerable people on the way to a maturity mothers should model. But the staging of this little family drama-within-a-drama suggests that other outcomes are just as likely when female maturity is a horror to be avoided at all costs and when a little girl is always a reminder to her mother of a lost glorious time when a cute smile and a lisped endearment were more than enough to win the breadwinner's love. By the time Crowe leaves this noir suburban interlude, the pairing of "femme" with "fatale" looks almost inevitable.

The darkest moment, comes, however, as an intrusion into the otherwise happy resolution of Cole's problems. Helped by Crowe's faith in him, and stoically taking on his mission to act as the advocate of murder victims, the little boy at last confides in his good, and long-suffering, mother. But his confession of his miraculous ability is interrupted, as they wait in stalled traffic, by yet another ghost. This one is a female bicyclist who was crushed between a car and a truck in downtown traffic. She is still wearing her pitifully inadequate, but standard, safety helmet on her crushed skull. Blood slowly drips down her angry face. Like all the other ghosts, she looks insistent in her pursuit of justice. Like all the others, she was sold out. She merely taps on Cole's mother's car window, but we might mentally supply her with some dialogue to the effect that it is ridiculous to expect bicyclists to be protected by helmets and bike lanes when the traffic they must negotiate includes not only so many cars that most drivers find it impossible to be aware of everything on the road, but also an ever-increasing number of SUVs and other large vehicles from which drivers cannot even see bicycles and pedestrians. Is this woman a murder victim like all the others? Context suggests she is. Like the others she was done in by the denial that creates an atmosphere even more noxious than the pollution surrounding us.

Meanwhile, Crowe receives his final lesson concerning the pervasive denial that structures his world. He has been returning intermittently throughout the film to his home, where he always finds his wife distant and uncommunicative, apparently lonely. As before his demise, he takes a proprietary and paternal interest. He is somewhat more moved when he realizes that she is being courted by her employee at the antique shop she had opened just before his death, but there seems minimal cause for concern as she remains chastely withdrawn, watching a video of their wedding obsessively. At long last, Crowe recognizes that the reason his wife is growing away from him is that he is dead. His quiet acceptance of the gradual dissipation of her mourning and her tentative interest in the other, younger and deferential, man signal that he may have also come to see what the audience could all along, that he was not the protective patriarch to his patients or to his wife that he thought he was and that it is time for the old ways to change. While the film never goes so far as to make explicit its meanest dark joke, that the best psychiatrist is a dead psychiatrist, it does drive the point home in its conclusion that the patriarchal system is moribund and the patriarchs who held it in place now only put an unbearable weight of deadness on the rest of us. Dead white males, indeed.

It was not always thus, the film reminds us. Once there were men who saw to the center of truth in ways that we apparently no longer can. In telling this cautionary tale, the film uses the ability to see the dead in ways that draw on the imagery of the Modernist masters, Eliot and Joyce in particular, and by doing so evokes their underlying philosophical vision of the bourgeois world as "deathly," as that other exemplary Modernist D. H. Lawrence always put it. *The Sixth Sense* gives this sort of critique of bourgeois materialism a millennial twist by looking at specifically contemporary problems: the failure of the nuclear family, the unhappy or insane domestic woman, the abused child, the father's gun representing a subconscious deadly hostility toward the children who entrap him into service to domesticity, and finally the deadly car against which our feeble gestures of protectiveness are utterly ineffectual. But Shyamalan's film goes beyond mere updating of elite Modernist horror at consumerist culture and its discontents.

In the Modernist's world awareness of the emptiness of bourgeois values was the province of the superior person. Expressing knowledge was a sign of power, even when one conferred that power on oneself. In ours it is the mark of the crank. As the heroine of Ruth Ozeki's *My Year of Meats* says, to explain why it took horrific tragedies to force her to face the toxicity of American meat products,

> [I]gnorance is an act of will, a choice that one makes over and over again, especially when information overwhelms and knowledge has become

synonymous with impotence. . . . If we can't act on knowledge, then we can't survive without ignorance. So we cultivate the ignorance, go to great lengths to celebrate it, even. The *faux*-dumb aesthetic that dominates TV and Hollywood *must* be about this. Fed on a media diet of really bad news, we live in a perpetual state of repressed panic. We are paralyzed by bad knowledge, from which the only escape is playing dumb. Ignorance becomes empowering because it enables people to live. Stupidity becomes proactive, a political statement. Our collective norm. (334, emphasis Ozeki's)

In this sense the dream of Goth is also an awakening. Goths escape the willed stupidity of the American Dream to find in the nightmare of fallen knowledge a becoming that is also a coming to knowledge with no goal beyond intimacy with life's dark side. They refuse end goals, remaining, instead, fascinated with natural decay and the falling apart of all things that current mainstream values formed. By valorizing perversion and artifice for its own sake, they express their desire for a regime of endless desire.

Goths are far from the only Deleuzoguattarian subculture of our times, but that they function as agents of deterritorialization seems beyond dispute. The terrains of American life mapped out by a therapy culture always there to help facilitate greater and greater conformity, to help us ignore the social and global as we focus increasingly myopically on the idealized suburban family and an absurd fantasy of the childhood innocence it supposedly protects, are violently deterritorialized by the young Goths who simply walk around the lies laid out in front of them as they wander in search of intensities. The overcoding effected by a permutation of consumer capitalism that demands we interpret passion as a death drive and consensual sex as assault so that we can forego lawless bodily pleasure in favor of market-driven accumulation is stripped away by Goth styles that celebrate not pretty, sanitized sensuality but the terrible beauty of the grotesque and tragically mortal. Deleuze and Guattari assert,

> It should be said that one can never go far enough in the direction of deterritorialization. . . . And when we consider what there is of a profoundly artificial nature in the perverted reterritorializations, but also in the psychotic reterritorializations of the hospital; or even the familial neurotic reterritorializations, we cry out "More perversion! More artifice!"—to a point where the earth becomes so artificial that the movement of territorialization creates of necessity and by itself a new earth. . . . That is what the completion of the process is: not a promised and a pre-existing land, but a world created in the process of its tendency, its coming undone, its deterritorialization. (*Anti-Oedipus*, 321–22)

When they make style into a religion and religion into a style, when they appropriate commercialism before it can appropriate them, when they refuse abstinence culture without refusing awareness of the deadly dangers sexuality in these plague years threatens, when they resurrect and infuse with frightening new energies the Darkwave counterculture of the sixties, when they express sexual desire as the urge to dismantle the masculine body of power and become woman or girl, when they persist despite cultural erasure in a darkness they love, when they celebrate masochism as a revolutionary and spiritual force, and when they create fluid identities through a maelstrom fusion of all that the dominant culture considers binary opposites, Goths take deterritorialization beyond limits; they come undone. Goth can do nothing more in keeping with its values than sliding always more deeply into decline, down into the underground, spreading rhizomatically, dissolving shape into a continual becoming. For to come undone is to become. Long may Goth's dark empire decline!

APPENDIX
A Discography of Goth Rock Artists
by Don Anderson

As far back as I can remember I have always been fond of dark and depressing music. I never considered myself a depressed individual. The passion contained in a sad song simply spoke to me more than a happy jingle. I feel there is something noble, honest, and even proud about writing sad music. It's a strong position to take, a kind of backward machismo. "We are sadder than you," one could proclaim. My own involvement in dark music began when I first started playing guitar. While I was what one would call a Metal-head, I still retained a deep love for the slower doom bands. Eventually my tastes expanded and I discovered Goth rock. I became a fan of bands such as Fields of the Nephilim, The Sisters of Mercy, Christian Death, and The Cure. I was attracted to how original each band was, writing music that was transcendent in its sadness and mysticism. Later, when I began working with the band Agalloch in 1996, both the band and I insisted on integrating influences of Goth rock into our sound. To this day, three albums later, Agalloch is still a dark and depressing band, and that couldn't make me happier.

Attempting to design a discography concerned with a specific genre of music that fairly and accurately represents the artists and their respective recordings is a challenging, even daunting, task. It is impossible to avoid assigning certain artists to general categories, which ultimately belies the originality of the music. One soon finds this attempt is in vain because categories of music, especially music composed in these postmodern times, begin to collapse. This is due in part to musical crossbreeding and the exponential growth of information providing access to any style of music imaginable. We can no longer depend on a single descriptor to signify a particular sound.

Nowhere are these problems more apparent than in trying to form a discography of Goth rock. The term "Goth" is used in so many ways and has origins in so many different areas, such as literary history, medieval history, architecture, and fashion, that it is often unclear what one means by the term. There exist so many offshoots and lines of flight within Goth music that creating a discography is further problematized. For example, could not Led Zeppelin be considered Goth, what with their interests in the occult and Aleister Crowley, not to mention their Byron-esque lyrical themes that would not have been out of place in the eighteenth-century English Gothic revival? Yet I am confident one would be hard pressed to find a self-described Goth prepared to accept Led Zeppelin as a Goth band. How does one treat a band such as Fields of the Nephilim, who, most fans would argue, were a pivotal and influential quintet in the mid-late '80s Goth scene, but who dressed in Western garb inspired by Sergio Leone's spaghetti Westerns? If one of the primary prerequisites for Goth acceptance is a dark sound and look, then almost every genre of music is in some way guilty of Goth tendencies.

So I have thrown my arms up in desperation and surrendered to categories and labels. The contemporary discourse on Goth rock makes so much use of these terms I thought it irresponsible not to at least approach the bands with some sort of description. Nonetheless, within the discography itself, I have chosen to employ my own categories, which are less polarized and do not enforce a rigid musical dress code. I have opted to host bands under the following buzzword-free categories: "Traditional, Contemporary, and Classic," "On the Periphery," and "Guilty by Association." The first includes those bands universally recognized as being an integral part of Goth music's oeuvre. "On the Periphery" considers those bands that never claimed to be Goth, yet include former members of traditional Goth bands or have recourse to typical Goth themes. Those bands that are "Guilty by Association" normally get lumped in by fans of Goth rock, although the groups themselves may never have expressed a fondness for Goth, dressed like Goths, or even followed typical Goth themes. Blame this category on Goth fans whose school backpacks display both Bauhaus and the Smiths patches and buttons.

This discography is far from exhaustive. A complete discography would require a book in and of itself. It is meant purely to introduce Goth rock and to further emphasize the totality of the scene and its place within popular music. Under each band name both full-length releases and EPs are listed in order of release. To conserve space, I have omitted released singles, most live albums, and most greatest-hits collections.

Below is a list of the many subgenres of Goth rock as well as those often found in the company of Goth rock. I have described each genre and its relation to the phenomenon of the Goth music scene.

Goth Rock

The descriptor "Goth" as applied to rock music could easily be traced further back than is necessary for this study. However, "Goth rock" traditionally refers to music made from the mid-seventies to the present encompassing dark, morose themes such as death, tragic love, vampirism, sexual perversity, apocalyptic religion, Satanism, the occult, and so on. Goth is an incredibly broad term with a wide range of use. For the purposes of this discography, I will focus on groups active from the mid-seventies to the present.

Darkwave, Ambient, Neo-Classical

This genre normally adheres to a strictly minimalist approach. Keyboards are used heavily. Sometimes light percussion may be used. Examples are groups like Raison D'Etre, Lycia, Amon, Mortiis, and Arcana. Raison D'Etre's music is classically inspired with distinct movements, changes, strings, and chants. Amon's work is often labeled "isolationist" due to its incredibly sparse and minimalist nature.

Industrial

Though many would argue (and probably with good reason) that Industrial is not Goth, these two genres often converge and share similar themes. Industrial is characterized by unorthodox percussive elements, ranging from machine and metal sounds to overdistorted electronic drum beats. The music is heavily influenced by the industrial revolution; influences on the early British Industrial scene came directly from the first industrialized cities in England. Groups such as Throbbing Gristle, SPK, and Coil are ideal starting points for what was eventually termed Industrial. The genre actually takes its name from Throbbing Gristle's own label, Industrial Records.

Noise, Power Electronics

Often confused with Industrial music, Noise is normally less beat-driven and has more in common with modern classical composers such as Karlheinze Stockhausen, John Cage, and Iannis Xenakis. It is difficult to pinpoint the exact starting point of Noise. However, Japan's Merzbow marks its genesis within the independent music scene outside of classical music. England's Whitehouse, with its harsh soundscapes and incredibly violent and misogynist lyrics, is another starting point. Noise as an established genre reached its apex in the 1990s with an array of independent labels like Crionic Mind, Eibon, Triumvirate, Relapse/Release, Extreme, and many others. Noise is quite removed from Goth, although many of Goth's traditional themes are still prevalent. The more violent sides of sex and death are explored. This genre is as extreme and harsh as music has become.

Goth Metal

As Heavy Metal began to incorporate influences from groups like Joy Division, The Sisters of Mercy, and Bauhaus, a hybrid of Heavy Metal and Goth began to emerge. The music is often more guitar-driven and heavier than that of most Goth bands. The group Paradise Lost, which began as what some people would term Doom Metal, eventually morphed into what sounds like a love child of Metallica and The Sisters of Mercy. Other bands, such as Type O Negative and My Dying Bride, have always pinned their lyrics on death, tragic love, and suicide. The music is very slow and melodic, and makes greater use of keyboards and also "outside metal" instruments like the violin. This offshoot of Metal has become firmly established with bands like Theatre of Tragedy and album covers that display images of sexually provocative photography, nocturnal and romantic themes, and even the occasional band member made up as a corpse.

Apocalyptic Folk, Neo-Folk

This style of music is still rather young, though its influences date as far back as the early '60s. The greatest concentration of groups can be found on the English record label World Serpent. The term "Neo-Folk" was originally coined by the group Current 93, who midway through their career transitioned from an Industrial group to an eclectic combination of acoustic folk guitars, lullabies, and Gregorian chants. Thematically, Current 93's work revolves around the apocalypse, religion, and images of cats, stars, and moons. The groups Sol Invictus, Fire & Ice, and the early-nineties Death in June have been major figures in this style. The genre is more diverse than it may at first appear. One can easily trace influences ranging from American psychedelia to German Kraut and Progressive rock. This music resides more on the periphery of Goth, but many Goths express fondness for these generally very dark groups.

Traditional, Contemporary, and Classic Goth Rock

And Also the Trees

And Also the Trees. Reflex, 1984.
Virus Meadow. Reflex, 1986.
The Evening of the 24th. Reflex, 1987.
The Millpond Years. Normal, 1988.
Farewell to the Shade. Troy, 1989.
Green Is the Sea. Normal, 1991.
The Klaxon. Normal, 1993.
Angelfish. Mezentian, 1996.
Silver Soul. AATT, 1998.

Andi Sex Gang

Blind. Illuminated, 1985.
Ida Ho EP. Illuminated, 1985.
Arco Valley. Jungle, 1989.

God on a Rope. Cleopatra, 1993.
Western Songs for Children. Triple X, 1995.
Gabriel and the Golden Horn. Hollows Hill, 1999.
Faithful Covers. Dressed To Kill, 2000.
Last of England. Dressed To Kill, 2000.

Bauhaus

Bela Lugosi's Dead. Small Wonder, 1979.
In the Flat Field. 4AD Records, 1980.
Mask. Beggars Banquet, 1981.
Nature's Mortes — Still Lives. 4AD Records, 1981.
Press the Eject & Give Me the Tape (live). Beggars Banquet, 1982.
The Sky's Gone Out. Beggars Banquet, 1982.
Burning from the Inside. Beggars Banquet, 1983.
1979–1983, Volume 1. Beggars Banquet, 1986.
1979–1983, Volume 2. Beggars Banquet, 1986.
The Singles, 1981–1983. Beggars Banquet, 1989.
Swing the Heartache: The BBC Sessions. Beggars Banquet, 1989.

Chandeen

Red Letter Days. Hyperium, 1994.
Shaded by the Leaves. Hyperium, 1994.
Jutland. Hyperium, 1995.
Light within Time EP. Hyperium, 1995.
Strawberry Passion. Hyperium, 1995.
Papillon. Hyperium, 1996.
The Waking Dream. Hyperium, 1996.
Spacerider — Love at First Sight. Synthetic Symphony, 1998.
Bikes & Pyramids. Kalinkaland records, 2002.

Christian Death

Only Theatre of Pain. Epitaph, 1982.
Catastrophe Ballet. Nostradamus, 1984.
Ashes. Nostradamus, 1985.
Atrocities. Nostradamus, 1986.
The Scriptures. Jungle, 1987.
Sex, Drugs, & Jesus Christ. Jungle, 1988.
What's the Verdict EP. Jungle, 1988.
The Wind Kissed Pictures. Supporti, 1988.
All the Love All the Hate, Pt. 1. Jungle, 1989.
All the Love All the Hate, Pt. 2. Jungle, 1989.
The Iron Mask. Cleopatra, 1992.
Jesus Points the Bone at You. Jungle, 1992.

Skeleton Kiss. Cleopatra, 1992.
The Path of Sorrows. Cleopatra, 1993.
The Rage of Angels. Cleopatra, 1994.
Sexy Death God. Bullet Proof Records, 1994.
Prophecies. Cleopatra, 1996.
Pornographic Messiah. Cleopatra, 1998.
Insanus Ulita Prodito Miseric. Cleopatra, 1999.
Born Again Anti-Christian. Cleopatra, 2000.

Clan of Xymox

Clan of Xymox. 4AD, 1985.
Medusa. 4AD, 1987.
Twist of Shadows. Polygram, 1989.
Hidden Faces. Tess, 1997.
Creatures. Metropolis, 1999.
Live. Metropolis, 2000.
Notes from the Underground. Metropolis, 2001.
Subsequent Pleasures. Metropolis, 2001.
Remixes from the Underground. Metropolis, 2002.

Cocteau Twins

Garlands. 4AD, 1982.
Lullabies EP. 4AD, 1982.
Head over Heels. 4AD, 1983.
Peppermint Pig EP. 4AD, 1983.
Sunburst & Snowblind EP. 4AD, 1983.
The Spangle Maker EP. 4AD, 1984.
Treasure. 4AD, 1984.
Aikea-Guinea EP. 4AD, 1985.
Echoes in a Shallow Bay EP. 4AD, 1985.
Tiny Dynamine EP. 4AD, 1985.
Love's Easy Tears EP. 4AD, 1986.
The Moon & the Melodies. 4AD, 1986.
Victorialand. 4AD, 1986.
Blue Bell Knoll. 4AD, 1988.
Heaven or Las Vegas. 4AD, 1990.
Four Calendar Café. Mercury/Fontana, 1993.
Otherness EP. Mercury/Fontana, 1995.
Twinlights EP. Mercury/Fontana, 1995.
Milk & Kisses. Mercury/Fontana, 1996.

Corpus Delicti

Twilight. Glasnost Records, 1993.

Noxious. Glasnost Records, 1994.
Sylphes. Glasnost Records, 1994.
Obsessions. Cemetery Records, 1995.
Sarabands. Cleopatra, 1996.
Syn:drom. Seasons of Mist, 1998.

The Cure

Three Imaginary Boys. Polygram, 1979.
Boys Don't Cry. Elektra/Asylum, 1980.
Seventeen Seconds. Elektra/Asylum, 1980.
Faith. Elektra/Asylum, 1981.
Pornography. Elektra/Asylum, 1982.
Japanese Whispers. Polygram, 1983.
Concert: The Cure Live. Polygram, 1984.
The Top. Polygram, 1984.
The Head on the Door. Elektra/Asylum, 1985.
Staring at the Sea: The Singles, 1978–1985. Elektra/Asylum, 1985.
Kiss Me, Kiss Me, Kiss Me. Elektra/Asylum, 1987.
Disintegration. Elektra/Asylum, 1989.
Mixed Up. Elektra/Asylum, 1990.
Wish. Elektra/Asylum, 1992.
Paris Live. Elektra/Asylum, 1993.
Show Live. Elektra/Asylum, 1993.
Wild Mood Swings. Elektra/Asylum, 1996.
Galore: The Singles, 1987–1997. Elektra/Asylum, 1997.
Bloodflowers. Elektra/Asylum, 2000.

Dead Can Dance

Dead Can Dance. 4AD, 1984.
Spleen and Ideal. 4AD, 1986.
Within the Realm of a Dying Sun. Beggars Banquet, 1987.
The Serpent's Egg. Beggars Banquet, 1988.
Aion. 4AD, 1990.
Passage in Time. Beggars Banquet, 1991.
Into the Labyrinth. 4AD, 1993.
Toward the Within. 4AD, 1994.
Spiritchaser. Beggars Banquet, 1996.

Deep Red

The Awakening. Candyland Entertainment, 1996.
I Live. Candyland Entertainment, 1996.
Darkwaters. Osiris Soundworks, 2000.
Chimera. Osiris Soundworks, 2002.

Evanescence

Fallen. Wind-Up, 2003.

Faith & Disease

Beauty & Bitterness. Ivy Records, 1993.
Fortune His Sleep. Ivy Records, 1995.
Livesongs: Third Body. Ivy Records, 1996.
Insularia. Ivy Records, 1998.
Beneath the Trees. Projekt Records, 2000.

Faith & the Muse

Elyria. Tess Records, 1994.
Annwyn, beneath the Waves. Tess Records, 1995.
Evidence of Heaven. Neue Asthetik Multimedia, 1999.
Vera Causa: Night & Morning. Metropolis, 2001.

Fields of the Nephilim

Burning the Fields EP. Tower/Jungle, 1985.
Returning to Gehenna EP. Supporti Fonografici, 1986.
Dawnrazor. Beggars Banquet, 1987.
The Nephilim. Beggars Banquet, 1988.
Psychonaut EP. Situation Two, 1989.
Elizium. Beggars Banquet, 1990.
Earth Inferno. Beggars Banquet, 1991.
Laura. Contempo, 1991.
BBC Radio 1 Live in Concert. Windsong, 1992.
Revelations. Beggars Banquet, 1993.
From Gehenna to Here. Santeria, 2001.
Fallen. Jungle, 2002.

The Frozen Autumn

Pale Awakening. Weisser Herbst, 1995,
Fragments of Memories. Eibon Records, 1997.
The Pale Collection. Eibon Records, 2000.
Emotional Screening Device. Eibon Records, 2002.

Gene Loves Jezebel

Promise. Situation Two, 1983.
Immigrant. Relativity, 1985.
Discover. Geffen, 1986.
The House of Dolls. Geffen, 1987.
Kiss of Life. Geffen, 1990.

Heavenly Bodies. Savage, 1992.
From the Mouths of Babes: Some of the Best of Gene Loves Jezebel.
    Avalanche, 1995.
VII. Robinson Records, 1999.
Love Lies Bleeding. Triple X, 1999.
Voodoo Dollies. Beggars Banquet, 1999.
Giving up the Ghost. Triple X, 2001.

Genitorturers

120 Days of Genitorture. IRS Records, 1993.
Sin City. Cleopatra, 1998.
Machine Love. Cleopatra, 2000.
Flesh Is the Law EP. Phantom, 2002.

Ikon

The Echoes of Silence. Nile Records, 1994.
In the Shadow of the Angel. Metropolis, 1996.
The Final Experience. Apollyon, 1997.
Flowers for the Gathering. Metropolis, 1997.
A Moment in Time. Metropolis, 1997.
Ghost in My Head EP. Nile Records, 1998.
This Quiet Earth. Metropolis, 1998.
Subversion. Apollyon and Metropolis, 1998.
Lifeless EP. Apollyon, 1999.
On the Edge of Forever. Metropolis, 2001.

London after Midnight

Oddities. Metropolis, 1998.
Psycho Magnet. Magnet Metropolis, 1998.
Selected Scenes from the End of the World. Metropolis, 1998.

Loretta's Doll

Chemical Theater. World Serpent, 1993.
XXI Degrees. World Serpent, 1994.
War of the Worlds. World Serpent, 1996.
World of Tiers. World Serpent, 1996.
Nocturnal Arcade. World Serpent, 1998.
Creeping Sideways. World Serpent/Middle Pillar, 2001.

Love Like Blood

Anthology of an Agony. Deathwish Office, 1988.
Sinister Dawn EP. Deathwish Office, 1989.
Flags of Revolution. Deathwish Office, 1990.

Ecstasy EP. Deathwish Office, 1991.
Demimondes. Rebel Records, 1992.
An Irony of Fate. Rebel Records, 1992.
Kiss & Tell EP. Deathwish Office, 1992.
Flood of Love. Rebel Records, 1993.
Stormy Visions. Rebel Records, 1993.
Odyssee. Rebel Records, 1994.
Exposure. Rebel Records, 1995.
Taste of Damocles. Focusion, 1997.
The Love Like Blood EP. Hall Of Sermon GmbH, 1998.
Snakekiller. Hall of Sermon GmbH, 1998.
Enslaved + Condemned. Hall of Sermon GmbH, 2000.
Chronology of a Love Affair. Hall of Sermon GmbH, 2001.

Malice Mizer

Bara no Seidou. Midi-Nette, 2001.
Gardenia. Midi-Nette, 2001.
Merveille. Zai, 2001.
Amusement in Nothingness. Midi-Nette, 2002.
Midnight. Midi-Nette, 2002.
Voyage. Malice Mizer Records, 2002.

Marilyn Manson

Portrait of an American Family. Interscope, 1994.
Smells Like Children. Interscope, 1995.
Antichrist Superstar. Interscope, 1996.
Mechanical Animals. Interscope, 1998.
Holy Wood—In the Shadow of the Valley of Death. Interscope, 2000.
The Golden Age of Grotesque. Interscope, 2003.

Mephisto Waltz

Terra Regina. Cleopatra, 1993.
The Eternal Deep. Cleopatra, 1994.
Thalia. Cleopatra, 1995.
Immersion. Cleopatra, 1998.

The Mission

First Chapter. Mercury, 1987.
Gods Own Medicine. Mercury, 1987.
Children. Mercury, 1988.
Carved in Sand. Mercury, 1990.
Grains of Sand. Mercury, 1990.

Masque. Vertigo, 1992.
Sum & Substance. Vertigo, 1994.
Neverland. Equator/Sony, 1995.
Blue. Equator/Sony, 1996.
Resurrection. Cleopatra, 1999.
Everafter. Trojan, 2000.
Aura. PGND, 2001.

Murphy, Peter

Should the World Fail to Fall Apart. Beggars Banquet, 1986.
Love Hysteria. Beggars Banquet, 1988.
Deep. Beggars Banquet, 1990.
Holy Smoke. Beggars Banquet, 1992.
Cascade. Beggars Banquet, 1995.
A Retrospective. Beggars Banquet/Atlantic, 1995.
Recall. Red Ant, 1997.
Wild Birds (1985–1995). Beggars Banquet, 2000.

The Nefilim

Zoon. Beggars Banquet, 1996.

Nosferatu

The Hellhound EP. Possession, 1991.
Rise. Cleopatra, 1993.
Legend. Cleopatra, 1994.
The Prophecy. Cleopatra, 1994.
Prince of Darkness. 1996.
Lord of the Flies. Cleopatra, 1998.
Re Vamped. Cleopatra, 1999.
Reflections through a Darker Glass. Cleopatra, 2000.

Penis Flytrap

Tales of Terror. Bloody Daggre, 1998.
Music for Monsters. Black Plague, 2001.
Dismemberment. Black Plague, 2002.

Red Lorry Yellow Lorry

Talk about the Weather. Red Rhino, 1985.
Paint Your Wagon. Red Rhino, 1986.
The Singles, 1982–1987. Cherry Red, 1987.
Nothing Wrong. Situation Two, 1988.
Blow. Situation Two, 1989.
Blasting Off. Sparkhead/Release, 1991.

Rosetta Stone

Adrenaline. Cleopatra, 1993.
Foundation Stones. Cleopatra, 1995.
Friends & Executioners. Cleopatra, 1995.
The Tyranny of Inaction. Cleopatra, 1995.
Hiding in Waiting. Cleopatra, 1996.
Chemical Emissions. Cleopatra, 1998.
Unerotica: Reformatted Eighties Audio. Cleopatra, 2000.

Sex Gang Children

Naked MC. Sex, 1982.
Beasts EP. Illuminated, 1983.
Sebastiane EP. Illuminated, 1983.
Sex Gang Children LP. Sex, 1983.
Song and Legend. Illuminated, 1983.
Dirty Roseanne EP. D.E.A., 1986.
Blind. Cleopatra, 1992.
Play with Children. Cleopatra, 1992.
Dieche. Dressed to Kill, 1993.
Medea. Dressed to Kill, 1993.
Welcome to My World. Receiver, 1998.
Pop Up. Dressed to Kill, 1999.
Shout & Scream. Dressed To Kill, 1999.
Veil. Dressed to Kill, 1999.
Demonstration. Dressed to Kill, 2000.
Empyre & Fall. Triple X, 2001.
Helter Skelter. Dressed to Kill, 2001.
Wrath of God. Livid, 2001.
Bastard Art. Universal, 2002.

Siouxsie and the Banshees

The Scream. Geffen, 1978.
Join Hands. Geffen, 1979.
Kaleidoscope. Geffen, 1980.
Juju. Geffen, 1981.
Once upon a Time/The Singles. Geffen, 1981.
A Kiss in the Dreamhouse. Geffen, 1982.
Hyaena. Geffen, 1984.
Tinderbox. Geffen, 1986.
Through the Looking Glass. Geffen, 1987.
Peepshow. Geffen, 1988.

Superstition. Geffen, 1991.
Twice upon a Time/The Singles. Geffen, 1992.
The Rapture. Geffen, 1995.

The Sisters of Mercy

First & Last & Always. Elektra/Asylum, 1985.
Floodland. Elektra/Asylum, 1987.
Vision Thing. Elektra/Asylum, 1990.
Some Girls Wander by Mistake. Mercyful Release, 1992.
A Slight Case of Overbombing. Elektra/Asylum, 1993.

Southern Death Cult

Southern Death Cult. Beggars Banquet, 1983.

Sunshine Blind

Sunshine Blind. Demo Cassette, 1992–1994.
Love the Sky to Death. Scream Records, 1995.
Liquid. Energy Records, 1997.

Suspiria

The Great and Secret Show. Nightbreed, 1995.
Drama. Nightbreed, 1997.
Primitive Attentions. Nightbreed, 1997.

Switchblade Symphony

Serpentine Gallery. Cleopatra, 1995.
Clown. Cleopatra, 1996.
Bread & Jam for Frances. Cleopatra, 1997.
Scrapbook EP. Self-released, 1997.
The Three Calamities. Cleopatra, 1999.
Sinister Nostalgia. Cleopatra, 2001.

On the Periphery

Black Tape for a Blue Girl

Canaan

Cave, Nick & the Birthday Party

Cave, Nick & the Bad Seeds

The Cult

The Damned

Diamanda Galas

In the Nursery

Joy Division

Love Is Colder Than Death

New Order

Swans

This Mortal Coil

Type O Negative

Virgin Prunes

Guilty by Association

Angels of Light

Blood Axis

Coil

Current 93

Death in June

Depeche Mode

Devil Doll

Fire & Ice

Laibach

Legendary Pink Dots

Les Joyeaux de la Princess

Ministry

Morrissey

Mortiis

My Life with the Thrill Kill Kult

Nature & Organization

Nazka

Nine Inch Nails

Seigmen

Skinny Puppy

The Smiths

Slowdive

Sol Invictus

Sorrow

SPK

Strawberry Switchblade

Thanatos

Throbbing Gristle

Wumpscut

NOTES

Introduction

1. Following the lead of Gilles Deleuze and Félix Guattari's first academic popularizer, Ronald Bogue, I have chosen to avoid the "somewhat awkward . . . neologism" "Deleuzoguattarian" except when it seems absolutely necessary to clarity, preferring the more common adjective "Deleuzian" for some of the ideas associated with the collaborative, as well as the independent, work of Deleuze (*Deleuze and Guattari*, 9). As Bogue says in the introduction to his later text, *Deleuze on Literature*, because of the depth of the "integration of their styles and thought" from their first collaboration on, "it is impossible to separate Deleuze and Guattari either in their joint works or even in their individual projects after *Anti-Oedipus*," and so the most sensible approach for the scholar of Deleuze who will be citing several texts in the production of which Guattari did not collaborate seems to be to "treat Deleuze's works and the Deleuze-Guattari volumes both as constituents of Deleuze's *oeuvre*" (8).

2. Because I understand contemporary Goth subcultures as existing in rhizomatic relation to the Gothic tradition, I capitalize the word "Goth" in reference to these subcultures.

3. I agree with Joanne Addison and Michelle Comstock that "[r]esearch guidelines that are meant to prevent the exploitation of 'under-age' survey respondents . . . also serve to isolate youth and deny them the opportunity to speak for and contribute to accounts of their communities that are being constructed by others," and that this is particularly the case when one deals with youth with minoritized sexualities, "since most of them are not 'out' to their parents or guardians," whose presence at a formal interview is mandated by academic rules for work with human subjects (371). In both my earlier study of subcultures and here, I have forgone formal interviews in favor of unstructured conversations with young people. In finding young people with whom to talk I have relied heavily on my large acquaintance within rock and roll communities and among former students, some of whom I remain close to. These young people, often accompanying me on "fact-finding missions," as one liked to call them, helped me engage young people at subcultural events, concerts, cafés, and all-ages clubs in conversations about their lives. They also let it be known among their circle of acquaintance that I was writing a book representing specific subcultural groups, and that they might want to have input into it. Dozens of young people responded to these "calls" and came around to talk to me. Others emailed me on their own after seeing my webpage, and to them I did send out some preformulated questions. And

finally, on my own, I sought out young people whose personal style identified them to me as members of rock and roll subcultures and initiated conversations with them. Young people have consistently responded to me with seemingly earnest confidences and exhortations to report truthfully on their group. I think the information I have gathered from these conversations is as accurate as such research can be.

4. See my *New Millennial Sexstyles* for detailed and extensive discussion of this band and its audiences.

5. Edmundson dismisses "rants about AIDS and environmental disaster, framed in the apocalyptic Gothic mode," as useless, claiming they "spawn guilt and fear but contribute nothing to progress" (61). As is often the case in his discussions of social problems, he fails to recognize the validity of the outrage felt by adolescents who bear no responsibility for these problems that may take their lives, nor does he seem moved by the desperation of the young to impress upon their tormentors, the very generation to which he (and I) belong, some sense of guilt for the toxic world we have wrought.

6. Moynihan, a prominent member of Anton LaVey's Church of Satan, is considered by many to be a neo-fascist, although he often suggests that this is a misinterpretation of his political position. His adversarial relationship with the media, mocking attitude, and apparent love of sensation and notoriety make it nearly impossible to determine exactly what his politics are.

7. I was hired by Loyola University New Orleans to develop a minor in women's studies (among other duties) and soon found myself working to create a women's center at the school as well as acting as unofficial advisor to a large number of gay, lesbian, and bisexual students because they chose to make me their advocate. My off-campus social activities with students who saw their sexual and gender identifications as under censure drew me into the developing Goth scene.

8. See Shere Hite's *The Hite Report: Women and Love* (1987) for survey results that lead her to believe that in the late nineteen-eighties it is still the case that "the double standard lives" (183, 190). Although Hite, as usual, generalizes beyond the respondents to her survey, it seems important to note that she does offer compelling evidence that, within the bourgeoisie, women who pretend to be nearly asexual before marriage are more likely to win at the marriage-for-security game. One might also keep in mind that this is the message of most relationship advice books written at the end of the twentieth century: for example, Ellen Fein and Sherrie Schneider's *The Rules*.

9. And not just heterosex. As Gerhard documents throughout her study, lesbians often chafed under the same constraints. Gerhard quotes Gayle Rubin's 1981 essay "Talking Sex": "By conflating lesbianism (as sexual experience) with feminism (a political philosophy), the ability to justify lesbianism on grounds other than feminism dropped out of the discourse" (187).

10. Goths are first mentioned in Widdicombe and Wooffitt's text as subjects exemplifying resistance to subcultural identification (104).

11. Working from Stanley Cohen's theory of the demonization of subcultures, as elaborated throughout his *Folk Devils and Moral Panics*, Thornton argues that media campaigns against specific subcultures in fact encourage their proliferation (119–37).

12. The appendix to this book, provided by Don Anderson of the (nonfascist) Darkwave band Agalloch, contains a discography that should help orient the uninitiated to the basic players in Goth's musical nightscape.

13. The part of the book next most popular with my young Goth friends was chapter 1, especially its conclusion.

14. Some of Muggleton's informants do assert such identification. In his interview of "Tony and Beth," for instance, Tony firmly names himself and Beth "Gothics," but Beth disagrees, insisting this is inaccurate because "I am my own person." Muggleton has little to say about Tony's response ("Suffice to say that an unequivocal acceptance of a single label . . . occurred only rarely in the interviews as a whole") and concentrates on discussing the significance of Beth's (61–62). I think I had an advantage over Muggleton as an analyst of Goth in that, in the first round of conversations I had with young people in subcultures, a considerable number had come to talk to me *because* they considered themselves Goths. In fact, many stressed to me that they wanted to make sure my book represented them accurately. (Which is why I was able to use them as initial readers of sections.) So I did not have to either attribute to them an identity they resisted or else see Goth as a construct within which no one could be placed unless I disregarded what they had to say about themselves.

15. See Elizabeth Arias et al., "Annual Summary of Vital Statistics—2002" in *Pediatrics* for more on this trend. Among the report's shocking revelations is that "[f]or teens aged 15 to 19 years . . . [s]uicide was the third leading cause" of death (16). During the question and answer period following a book reading I gave to promote *New Millennial Sexstyles*, I offered the list of social ills included in the text above as the explanation of why "young people today are so depressed," and while their elders reacted with consternation, the young people present, including a large contingent of Goths, stood up and applauded. It was at this reading that the present book was born, when a young male Goth spontaneously hugged me and asked when I was going to "write a book about us to set the record straight."

I. Perils for the Pure

1. For the origins of this theory see Max Horkheimer and Theodor Adorno's "The Culture Industry: Enlightenment as Mass Deception."

2. The most extensive and reliable reporting on the culture war against Goths after Columbine is Jon Katz's remarkable web posting on *Slashdot*, "Voices from the Hellmouth" (April 26, 1999), in response to which Goths, mostly high school students, reported directly on their own experiences. In single-spaced ten-point type with one-inch margins, the discussion prints out at about three hundred and fifty-eight pages.

3. Given the media insistence that Kleibold and Harris were Goths, a striking feature of their friend Brooks Brown's first-person account of the Columbine shootings, *No Easy Answers: The Truth behind Death at Columbine*, is that the term "Goth" never appears in the text. This is not surprising in that Brooks repeatedly says that the shooters preferred German Industrial bands such as Rammstein and KDFDM (71, 100–101). While there sometimes is an overlap between the fan bases of Goth bands and such Industrial groups, Dave Thompson seems right to point out that they are "decidedly un-Gothic" (244). None of the music Brown mentions as appealing to himself or the "Punk and alternative crowd" (63) to which he belonged is typically understood to be Gothic.

4. See Katz's "Voices from the Hellmouth."

5. For a full history of Goth rock's two waves, see Dave Thompson, *The Dark Reign of Gothic Rock: In the Reptile House with The Sisters of Mercy, Bauhaus, and The Cure.*

6. See Janice M. Irvine, *Talk about Sex,* for an excellent history of abstinence education that emphasizes its rise during the 1980s and the triumph of the far Right in the 1990s.

7. The critically despised 2003 film *The Real Cancun* might be productively examined as a representation of how society now expects mainstream youth to express their sexuality. Modeled on MTV's notorious *Real World* series, the film follows sixteen young people on a spring break visit to Cancun. Notably, although the film was advertised as if it were sexploitation, most of it documents the young participants' prim avoidance of actual intercourse (and oral sex). They seem obsessed with establishing that they are not "sluts," constantly discussing their sexual purity, and in many cases asserting their virginity. While near nudity, simulated sex acts, feigned lesbianism, and other sorts of display are used to get attention, any sort of contact with unclothed (or condom-covered) genitalia is treated as utterly taboo. At the end of a drunken, stoned, and unsupervised week, the audience is given to understand that only two couples had sex. Those young people are angrily berated by the others.

8. My separation here of Kamen's opinions from those of her interview subjects stems from our dialogue about the text and the issues it raises, some of which is posted in the web-based journal *Rhizomes.*

9. My emphasis. The line comes from "Ted, Just Admit It," a song that begins with a sample of a radio interview with serial killer Ted Bundy. The song was later remixed by Trent Reznor for the soundtrack of Oliver Stone's film *Natural Born Killers,* in which the central characters, Mickey and Mallory, seem to be driven into a frenzy of murderous rage by the hypocrisy of a society that polices consensual teen sexuality so assiduously that Mickey is imprisoned for the statutory rape of Mallory, his slightly younger girlfriend who adores him, while her father's unwanted sexual domination of her is ignored.

10. See Beryl Satter's "The Sexual Abuse Paradigm in Historical Perspective" (446–47) for an overview of radical feminist advocacy of children's freedom of sexual expression.

11. In a study of small children's responses to a curriculum meant to help them defend themselves from molestation, N. Dickson Reppuci and Jeffrey J. Haugaard found that the warnings against "suspicious" people actually reinforced children's prejudices against members of groups minoritized because of race or class. My own conversations with teenagers and young adults about courtship practices have revealed an alarming tendency among the abstinent not only to reject potential partners for these reasons, but to moralize such choices. Remarks like "he wanted to go out with me and he didn't even have his own car" are common. The number of racist comments made by the abstinent is even more discouraging. And no wonder, since the findings of a 1997 study of the "Sex Respect" abstinence program popular with California schools show that it "portrays black youth, in text and illustrations, as promiscuous, irresponsible, and troubled" (Fuentes, 17).

12. Levine cites information from the *Journal of the American Medical Association,* the 1997 International AIDS Conference, the Centers for Disease Control and Prevention, and the National Institutes of Health (113, 271).

13. For a startling and succinct comparison of American to British attitudes about adolescent sexuality, one can look at the way the popular 1999 British TV series *Queer as Folk* was revised for the American audience. The British version focuses on the comic sexual affair between Stuart, a twenty-nine-year-old gay dance club Don Juan, and fifteen-year-old Nathan, who becomes smitten with him after a one-night stand. Central to the development of Stuart's character is his refusal to sentimentalize sexual encounters, which causes him to refuse to take Nathan's absurdly overdramatized feelings seriously. The general attitude of the series seems to be the same, as it includes numerous jokes at Nathan's expense. The overall message seems to be that the confusion of sex with love is a sign of immaturity. In the American version of the series, aired the next year, Stuart's character, now called Brian, is less appealingly presented as someone with whose perspective the series does not always agree. But most surprisingly, Nathan is translated into an almost legal seventeen-year-old. And this despite the fact that survey after survey tells us that fifteen is the age when most Americans begin to have sex.

2. In Memoriam Darkwave Hippies

1. For pertinent feminist discussions of the gendering of Punk, see Lauraine Leblanc's *Pretty in Punk: Girls' Gender Resistance in a Boys' Subculture* (especially 50–56 and 104–33), Gina Arnold's *Route 666: On the Road to Nirvana,* and Gillian Gaar's *She's a Rebel: The History of Women in Rock & Roll.* Of course, when it emerged from Punk Goth seemed still in many ways indistinguishable from it, and many similarities do remain to this day, which is why mainstream observers are often confused when they try to distinguish between members of the two subcultures. Attitude toward gender is one of the strongest and most consistent markers of difference between Punk and Goth.

2. See Baddeley's *Goth Chic,* 69–71, for more on Lovecraft's status in Goth.

3. The song "Dragula" provides background music for the chasing the white rabbit scene in *The Matrix.*

4. This theme gets a gender reversal in Carter's *The Infernal Desire Machines of Doctor Hoffman* (1972), in which a young man gruesomely destroys his dream girl after many horrible sensual adventures.

5. I have written extensively about the majoritist feminist view of S/M in *Male Masochism* and *New Millennial Sexstyles.* See also the writings of Pat Califia, Dorothy Allison, and Karmen MacKendrick.

6. For example, Carter's 1974 short story collection, *Fireworks: Nine Profane Pieces,* concentrates on tales of sadism and masochism, often highly romanticized. They are deliberately in the tradition of what, in the afterword, she calls "Gothic tales, cruel tales, tales of wonder, tales of terror" (132). She explains that they were inspired by her recognition, upon her return from two years in Japan, that "[w]e live in Gothic times" (132–33).

7. See, for example, the depictions of incestuous rape and other atrocities in Finley's collection *Shock Treatment.* Lauraine Leblanc's perceptive discussion of Punk's relation to S/M symbology is also useful in correcting misunderstandings (37–47).

8. A large number of feminist texts persuasively argue the opposite. Susan Bordo's *Unbearable Weight: Feminism, Western Culture, and the Body* and Sharlene Hesse-

Biber's *Am I Thin Enough Yet? The Cult of Thinness and the Commercialization of Identity* are among the best.

9. Neil Jordan's 1984 film version foregrounds the tale's concern with female coming of age by using as a frame a modern girl's retreat to her room to suffer the cramps that accompany her first menstruation. Carter's story, set in a fairy-tale past, mentions that the protagonist has "just started her woman's bleeding," but that is not the occasion for the narrative.

3. That Obscure Object of Desire Revisited

1. Anonymous e-mail correspondent, September 8, 1998. It is worth noting that Brite's appeal is far from being limited to Goths. For example, Jason Walton, a musician so enamored of Brite's fiction that he chose to perform under the name of one of her characters (Nothing), writes me that "although I love Brite's work, the 'mainstream Gothic' characters and their affinity for pop culture somewhat puts me off" (e-mail, January 8, 2001). One might also do well to note that there are, of course, Goths who aren't interested in Brite's work and even some to whom she is unknown.

2. Less than a decade ago, as I discuss throughout *Male Masochism*, the consensus among academics studying gender seemed to be that this sexual orientation was merely a cover obscuring (to all but the analyst's eye) a sneaking misogyny. The title of a chapter in Lynn S. Chancer's *Sadomasochism in Everyday Life* succinctly states the view of the relation between S/M and gender politics most commonly expressed in feminist theory at the twentieth century's end: "Engendering Sadomasochism: Dominance, Subordination, and the Contaminated World of Patriarchy."

3. See *Kafka: Toward a Minor Literature*, especially chapter 3, "What Is a Minor Literature?" (16–27), and *A Thousand Plateaus* (100–10) for further discussion of this concept. In *Deleuze on Literature*, Ronald Bogue explains Deleuze and Guattari's understanding of "Kafka's depiction of power as consonant with Foucault's analyses of power in *Discipline and Punish* and *The History of Sexuality, Vol. 1*" (81). In fact, as early as his first book, *Madness and Civilization*, Foucault was drawing on Nietzsche's *On the Genealogy of Morals* to describe how culture and society code experience and create identities and subjectivities; Foucault makes this explicit in his 1971 essay "Nietzsche, Genealogy, History."

4. Ligotti's collaboration with the band Current93 on the CD *I Have a Special Plan for This World* brought him to the attention of many in the Goth music scene. Ligotti emphasizes his work's connections to Lovecraft in the dedication to his own short story "The Last Feast of Harlequin."

5. Some of the lyrics of Nine Inch Nails songs, as well as those of The Cure, can be read as sadistic, rather than masochistic. But, as I discuss at some length in *New Millennial Sexstyles*, music critics nearly uniformly described Trent Reznor's persona on stage and in his songs as masochistic, and with good reason.

6. The most extreme version of this may be Anne Mellor's reading of Victor Frankenstein's passionate attachment to his monster as a cover for his misogynous desire to rid the world of women, which, as Judith Halberstam observes, "runs the risk of sounding homophobic and misunderstands the relation between homosexuality, textuality, and patriarchy" (*Skin Shows*, 42).

7. I thank Michael Bibby for bringing to my attention the likelihood that Brite's

choice of title was also influenced by the popularity, in Goth circles, of the Australian Industrial rock project Scraping Foetus off the Wheel, in which "angry woman in rock" and Punk icon Lydia Lunch was involved.

8. The term "slash" derives from the slash mark "/" between the initials K (for Kirk) and S (for Spock); the label "K/S" indicated "to those purchasing by mail amateur fanzines (or 'zines) that the stories, poems, and artwork published there concern[ed] a same sex relationship between the two men" (Penley, 137). The term was rapidly generalized to apply to stories about any characters.

9. Comically, I read it first during an airplane trip, and the passenger next to me, after looking for a few minutes over my shoulder at the page I was reading, rang the call button and asked the flight attendant's permission to change seats. Her request was accommodated. Among other things, I remain grateful to Brite for the additional leg room.

10. Halberstam claims, "Gothic fiction is a technology of subjectivity, one which produces the deviant subjectivities opposite which the normal, the healthy, and the pure can be known" (*Skin Shows*, 2). She observes that minoritized racial status is one of the primary attributes assigned to the deviant or monster. However, the application of her theory to Brite's novel is problematized by Tran's role as victim rather than monster.

11. The difference between Brite's depiction of male and female experiences of sexuality is perhaps best illustrated by the contrast between Michael's harrowing initiation into sex through violent incest and the incestuous experiences of Jessy, who demands sex with her father. The intimidated man puts up a little resistance and then "let[s] her lay him out and undo his trousers and straddle him" (*Lost*, 79). Almost all heterosexual encounters in Brite's fiction are woman-superior in more ways than one.

12. Numerous Asian American writers have described the damage done to males within their racial group by the concept of the model minority and by the perception of them as effeminate by those outside the group. Probably the most outraged voices are those of Frank Chin, Jeffery Paul Chan, Lawson Fusao Inada, and Shawn Wong in their introduction to the Mentor edition of *Aiiieeeee! An Anthology of Asian-American Writers*. Despite Frank Chin's notorious condemnation of this text, David Henry Hwang's play *M. Butterfly* also covers the issue very well, as does David Mura's *Where the Body Meets Memory*. More on this in the final chapter.

4. Boys Don't Cry

1. Straight Edge Punks, a fairly large contingent in the U.S. and Britain, adopt particularly rigid codes of sexual purity, frowning on casual sex for males as well as females.

2. See Missy Suicide's *SuicideGirls* for a better sense of the girls' self-presentation and their articulations of Punk and Goth identities.

3. I refer to Brandon Teena here as "s/he" because the documentary gives us fragmentary images from both her life as Teena Brandon and his life as Brandon Teena; however, in my view, transsexual gender identities have as much validity as any others. Just as I am female because I perceive myself to be female, so was Brandon Teena male because he perceived himself to be male. For this reason, I refer to him with the male pronoun throughout the rest of this essay.

4. I do not mean to imply here that lesbianism and glamour are mutually exclusive. Far from it. Still, just as Hollywood beauties like Swank and Sevigny are not representative of the general population of young women, they are not representative of typical lesbians. Nor is exhibitionism aimed at arousing males the most common form of lesbian sexual expression, despite what soft-core pornography often seems to suggest.

5. Throughout the responses to "Voices from the Hellmouth," the terms "geek" and "Goth," as well as "nerd," are used interchangeably.

5. Heterosexualizing the Femme Boy

1. The stage play ends with Laura's sexual invitation to Tom, but the film concludes with a flash-forward to Tom's attendance at his class's ten-year reunion, at which he receives a letter from Laura expressing her regret that their affair, which she now understands to have been immoral, ended her marriage in "disgrace." In contrast to her tragic fate, he is now happily married.

2. An interesting variation on this trend is represented by radical lesbian Pearl Time's Child's charming self-published journal *The Auto Biography of Deborah Carr*, in which she uses Deborah Kerr's role in the film as her departure point for extensive musing on the meaning of her own life. (The title and narrative structure of the book play on Gertrude Stein's *Autobiography of Alice B. Toklas*, because Pearl Time's Child named her car after her favorite actress.) The book begins by quoting the entire conclusion of the play and then goes on to discuss the author's girlhood infatuation with Kerr. For Pearl Time's Child, Kerr's film persona exemplifies a kindliness whose expression is explicitly not only gay-friendly, but also associated with the gentleness and maternal values cultural feminists often attribute to women. Time's Child seems to identify so strongly with Tom that she reads the play and film as an acceptable equivalent to a lesbian love story, since its most important narrative detail is the sympathy Laura/Kerr offers to an adolescent who cannot conform to gender norms.

3. Parker Tyler, who calls the film a "crudely inept charade," takes particular exception to it on the grounds that it seems to occur to no one within the film, nor to the filmmakers, that the persecution of Tom would be "just as much of an outrage" if he were actually gay, not just mistakenly assumed to be (249, 246).

4. As a director, Rob Schmidt has so far concentrated on providing nightmare visions of American families and the struggles of their victims to escape. His work to date includes a failed television pilot, *An American Town*, about dark secrets in a deceptively bucolic location; the 1999 film *Saturn*, the tale of a young man who must take care of his incontinent, dependent elderly father and whose sense of entrapment drives him to rebel through dealing drugs and taking up with an anti-social drug-addicted woman; and *Wrong Turn* (2003), a horror film placed in the same fervently anti-patriarchal family genre as Wes Craven's *The Hills Have Eyes* and Tobe Hooper's *The Texas Chainsaw Massacre*, by its use of an inbred, ultra-masculinist, male-dominated family as the center of the terror.

5. The classic motif of the tragic woman whose concern with providing a father to her children causes them all to be trapped by a sociopath appears memorably in *Night of the Hunter*, similarly counteracting potential audience condemnation of the mother as inappropriately sexy, a real danger given Shelley Winters's sizzling screen presence in the role.

6. *American Beauty* contrasts the sterility of the Burnhams' bedroom to the intensity of Carolyn Burnham's affair with Buddy Kane, "The Real Estate King," her more successful rival who elicits her passion through masterful sexual domination.

7. In *Dialogues II*'s first section Deleuze and Parnet alternate as authors. After that, they co-author.

6. Identity Hunter A

1. While Asian American studies have become increasingly inclusive in the last decade, this discussion focuses on people of Chinese, Japanese, Korean, Vietnamese, and Philippine heritage, as opposed to people of East Indian heritage, because the U.S. media's representation of men from the former groups has been markedly different from that of men of Indian heritage.

2. I have chosen to discuss Asian American Goths, rather than any other raced subjects who identify as Goths, not only because they are represented in the subculture in larger numbers so far than any other group deemed nonwhite, but also because the ways that they participate in Goth seem most strikingly to address issues raised by racialization as it is articulated in American cultures. Nonetheless, those interested in intersections of Goth and race should certainly look at the fairly substantial participation of Latinos/Latinas and African Americans and the growing involvement of Native Americans in Goth subcultures. Of particular interest is the Flagstaff, Arizona–based Navaho Goth band Black Fire.

3. The lyrics of "China Girl," co-written with and first recorded by Iggy Pop on his album *The Idiot*, are extremely ambiguous, suggesting fear of racism as much as they do racism, so I can only conclude that the central topic of the singer's romantic relationship to a Chinese girl was in itself enough to make many listeners decide the song must be about using her in a sadistic manner. It is as if a sort of tar of sexual corruption covers the Asian woman and is assumed to adhere to anyone who touches her.

4. The term "model minority," used in almost all late-twentieth-century and later discussions of Asian American racial and ethnic identity, reflects a vision of Asian Americans as peacefully compliant with the mainstream and assimilationist in attitude. See Stacey Lee's *Unraveling the "Model Minority" Stereotype: Listening to Asian-American Youth* for a useful account of the impact of this myth on current teens.

5. Both *Vampire Hunter D* and Eastwood's "Man with No Name" seem to be influences on Shinichirō Watanabe's 1998 underground hit television series *Cowboy Bebop*, which presents in a postmodern, parodic fashion the adventures of a cynical and laconic futuristic bounty hunter.

6. Anderson/Neo is marked as a Goth by his profession, as the overlap of the terms "nerd," "geek," and "Goth" in the responses to "Voices from the Hellmouth," and on many Goth websites, suggests, and also by the marked similarity of his professional and recreational interests and those of Zach in Brite's *Drawing Blood*. His preferred attire of a black trench coat also associates him with the Goth subculture, as does the film's stylistic borrowings from William Gibson's cyberpunk classic short story "Johnny Mnemonic," also made into a film starring Reeves.

7. See Chela Sandoval's *Methodology of the Oppressed*, 87–88, for further discussion of the status of "non-European peoples of color" as the quintessential revolutionary class in contemporary global politics.

8. Included within her book *Ecstasy Unlimited*.

9. Connections between rave culture and Deleuze and Guattari are made not only by academics but by the producers of rave music themselves, as Reynolds discusses. The rave record label Mille Plateaux is one instance of this, as is the explicitly Deleuzian music of DJ Spooky.

Conclusion

1. Just as authors Deleuze and Guattari rightly call minoritarian, such as Kafka, do not become any less so once their work has become canonical and is often interpreted by critics in ways aligned with discourses of power, so films made in the minoritarian spirit lose nothing of their capacity to spark resistance if they achieve financial success.

2. An illustrative comparison would be to Stanley Kubrick's 1980 film interpretation of a Stephen King horror novel, *The Shining*. In the film, the suspense derives primarily from the dangers a psychic little boy faces when his parents take him to a haunted hotel where all that was ordinary about their home life breaks down. Here, as in hundreds of other classic horror films, the end of horror means a return to normality pretty much as mainstream America defines it.

BIBLIOGRAPHY

Abel, Marco. "Don DeLillo's 'In the Ruins of the Future': Literature, Images, and the Rhetoric of *Seeing 9/11*." *PMLA* 118.3 (2003): 1236–50.

ACLU (American Civil Liberties Union). "Ohio ACLU Defends Students Suspended over Gothic-Themed Web Site." *American Civil Liberties Union Freedom Network*, May 3, 1999. http://www.aclu.org/news/1999/n050399a.html, accessed September 29, 2004.

Addison, Joanne, and Michelle Comstock. "Virtually Out: The Emergence of a Lesbian, Bisexual, and Gay Youth Cyberculture." In *Generations of Youth: Youth Cultures and History in Twentieth-Century America*, ed. Joe Austin and Michael Nevin Willard, 367–78. New York: New York University Press, 1998.

Adorno, Theodor. "On the Fetish Character in Music and the Regression of Listening." In *The Culture Industry: Selected Essays on Mass Culture*, 26–52. London: Routledge, 1991.

American Beauty. Directed by Sam Mendes. DreamWorks, 1999.

Anderson, Melissa. Review of *The Brandon Teena Story* and *Boys Don't Cry*. *Cineaste* 25.2 (2000): 54–56.

Anderson, Robert. *Tea and Sympathy*. New York: Random House, 1953.

Arias, Elizabeth, Marian F. MacDorman, Donna M. Strobino, and Bernard Guyer. "Annual Summary of Vital Statistics—2002." *Pediatrics* 112.6 (2003): 1215–30.

Arnold, Gina. *Route 666: On the Road to Nirvana*. New York: St. Martin's, 1993.

Aronson, Amy, and Michael Kimmel. "The Saviors and the Saved: Masculine Redemption in Contemporary Film." In *Masculinity: Bodies, Movies, Culture*, ed. Peter Lehman, 43–50. New York and London: Routledge, 2001.

"Back to School: Guide to New York." Beginner's Guide to New York, *Village Voice*, August 28, 2001: 91–105.

Bad Girl. Directed by Marielle Nitoslawska. Desire Films, 2001.

Baddeley, Gavin. *Goth Chic: A Connoisseur's Guide to Dark Culture*. London: Plexus, 2002.

Band, Carol. "Do As I Say . . . Not As I Did." *Portland Parent*, July 2001: 14–17.

BeanThere. "'What People Say' Isn't the Problem." Contribution to discussion of "Voices from the Hellmouth," by Jon Katz. *Slashdot*, April 26, 1999. http://slashdot.org/comments.pl?sid=17046&cid=1915801, accessed November 1, 2004.

———. "Working Class Hero." Contribution to discussion of "Voices from the Hell-

mouth," by Jon Katz. *Slashdot*, April 26, 1999. http://slashdot.org/comments.pl?
sid=17046&cid=1915800, accessed November 1, 2004.

Berger, Joshua, and Eric Lengvenis. "NineInchNails." *Plazm* 7 (1994): 48–51.

Blodgett, Harriet. "Fresh Iconography: Subversive Fantasy by Angela Carter." *Review
of Contemporary Fiction* 14.3 (1994): 49–55.

Bogue, Ronald. "Becoming Metal, Becoming Death . . ." In *Deleuze's Wake: Tribute
and Tributaries*, 83–108. Albany: State University of New York Press, 2004.

———. *Deleuze and Guattari*. New York and London: Routledge, 1989.

———. *Deleuze on Cinema*. New York and London: Routledge, 2003.

———. *Deleuze on Literature*. New York and London: Routledge, 2003.

Bonca, Cornel. "In Despair of the Old Adams: Angela Carter's *The Infernal Desire Machines of Doctor Hoffman*." *Review of Contemporary Fiction* 14.3 (1994): 56–62.

Bordo, Susan. *Unbearable Weight: Feminism, Western Culture, and the Body*. Berkeley and Los Angeles: University of California Press, 1995.

Botting, Fred. *Gothic*. London and New York: Routledge, 1996.

Bowling for Columbine. Directed by Michael Moore. United Artists, 2002.

Boys Don't Cry. Directed by Kimberly Peirce. 20th Century Fox, 1999.

The Brandon Teena Story. Directed by Susan Muska and Gréta Olafsdóttir. Zeitgeist
Films, 1998.

Brick, Howard. *Age of Contradictions: American Thought and Culture in the 1960s*.
Ithaca: Cornell University Press, 1998.

Brite, Poppy Z. "Angels." In *Wormwood*. New York: Bantam-Dell, 1994.

———. *The Crow: The Lazarus Heart*. New York: HarperPrism, 1998.

———. *Drawing Blood*. New York: Bantam-Dell, 1993.

———. *Exquisite Corpse*. New York: Scribner, 1996.

———. Foreword to *The Nightmare Factory*, by Thomas Ligotti, ix–xx. New York:
Carroll & Graf, 1996.

———. *Lost Souls*. New York: Bantam-Dell, 1992.

———. *Plastic Jesus*. Burton, Mich.: Subterranean, 2000.

Brown, Brooks, and Rob Merritt. *No Easy Answers: The Truth behind Death at Columbine*. New York: Lantern, 2002.

Brown, Norman O. *Life against Death: The Psychoanalytical Meaning of History*.
Middletown, Conn.: Wesleyan University Press, 1959.

Brumberg, Joan Jacobs. *The Body Project: An Intimate History of American Girls*. New
York: Vintage, 1997.

Buchanan, Ian. *Deleuzism: A Metacommentary*. Durham and London: Duke University Press, 2000.

Burg, Michael S. Open letter. http://www.gothic.net/~mayfair/trenchcoat/posts/
michaelb.html (page no longer available).

Butler, Judith. *Gender Trouble: Feminism and the Subversion of Identity*. New York
and London: Routledge, 1990.

The Butterfly Effect. Directed by Eric Bress and J. Macky Gruber. New Line Cinema,
2004.

Carter, Angela. "The Company of Wolves." In *The Bloody Chamber*. London: Penguin, 1979.

———. *Expletives Deleted: Selected Writings*. London: Vintage, 1993.

———. *Fireworks: Nine Profane Pieces*. New York: Penguin, 1974.

———. *Heroes and Villains*. London: Penguin, 1969.

———. *Love*. Revised edition. London: Chatto and Windus, 1987.

———. *The Magic Toyshop*. London: Virago, 1967.

———. *Nothing Sacred: Selected Writings*. London: Virago, 1982.

———. *The Sadeian Woman*. New York: Pantheon, 1978.

———. *Several Perceptions*. London: Virago, 1968.

———. *Shadow Dance*. Harmondsworth: Penguin, 1966.

Cash, Johnny. "A Boy Named Sue." *At San Quentin (Live)*. Sony, 1969.

Chancer, Lynn S. *Sadomasochism in Everyday Life: The Dynamics of Power and Powerlessness*. New Brunswick, N.J.: Rutgers University Press, 1992.

Chesler, Phyllis. *Women and Madness*. New York: Avon, 1972.

Cheung, King-Kok. "Art, Spirituality and the Ethic of Care: Alternative Masculinities in Chinese American Literature." In *Masculinity Studies and Feminist Theory*, ed. Judith Kegan Gardiner, 261–89. New York: Columbia University Press, 2002.

Chin, Frank, et al. "Introduction: Fifty Years of Our Whole Voice." In *Aiiieeeee! An Anthology of Asian-American Writers*, ed. Frank Chin, Jeffery Chan, Lawson Fusao Inada, and Shawn Wong, 1–38. 1983; New York: Mentor, 1991.

Chua, Peter, and Diane C. Fujino. "Negotiating New Asian-American Masculinities: Attitudes and Gender Expectations." *Journal of Men's Studies* 7.3 (1999): 391–413.

Cixous, Hélène, and Catherine Clément. *The Newly Born Woman*. Trans. Betsy Wing. Minneapolis: University of Minnesota Press, 1986.

Clum, John M. *"He's All Man": Learning Masculinity, Gayness, and Love from American Movies*. New York: Palgrave, 2002.

Cohen, Stanley. *Folk Devils and Moral Panics: The Creation of the Mods and Rockers*. London: MacGibbon and Kee, 1972.

Colebrook, Claire. *Gilles Deleuze*. London and New York: Routledge, 2002.

———. *Understanding Deleuze*. London and New York: Routledge, 2002.

The Company of Wolves. Directed by Neil Jordan. Cannon International, 1984.

Cool, Lisa Collier. "The Secret Sex Lives of Kids." *Ladies' Home Journal*, March 2001: 156–59.

Cooper, Dennis. *Period*. New York: Grove, 2000.

Coover, Robert, "A Passionate Remembrance." 1992. Reprint, *Review of Contemporary Fiction* 14.3 (1994): 9–10.

Cox, Lauren. "Oh Father! A Girl's Guide to Getting Back at Your Parents." In "I Hate My Parents," special issue of *While You Were Sleeping* 23 (2003): 45–46.

Crime and Punishment in Suburbia. Directed by Rob Schmidt. Metro-Goldwyn-Mayer, 2000.

Crimes of Passion. Directed by Ken Russell. Anchor Bay, 1984.

The Crow. Directed by Alex Proyas. Miramax, 1994.

The Crying Game. Directed by Neil Jordan. Miramax, 1992.

Cunningham, Douglas A. "Stalling Zion: Hegemony through Racial Conflict in *The Matrix*." *Rhizomes* 7: *Theory's Others*, 2003. http://www.rhizomes.net, accessed September 29, 2004.

The Cure. "Boys Don't Cry." *Boys Don't Cry*. Electra/Asylum, 1980.

———. "Shiver and Shake." *Kiss Me Kiss Me Kiss Me*. Electra/Asylum, 1987.

———. "Torture." *Kiss Me Kiss Me Kiss Me*. Elektra/Asylum, 1987.

Dagon. Directed by Stuart Gordon. Trimark, 2001.

Dark, Jane. "Hacking the 'Matrix' Master Code: Reloaded Questions." *Village Voice*, May 14–20, 2003: 35–36.

Davenport-Hines, Richard. *Gothic: Four Hundred Years of Excess, Horror, Evil, and Ruin*. New York: Farrar, Straus and Giroux, 1998.

Deleuze, Gilles. *Cinema 1: The Movement-Image*. Trans. Hugh Tomlinson and Barbara Habberjam. Minneapolis: University of Minnesota Press, 1986.

———. *Cinema 2: The Time-Image*. Trans. Hugh Tomlinson and Robert Galeta. Minneapolis: University of Minnesota Press, 1989.

———. *Desert Islands and Other Texts, 1953–1974*. Ed. David Lapoujade. Trans. Michael Taormina. Cambridge, Mass.: MIT Press, 2004.

———. *Difference and Repetition*. Trans. Paul Patton. New York: Columbia University Press, 1994.

———. *Foucault*. Trans. and ed. Seán Hand. Minneapolis: University of Minnesota Press, 1988.

———. *Masochism: An Interpretation of Coldness and Cruelty*. Trans. Jean McNeil. New York: Georges Braziller, 1971.

Deleuze, Gilles, and Félix Guattari. *Anti-Oedipus: Capitalism and Schizophrenia*. With a preface by Michel Foucault. Trans. Robert Hurley, Mark Seem, and Helen R. Lane. Minneapolis: University of Minnesota Press, 1983.

———. *Kafka: Toward a Minor Literature*. Trans. Dana Polan. Minneapolis: University of Minnesota Press, 1986.

———. *Nomadology: The War Machine*. Trans. Brian Massumi. New York: Semiotext(e), 1986.

———. *A Thousand Plateaus: Capitalism and Schizophrenia*. Trans. Brian Massumi. London: Athlone, 1988.

———. *What Is Philosophy?* Trans. Hugh Tomlinson and Graham Burchell. New York: Columbia University Press, 1994.

Deleuze, Gilles, and Claire Parnet. *Dialogues II*. Trans. Hugh Tomlinson and Barbara Habberjam; "The Actual and the Virtual" trans. Eliot Ross Albert. New York: Columbia University Press, 2002.

Derek. "I Feel Sorry for This S-O-Bs!" Contribution to discussion of "Voices from the Hellmouth," by Jon Katz. *Slashdot*, April 26, 1999. http://slashdot.org/comments. pl?sid=17046&cid=1916003, accessed September 29, 2004.

The Donnas. "Forty Boys in Forty Nights." *The Donnas Turn 21*. Lookout! Records, 2001.

Donnie Darko. Directed by Richard Kelly. 20th Century Fox, 2001.

Dostoyevsky, Fyodor. *Crime and Punishment*. Trans. Sidney Monas. New York: New American Library, 1968.

Dracula: Pages from a Virgin's Diary. Directed by Guy Madden. Zeitgeist Films, 2002.

Dunn, Kevin J. "Head Down." *Village Noize* 6.16 (1994): 26–30.

Dworkin, Andrea, and Catherine MacKinnon. "Questions and Answers." In *Making Violence Sexy: Feminist Views on Pornography*, ed. Diana E. H. Russell, 78–96. New York: Teacher's College Press, 1993.

Ebert, Roger. Review of *Crime and Punishment in Suburbia*. September 22, 2000. http://www.suntimes.com/ebert/ebert_reviews/2000/09/092201.html, accessed September 29, 2004.

Echols, Alice. *Daring to Be Bad: Radical Feminism in America, 1967–1975*. Minneapolis: University of Minnesota Press, 1989.

Edmundson, Mark. *Nightmare on Main Street: Angels, Sadomasochism, and the Culture of Gothic*. Cambridge, Mass.: Harvard University Press, 1997.

Edward Scissorhands. Directed by Tim Burton. 20th Century Fox, 1990.

Elder, Preston A. Open letter, April 22, 1999. http://www.goth.net/colorado.html, accessed November 1, 2004.

Eng, David L. *Racial Castration: Managing Masculinity in Asian America*. Durham and London: Duke University Press, 2001.

Enter the Dragon. Directed by Robert Clouse. Warner Brothers, 1973.

Eurythmics. "Sweet Dreams." *Sweet Dreams*. RCA, 1983.

Far from Heaven. Directed by Todd Haynes. Clear Blue Sky, 2002.

Feinberg, Leslie. *Trans Liberation: Beyond Pink or Blue*. Boston: Beacon, 1999.

Feng, Peter. "Redefining Asian American Masculinity: Steven Okazaki's 'American Sons.'" *Cineaste* 22.3 (1996): 27–29.

The Filth and the Fury. Directed by Julien Temple. Universal Pictures, 2000.

Finckenauer, James. *Scared Straight! and the Panacea Phenomenon*. Englewood Cliffs, N.J.: Rutgers University Press, 1982.

Finley, Karen. *Shock Treatment*. San Francisco: City Lights, 1990.

Foucault, Michel. "Clarifications on the Question of Power." In *Foucault Live*, ed. Sylvère Lotringer, trans. John Johnston, 179–92. New York: Semiotext(e), 1989.

——. "Contemporary Music and Its Public." *CNAC Magazine* 15 (1983). Reprinted in *Politics, Philosophy, Culture*, ed. Lawrence D. Kritzman, 314–22. New York and London: Routledge, 1988.

——. *The History of Sexuality, Volume 1: An Introduction*. Trans. Robert Hurley. New York: Vintage, 1980.

——. "An Interview: Sex, Power and the Politics of Identity." *Advocate*, August 7, 1984: 26–30, 58.

——. "Is It Useless to Revolt?" *Le Monde*, 1979. Reprinted in *Religion and Culture*, ed. Jeremy R. Carrette, trans. James Bernauer, 131–34. New York and London: Routledge, 1999.

——. "Nietzsche, Genealogy, History." In *Hommage à Jean Hyppolite*, by Suzanne Bachelard et al., 145–72. Paris: Presses Universitaires de France, 1971. Reprinted in *The Foucault Reader*, ed. Paul Rabinow, trans. Donald F. Bouchard and Sherry Simon, 74–100. New York: Pantheon, 1984.

——. *Remarks on Marx: Conversations with Duccio Trombadori*. Trans. R. James Goldenstein and James Cascaito. New York: Semiotext(e), 1991.

——. "Sexual Choice, Sexual Act: Foucault and Homosexuality." Trans. James O'Higgins. *Salmagundi*, 1983. Reprinted in *Politics, Philosophy, Culture*, ed. Lawrence D. Kritzman, 286–303. New York and London: Routledge, 1988.

——. "Sexual Morality and the Law." Trans. James Sheridan. In *Politics, Philosophy, Culture*, ed. Lawrence D. Kritzman, 271–85. New York and London: Routledge, 1988.

French, Brandon. *On the Verge of Revolt: Women in American Films of the Fifties*. New York: Frederick Unger, 1978.

Fuentes, Annette. "No Sex Ed: Congress Pushes Abstinence in the Schools." *In These Times*, December 18, 1997: 16–18.

Gaar, Gillian. *She's a Rebel: The History of Women in Rock & Roll*. Seattle: Seal, 1992.

Gaines, Donna. *Teenage Wasteland: Suburbia's Dead End Kids*. 1990. Reprint, Chicago: University of Chicago Press, 1998.

Gallant, Chris. "Quoting the Raven, Philosophies of Composition and the Female Corpse as Objet d'Art: The Influence of Edgar Allan Poe." In *Art of Darkness: The Cinema of Dario Argento*, ed. Chris Gallant, 75–83. Guildford: Fab, 2000.

Gerhard, Jane. *Desiring Revolution: Second-Wave Feminism and the Rewriting of American Sexual Thought, 1920 to 1982*. New York: Columbia University Press, 2001.

Gilbert, Sandra M., and Susan Gubar. *The Madwoman in the Attic: The Woman Writer and the Nineteenth-Century Literary Imagination*. New Haven: Yale University Press, 1979.

Gold, Jonathan. "Love It to Death." *Rolling Stone*, September 8, 1994: 50–54, 88.

Guattari, Félix. "Four Truths for Psychiatry." Trans. Chet Wiener. 1985. Reprinted in *Soft Subversions*, ed. Sylvère Lotringer, 262–67. New York: Semiotext(e), 1996.

———. "In Order to End the Massacre of the Body." Trans. Jarred Becker. 1973. Reprinted in *Soft Subversions*, ed. Sylvère Lotringer, 29–36. New York: Semiotext(e), 1996.

Halberstam, Judith. *Female Masculinity*. Durham and London: Duke University Press, 1998.

———. *Skin Shows: Gothic Horror and the Technology of Monsters*. Durham and London: Duke University Press, 1998.

———. "The Transgender Gaze in *Boys Don't Cry*." *Screen* 42:3 (2001): 294–98.

Halperin, David M. *Saint Foucault: Towards a Gay Hagiography*. New York: Oxford University Press, 1995.

Hamilton, Laurell K. *Narcissus in Chains*. New York: Jove, 2002.

Hattenhauer, Darryl. *Shirley Jackson's American Gothic*. Albany: State University of New York Press, 2003.

Heath, Chris. "The Love Story of Marilyn Manson." *Rolling Stone*, October 15, 1998: 36–38.

Hebdige, Dick. *Subculture: The Meaning of Style*. London and New York: Routledge, 1979.

Henderson, Lisa. "The Class Character of *Boys Don't Cry*." *Screen* 42.3 (2001): 299–303.

Hesse-Biber, Sharlene. *Am I Thin Enough Yet? The Cult of Thinness and the Commercialization of Identity*. New York: Oxford University Press, 1997.

Hite, Shere. *The Hite Report: Women and Love; A Cultural Revolution in Progress*. New York: Alfred A. Knopf, 1987.

Hodkinson, Paul. *Goth: Identity, Style, and Subculture*. Oxford and New York: Berg, 2002.

Hollibaugh, Amber L. "Seducing Women into 'A Lifestyle of Vaginal Fisting': Lesbian Sex Gets Virtually Dangerous." In *Policing Public Sex: Queer Politics and the Future of AIDS Activism*, ed. Dangerous Bedfellows, 321–36. Boston: South End, 1996.

Holmlund, Chris. *Impossible Bodies: Femininity and Masculinity at the Movies*. New York and London: Routledge, 2002.

Hongo, Garrett. *Volcano: A Memoir of Hawai'i*. New York: Alfred A. Knopf, 1995.

Horkheimer, Max, and Theodor Adorno. "The Culture Industry: Enlightenment as Mass Deception." In *The Dialectic of Enlightenment*. Trans. John Cunning. 1944. Reprint, New York: Continuum, 2001.

Hwang, David Henry. *M. Butterfly*. New York: Penguin, 1989.

Irvine, Janice. *Talk about Sex: The Battles over Sex Education in the United States*. Berkeley and Los Angeles: University of California Press, 2002.

Jameson, Fredric. "The End of Temporality." *Critical Inquiry* 29.4 (2003): 695–718.

Jane's Addiction. "Ted, Just Admit It." *Nothing's Shocking*. Warner, 1988.

Jardine, Alice A. *Gynesis: Configurations of Woman and Modernity*. Ithaca: Cornell University Press, 1985.

Jenkins, Henry. "Testimony before the U.S. Senate Commerce Committee, May 4, 1999." http://commerce.senate.gov/hearings/0504jen.pdf, accessed September 29, 2004.

Jesse. "You People Are Kidding." Contribution to discussion of "Voices from the Hellmouth," by Jon Katz. *Slashdot*, April 27, 1999. http://slashdot.org/comments.pl?sid=17046&cid=1916072, accessed September 29, 2004.

Joplin, Janis. "Me and Bobby McGee." *Pearl*. Sony, 1971.

Kamen, Paula. *Her Way: Young Women Remake the Sexual Revolution*. New York: Broadway, 2002.

Kamen, Paula, and Carol Siegel. "Dialogue." *Rhizomes 7: Theory's Others*, 2003. http://www.rhizomes.net, accessed September 29, 2004.

Kaplan, E. Ann. "Is the Gaze Male?" In *Feminism and Film*, ed. E. Ann Kaplan, 119–38. Oxford: Oxford University Press, 2000.

Katz, Jon. "Voices from the Hellmouth." *Slashdot*, April 26, 1999. http://slashdot.org/articles/99/04/25/1438249.shtml, accessed September 29, 2004.

Kaufman, Linda S. *Bad Girls and Sick Boys: Fantasies in Contemporary Culture*. Berkeley and Los Angeles: University of California Press, 1998.

Kellerman, Faye. *The Forgotten*. New York: Avon, 2001.

Kennedy, Barbara M. *Deleuze and Cinema: The Aesthetics of Sensation*. Edinburgh: Edinburgh University Press, 2002.

Kingston, Maxine Hong. *The Woman Warrior: Memoirs of a Girlhood among Ghosts*. New York: Vintage, 1989.

Kipnis, Laura. *Ecstasy Unlimited: On Sex, Capital, Gender, and Aesthetics*. Minneapolis: University of Minnesota Press, 1993.

Lacan, Jacques. *Le Séminaire Livre XX: Encore*. Paris: Editions du Seuil, 1975.

Lady Chaos. Open letter. http://www.gothic.net/%7Emage/goth/scouts/state/ (page no longer available).

Leblanc, Lauraine. *Pretty in Punk: Girls' Gender Resistance in a Boys' Subculture*. New Brunswick, N.J.: Rutgers University Press, 2001.

Lee, Chang-rae. *A Gesture Life*. New York: Penguin, 1999.

Lee, Stacey. *Unraveling the "Model Minority" Stereotype: Listening to Asian-American Youth*. New York: Teacher's College Press, 2001.

Lennon, John. "Working Class Hero." *John Lennon/Plastic Ono Band*. Apple Records, 1970.

Lerner, Sharon. "An Orgy of Abstinence: Federal Funding Pushes No-Sex Education into the Mainstream." *Village Voice*, August 7, 2001: 34–37.

Levin, Julia. Review of *Crime and Punishment in Suburbia*. *Filmcritic.com*, 2001.

http://filmcritic.com/misc/emporium.nsf/84dbbfa4d710144986256c290016f76e/
a06ef69005722fb4882569cb00129610?OpenDocument&Highlight=0,crime,
punishment, accessed September 29, 2004.

Levine, Judith. *Harmful to Minors: The Perils of Protecting Children from Sex*. Minneapolis: University of Minnesota Press, 2002.

Levy, Shawn. *Ready, Steady, Go! The Smashing Rise and Giddy Fall of Swinging London*. New York: Broadway, 2002.

Ligotti, Thomas. "Eye of the Lynx." In *The Nightmare Factory*, 71–78. New York: Carroll & Graf, 1996.

Ling, Jinqi. "Identity Crisis and Gender Politics: Reappropriating Asian American Masculinity." In *An Interethnic Companion to Asian American Literature*, ed. King-Kok Cheung. 312–37. Cambridge: Cambridge University Press, 1997.

Lippman, Laura. *In Big Trouble*. New York: Avon, 1999.

Luke, Allan. "Representing and Reconstructing Asian Masculinities: This Is Not a Movie Review." *Social Alternatives* 16.3 (1997): 32–34.

Ma Vie en Rose. Directed by Alain Berliner. Sony Pictures, 1997.

MacKendrick, Karmen. *Counterpleasures*. Albany: State University of New York Press, 1999.

Manson, Marilyn. *Dope Hat*. Music video, directed by Richard Kern, 1995.

———. *Sweet Dreams (Are Made of This)*. Music video, directed by Dean Karr, 1996.

Marcus, Greil. *Lipstick Traces: A Secret History of the Twentieth Century*. Cambridge, Mass.: Harvard University Press, 1989.

Marcuse, Herbert. *Eros and Civilization: A Philosophic Inquiry into Freud*. Boston: Beacon, 1974.

———. *An Essay on Liberation*, Boston: Beacon, 1971.

Marwick, Arthur. *The Sixties: Cultural Revolution in Britain, France, Italy, and the United States, c. 1958–1974*. Oxford and New York: Oxford University Press, 1998.

Massé, Michelle. *In the Name of Love: Women, Masochism, and the Gothic*. Ithaca and New York: Cornell University Press, 1992.

The Matrix. Directed by Andy Wachowski and Larry Wachowski. Warner Brothers, 1999.

The Matrix Reloaded. Directed by Andy Wachowski and Larry Wachowski. Warner Brothers, 2003.

The Matrix Revolutions. Directed by Andy Wachowski and Larry Wachowski. Warner Brothers, 2003.

McCabe and Mrs. Miller. Directed by Robert Altman. Warner Brothers, 1971.

McRobbie, Angela. *Feminism and Youth Culture*. 2nd ed. New York and London: Routledge, 2000.

McWhorter, Ladelle. *Bodies and Pleasures: Foucault and the Politics of Normalization*. Bloomington: Indiana University Press, 1999.

Meat Puppets. "Two Rivers." *Up on the Sun*. Rykodisc USA, 1985.

Mellor, Anne K. *Mary Shelley: Her Life, Her Fiction, Her Monsters*. London and New York: Routledge, 1988.

Mercer, Mick. *Hex Files: The Goth Bible*. Woodstock, N.Y.: Overlook, 1997.

———. *21st Century Goth*. London: Reynolds and Hearn, 2002.

Messerschmidt, James W. *Masculinities and Crime: Critique and Reconceptualization of Theory.* Lanham, Md.: Rowman & Littlefield, 1993.

"MH." Review of *Crime and Punishment in Suburbia* for the Political Film Society. 2000. http://www.geocities.com/~polfilms/crimepunishment.html, accessed September 29, 2004.

Modest Mouse. "Trailer Trash." *The Lonesome Crowded West.* Up, 1997.

Moers, Ellen. *Literary Women.* Garden City, N.J.: Doubleday, 1977.

Moynihan, Michael, and Didrik Søderlind. *Lords of Chaos: The Bloody Rise of the Satanic Metal Underground.* Venice, Calif.: Feral House, 1998.

Muggleton, David. *Inside Subculture: The Postmodern Meaning of Style.* Oxford: Berg, 2000.

Mura, David. *Where the Body Meets Memory: An Odyssey of Race, Sexuality, and Identity.* New York: Doubleday, 1995.

My Life with the Thrill Kill Kult. "China De Sade." *13 above the Night.* Interscope, 1993.

Natural Born Killers. Directed by Oliver Stone. Warner, 1994.

Nguyen, Viet Thanh. "The Remasculinization of Chinese America: Race, Violence, and the Novel." *American Literary History* 12.2 (2000): 130–57.

Nine Inch Nails. "Closer." *The Downward Spiral.* Nothing/TVT/Interscope, 1994.

———. *Closer.* Music video, directed by Mark Romanek, 1994.

———. *Happiness in Slavery.* Music video, directed by Jonathan Reiss, 1992.

———. "Reptile." *The Downward Spiral.* Nothing/TVT/Interscope, 1994.

———. "Sanctified." *Pretty Hate Machine.* TVT, 1989.

———. "Sin." *Pretty Hate Machine.* TVT, 1989.

———. "Twist." *Demos and Remixes.* Bootleg recording, 1988–92, 1992.

Opel, Andy. "*Paradise Lost I & II:* Documentary and the Monster of Justice." Paper presented to the Society for Cinema and Media Studies Conference, Atlanta, March 5, 2004.

Ozeki, Ruth L. *My Year of Meats.* New York: Penguin, 1998.

Paradise Lost: The Child Murders at Robin Hood Hills. Directed by Joe Berlinger and Bruce Sinofsky. Home Box Office, 1996.

Paradise Lost II: Revelations. Directed by Joe Berlinger and Bruce Sinofsky. Home Box Office, 2001.

Patton, Cindy. *Fatal Advice: How Safe-Sex Education Went Wrong.* Durham and London: Duke University Press, 1996.

Penley, Constance. "Brownian Motion: Women, Tactics, and Technology." In *Technoculture,* ed. Constance Penley and Andrew Ross, 135–62. Minneapolis: University of Minnesota Press, 1991.

"Perkygoff Manifesto." *Encyclopedia Gothica.* http://www.waningmoon.com/gothica/articles/6660047.shtml, accessed September 29, 2004.

Petrosino, Anthony, Carolyn Turpin-Petrosino, and James O. Finckenauer. "Well-Meaning Programs Can Have Harmful Effects! Lessons from Experiments of Programs Such as Scared Straight." *Crime and Delinquency* 46.3 (2000): 354–79.

Pimpbot3k. "Cheerleader/Band Geek." Contribution to discussion of "Voices from the Hellmouth," by Jon Katz. *Slashdot,* April 27, 1999. http://slashdot.org/comments.pl?sid=17046&cid=1915321, accessed September 29, 2004.

Pipher, Mary. *Reviving Ophelia: Saving the Selves of Adolescent Girls*. New York: Putnam, 1994.

Planned Parenthood. *Abstinence*. New York: Planned Parenthood Publications, 2001.

———. *Sexually Transmitted Infections*. New York: Planned Parenthood Publications, 2001.

Powers, Ann. *Weird Like Us: My Bohemian America*. New York: Da Capo, 2000.

Queen, Carol. *Real Live Nude Girl: Chronicles of a Sex-Positive Culture*. San Francisco: Cleis, 2002.

Queer as Folk. Directed by Sarah Harding and Charles McDougall. C1TV Entertainment Television, 1999.

Queer as Folk. Directed by Russell Mulcahy. Showtime, 2000.

Rapping, Elayne. *Media-Tions: Forays into the Culture and Gender Wars*. Boston: South End, 1994.

The Real Cancun. Directed by Rick Oliveira. New Line Cinema, 2003.

Reed, Lou. "Venus in Furs." *The Velvet Underground and Nico*. Polydor, 1967.

Reimer, Susan. "Children Don't Outgrow Need for Support." *Baltimore Sun*. Reprinted in *Sunday Oregonian*, July 22, 2001: F5.

Reitman, Janet. "The Killing Joke." *Rolling Stone*, May 13, 2004: 62–67.

Reppucci, N. Dickson, and Jeffrey J. Haugaard. "Prevention of Child Sexual Abuse: Myth or Reality." *American Psychologist* 44.10 (1989): 1266–75.

Revolting Cocks. "Da Ya Think I'm Sexy." *Linger Ficken' Good*. Reprise, 1993.

Reynolds, Simon. *Blissed Out: The Raptures of Rock*. London: Serpent's Tail, 1990.

———. *Generation Ecstasy: Into the World of Techno and Rave Culture*. 1998. Reprint, New York and London: Routledge, 1999.

Rice, Anne. *Interview with the Vampire*. New York: Ballantine, 1976.

Rotary Connection. "Ruby Tuesday." *The Rotary Connection*. MCA, 1967.

Russo, Vito. *The Celluloid Closet: Homosexuality in the Movies*. Revised ed. New York: Harper and Row, 1987.

Said, Edward W. *Orientalism*. New York: Random House, 1979.

Sandoval, Chela. *Methodology of the Oppressed*. Minneapolis: University of Minnesota Press, 2000.

Satter, Beryl. "The Sexual Abuse Paradigm in Historical Perspective: Passivity and Emotion in Mid-Twentieth Century America." *Journal of the History of Sexuality* 12.3 (2003): 424–64.

Sedgwick, Eve Kosofsky. *Tendencies*. Durham and London: Duke University Press, 1993.

Shary, Timothy. *Generation Multiplex: The Image of Youth in Contemporary Cinema*. Austin: University of Texas Press, 2002.

Shawcross, E. L. *Devils Speak of Bloody Angels*. Nine Inch Nails fan website. Originally at http://www.student.uwa.edu.au/~dreamgod/trent/toc.html, where I accessed it in 2001; now at http://www.mtrez.net/old/trent/toc.html, accessed September 29, 2004.

The Shining. Directed by Stanley Kubrick. Warner Brothers, 1980.

Siegel, Carol. *Male Masochism: Modern Revisions of the Story of Love*. Bloomington: Indiana University Press, 1995.

———. *New Millennial Sexstyles*. Bloomington: Indiana University Press, 2000.

Sinfield, Alan. *Gay and After*. London: Serpent's Tail, 1998.

The Sixth Sense. Directed by M. Knight Shyamalan. Buena Vista, 1999.

Smith, Patricia Juliana. "All You Need Is Love: Carter's Novel of Sixties Sex and Sensibility." *Review of Contemporary Fiction* 14.3 (1994): 24–29.

Smiths. "Is It Really So Strange?" *Louder than Bombs*. Sire, 1987.

Stevens, David. *The Gothic Tradition*. New York: Cambridge University Press, 2000.

Stewart, Rod. "Da Ya Think I'm Sexy." *Blonds Have More Fun*. Warner Brothers, 1978.

Suicide, Missy. *SuicideGirls*. Venice, Calif.: Feral House, 2004.

Swan, Rachel. Review of *Boys Don't Cry*. *Film Quarterly* 54.3 (2001): 47–52.

Taormino, Tristan. *Down and Dirty Sex Secrets: The New and Naughty Guide to Being Great in Bed*. New York: Regan, 2003.

Tea and Sympathy. Directed by Vincente Minnelli. Metro-Goldwyn-Mayer, 1956.

Thompson, Dave. *The Dark Reign of Gothic Rock: In the Reptile House with The Sisters of Mercy, Bauhaus, and The Cure*. London: Helter Skelter, 2002.

Thompson, Kristin. "Fantasies, Franchises, and Frodo Baggins: *The Lord of the Rings* and Modern Hollywood." *Velvet Light Trap*, no. 52 (2003): 45–63.

Thornton, Sarah. *Club Cultures: Music, Media, and Subcultural Capital*. 1995. Reprint, Hanover and London: Wesleyan University Press, 1995.

Time's Child, Pearl. *The Auto Biography of Deborah Carr*. Ashland, Oregon: n.p., 1983.

Toth, Csaba. "'Like Cancer in the System': Industrial Gothic, Nine Inch Nails, and Videotape." In *Gothic: Transmutations of Horror in Late Twentieth Century Art*, ed. Christoph Grunenberg, 118–79 (pagination is reversed). Cambridge, Mass.: MIT Press, 1997.

Tyler, Parker. *Screening the Sexes: Homosexuality in the Movies*. New York: Da Capo, 1993.

Vampire Hunter D (*Kyûketsuki Hunter D*). Directed by Toyoo Ashida and Carl Macek. Manga Films S. L., 1985.

Vampire Hunter D: Bloodlust. Directed by Yoshiaki Kawajiri and Tai Kit Mak. Manga Films S. L., 2000.

Vasquez, Jhonen. *Johnny the Homicidal Maniac: Director's Cut*. New York: Slave Labor Publications, 1999.

Voodoo@aimnet.com. Open letter. http://www.gothic.net/~mayfair/trenchcoat/posts/voodoo.txt (page no longer available).

Walker, Tim. "School's Out." *Teaching Tolerance*, no. 21 (2002): 25–29.

Walser, Robert. "Clamour and Community in the Music of Public Enemy." In *Generations of Youth: Youth Cultures and History in Twentieth-Century America*, ed. Joe Austin and Michael Nevin Willard, 293–310. New York and London: New York University Press, 1998.

Wang, Athena. "Asian and White Boys' Competing Discourses about Masculinity: Implications for Secondary Education." In "Boys, Men, Masculinity and Schooling," special issue, *Canadian Journal of Education* 25.2 (2000): 113–25.

Warner, Michael. *The Trouble with Normal: Sex. Politics, and the Ethics of Queer Life*. Cambridge, Mass.: Harvard University Press, 1999.

Watt, Paul, and Kevin Stenson. "'It's a Bit Dodgy around There': Safety, Danger,

Ethnicity and Young People's Use of Public Space." In *Cool Places: Geographies of Youth Cultures*, ed. Tracey Skelton and Gill Valentine, 249–65. London and New York: Routledge, 1998.

Weiss, Mike. "Biological Didn't Bother: Music to Hate Your Parents To." In "I Hate My Parents," special issue of *While You Were Sleeping* 23 (2003): 76–77.

The Whip. Various artists. Cleopatra, 1993.

The Who. "My Generation." *My Generation.* Towser Tunes/Fabulous Music, 1965.

Widdicombe, Sue, and Robin Wooffitt. *The Language of Youth Subcultures: Social Identity in Action.* London: Harvester Wheatsheaf, 1995.

Williams, Anne. "Edifying Narratives: The Gothic Novel, 1764–1997." In *Gothic: Transmutations of Horror in Late Twentieth Century Art*, ed. Christoph Grunenberg, 151–118 (pagination is reversed). Cambridge, Mass.: MIT Press, 1997.

Williams, Linda. *Hard Core: Power, Pleasure, and the "Frenzy of the Visible."* Berkeley and Los Angeles: University of California Press, 1989.

Winter, Jessica. "Criminal Lovers." Review of *Crime and Punishment in Suburbia. Village Voice* on-line, September 13–19, 2000. http://www.villagevoice.com/issues/0037/winter.php, accessed September 29, 2004.

Wolf, Sheila. "Girls Will Be Boys: From Heretic to Heroine." *Propaganda* 26 (2001): 24–27.

Wong, Sau-ling C., and Jeffrey J. Santa Ana. "Gender and Sexuality in Asian American Literature." *Signs* 25.1 (1999): 171–226.

Wong, Shawn. *Homebase.* New York: Plume, 1991.

Zhong, Xueping. *Masculinity Besieged? Issues of Modernity and Male Subjectivity in Chinese Literature of the Late Twentieth Century.* Durham and London: Duke University Press, 2000.

Zombie, Rob. *Dragula.* Music video, directed by Rob Zombie, 1999.

Zwerdling, Alex. *Virginia Woolf and the Real World.* Berkeley and Los Angeles: University of California Press, 1986.

INDEX

Abel, Marco, 99
Abortion, 7, 47, 83
Abstinence, 9, 32–48, 72, 93, 96, 155, 166–67
ACLU, 31
Acker, Kerry, 10
Addison, Joanne, and Michelle Comstock, 183n3
Aiiieeeee! An Anthology of Asian-American Writers, 140–41, 144, 191n12
American Beauty, 126–28, 133–34, 160
Anderson, Melissa, 105, 108, 112
Anorexia, 63–64
Arias, Elizabeth, Marian F. MacDorman, Donna M. Strobino, and Bernard Guyer, 187n15
Arnold, Gina, 189n1
Aronson, Amy, and Michael Kimmel, 119, 124–25
AZN Goth, 143

Bad Girl, 33–34
Baddeley, Gavin, 7, 9, 12, 18, 53, 55, 56, 78, 88, 93, 96, 122, 130, 134, 138, 139, 147, 157
Band, Carol, 40
Batcave, 63, 157
Bauhaus, 24, 79
Beetlejuice, 90, 157
Berger, Joshua, and Eric Lengvenis, 89
Blade, 150
Blodgett, Harriet, 57
Bogue, Ronald, 92, 129, 130, 185n1, 190n3

Bonca, Cornell, 57
Bordo, Susan, 189n8
Botting, Fred, 5–6
Bowie, David, 140, 141
Bowling for Columbine, 10
Boys Don't Cry (film), 10, 97–115, 116, 129
"Boys Don't Cry" (song), 97, 100–103
Brandon Teena Story, The, 98–115
Brick, Howard, 55, 56, 67
Brite, Poppy Z., 48, 70, 72–92, 109, 123, 138, 145, 193n6
Brown, Brooks, and Rob Merritt, 32–33, 111
Brown, Norman O., 7
Brumberg, Joan Jacobs, 85
Buchanan, Ian, 28
Burg, Michael S., 31
Burton, Tim, 20, 157, 160
Butler, Judith, 129

Car culture, 47, 55, 159–60
Carter, Angela, 12, 50, 56–71, 72, 77
Cash, Johnny, 110
Chancer, Lynn S., 190n2
Chesler, Phyllis, 39
Cheung, King-Kok, 145
Chin, Frank, 140–41, 144, 150, 191n12
Christian Death, 123
Chua, Peter, and Diane C. Fujino, 142
Cixous, Hélène, and Catherine Clément, 91–92
Closer, 3, 80, 86, 89
Clubs/Clubbing, 4, 6, 10–11, 15, 20,

CAROL SIEGEL,

Professor of English and American Studies at Washington State University, Vancouver, is author of *Male Masochism: Modern Revisions of the Story of Love* and *New Millennial Sexstyles* (both from Indiana University Press) and *Lawrence among the Women: Wavering Boundaries in Women's Literary Traditions*, as well as various articles on Modernist and Victorian literature, gender theory, film, and rock music. She also co-edits the journals *Genders* and *Rhizomes*.